A(

a cleric off the leash

To
Richard & Nicola
to help you sleep

Colin

*A*CTION!

a cleric off the leash

COLIN HODGETTS
autobiography

ISBN-13: 978-1535433693
ISBN-10: 1535433698

Contents

Chapter One

Setting out my stall

THE COMPUTER HUMS TUNELESSLY. A pristine Word page, set on a powder blue ground, a little lighter than the blue of my eyes – though it is some time since they were the objects of a compliment – challenges me to begin my tale. But why does this backlit blank offer no clue as to where I should start? The machine hums as it waits, and won't wait long before a nap calls. In the days of a Bic and paper one could doodle, scratching for inspiration, like a cockerel raking through dust and gravel, until the rooster retired to rest and the cows came home.

Imminent dormition is a pressure. Feeling also, rather irrationally, that the machine is judging me is an even greater pressure. I become impatient. What if I let my digits loose on the keys, just to see what comes of their tap dance?

Denys Turner opens the Preface to his study of Julian of Norwich with this declaration: 'Some of my academic colleagues seem to know what they think before they talk. Others, among whom I count myself, need to talk in order to know what they think. As with speech, so with writing.' Or, as Lewis Carroll put it, 'How do I know what I think till I see what I say?'

It is comforting to find that others are soused in the same pickle juice. In writing this memoir I hope to discover what I think about my life. We won't know that until we reach the final chapter. I have been prompted by friends to 'write it all up', though their motive is a mite unclear. Perhaps they imagine it will gain them a few measly morsels of peace and quiet. For me it is merely one more in the series of challenges to be undertaken before I gain the hand of the princess.

Most memoirs begin with the subject's antecedents and birth, and then trudge or meander through the ensuing decades. I am not tempted by this sequential approach. For if, as predicted, I am about to lose my short-term memory and experience a clearer recall of the distant past, mightn't it be safer to begin with the present and work backwards? Let's face it: I already have difficulty recalling names to put to faces, and difficulty digging up a common word, let alone a bon mot: the writing is on the clock. 'When the age is in the wit is out.'

I have been alerted to False Memory Syndrome. This is a condition in which you remember, or think you remember, events that never happened. Sometimes there is an innocent explanation for this. I think I remember preaching my first sermon at the age of two because of the many times I heard my mother tell her friends, 'And do you know, he preached his first sermon when he was only two. It was on the Marcan hypothesis. And it was only three weeks later that he took his first collection. He hadn't learnt yet to call it an offertory, but, as I say, he was only two.' When you've heard that sort of thing often enough you think you remember it.

False Memory Syndrome is not to be confused with Golden Memory Disorder. In this latter condition positive memories are enlarged at the expense of negative memories. Thus the summers of one's youth were always sunny, the sand clean and silver, the sea Mediterranean blue and temperate, the scones warm from the oven, the cream thickly clotted, the jam nothing but strawberries. Washed from the memory are wet days on a pebble beach, the water recently arrived from the Arctic, the fishpaste sandwiches curled and more sand than wiches, the tea orange and tasting of Thermos.

Preparations have been made for the task ahead. I have alerted myself to the dangers of cognitive bias, and will pay particular attention to the long list of memory errors and prejudices of which I am likely to fall foul. Can I avoid 'telescoping' and 'rosy retrospection'? I don't see that the 'self-relevance effect' is problematic in an autobiographical context. There are bound to be memory distortions: some details of events will be sharpened at the expense of others. There is the challenge of consistency, of not attaching present attitudes and behaviours to what happened in the past. You can be sure you won't find in me a tendency to defend and bolster the status quo, and I hope I won't claim more responsibility for successes than failures, if I can recall the failures, that is. Then what about the Lake Wobegon effect: overestimating one's desirable qualities and underestimating one's undesirable qualities, especially when measured against those of other people? (Named after Garrison Keillor's fictional town where 'all the children are above average'.) I'll try to resist that temptation and will do my best to be objective, but be warned: telling stories is an attractive enterprise and the embellishment of them creatively seductive.

My wife Julia and I spent ten days with a friend in Rome. It was a relief to exchange Hartland's wind and rain for sunshine and *vino de cassa*. We returned home to rain again, the positive side being that the demands of the outside world – repairing a gate and replacing damaged guttering – were on hold, so I had no excuse for not wrestling with the challenge of summoning up the ghost of a life past. When in Rome I gave some thought to how I might organize my experiences and memories. I even made some jottings with the uniball that has usurped the Bic.

Let us talk then of graves, of worms, and of epitaphs. Rome's catacombs represent the model I have just rejected. For these boneyards to accommodate a quarter of a million corpses plus, each site has up to five levels of tomb tunnels, the top one, the one we were exploring, being the earliest. When that level had its full quota of bodies a new set of tunnels was excavated underneath it. So the most recent burials are in the lowest level. The oldest is the most accessible, which is how things will soon be with me and other of my decomposing contemporaries.

From those tunnels that are open to visitors the bones have been removed so as to foil memento-lifters. I, too, am tempted to commit my 'skeletons' to a charnel-house with access barred, though creative things might be done with this osseous tissue, as in a church in Rome. In Santa Maria della Concezione, a Capuchin church, the bones of nigh on four thousand monks decorate the crypt walls. Some skeletons are intact and wear Franciscan habits. The individual bones of the majority have been used to create elaborate ornamental designs. I, too, shall play 'wid dem bones' of mine, my memories I hasten to add, for I wouldn't undertake the task ahead unless I thought I might have some fun creating patterns out of the past.

Capuchin ossuary

I visited this Capuchin ossuary with Alona, a former pupil, and we both grinned with delight in response to the creativity of the bone setters. Other visitors – they had to be American – expressed dismay and shock verging on horror. Too many people today are distanced from death and shrink from 'the enemy'. Medieval artists reminded an audience, much more familiar than us with corpses, of its seriousness. I have on my wall a Galleria Borghese poster of Caravaggio's painting of St. Jerome. On an open book a skull overlooks his work.

This *memento mori*, reminder of death, is frequently to be found in Christian medieval art. In the colonial US, Puritan tombstones were heavy with winged skulls, skeletons, or angels snuffing out candles – Halloween-like slabs intended to convey a similar meaning. Nowadays, unless we have had the misfortune to have been fighting in Iraq or Afghanistan, or are in the medical or undertaking professions, we will be unfamiliar with real corpses and know death only as trivialised by the Xbox and the camera lens, the latter capturing Scandinavian pathologists at their grisly – or is it gristly? – dissection.

When I paid an early-afternoon visit to Vinoba Bhave, Gandhi's successor, on a trip to India to take part in the Gandhi Centenary celebrations a few decades ago, he was in a cot practising his death, something he did every afternoon, preparing the nuns who attended him for his demise. On another occasion we stood on the banks of the Ganges fascinated by the public barbecuing of corpses. In Asia it seems that death, no stranger, bears a tiny sting.

As a clergyman I have perhaps been closer than most of those who are not in the medical or undertaking professions to individuals who are fading away or have closed the door on life. One of my responsibilities as a curate in Sixties Hackney was to be the Anglican chaplain to St Joseph's Hospice, run by Roman Catholic nuns, where Cicely Saunders, also an Anglican and my mentor, set a new benchmark for care of the dying.

Mother Teresa, a nun who established a shelter in a former Hindu temple in Calcutta (Kolkata) where the poor could die with dignity, wrote: 'A beautiful death is for people who lived like animals to die like angels – loved and wanted.' I visited it forty-four years ago, shortly after Malcolm Muggeridge had filmed there for TV, he claiming a 'miracle' as the crew had obtained excellent footage despite a ban on the use of lights. Mother Teresa has been criticized in the West for refusing to employ medicines and machines to extend life. She brushed this off. She was committed to quality in life and in the departing of it, not to longevity.

Why all this about death before we've got started on life? Because coming to terms with death and dying is one of the most important spiritual tasks that we can undertake. Even though I believe that death may mean total annihilation, with no rebirth and no resurrection, early on I decided that I had to face and accept it, for in that acceptance there can be freedom, freedom from fear, freedom from worry about what others may do to me, or say about me, freedom to live in the present and freedom to live this day as though my last. 'When one has learned to let go and let be, then one is well disposed, and he or she is always in the right place whether in society or in solitude.' (*Meister Eckhart*, tr. Matthew Fox.)

The downside of living in the present is said, by some contemporaries, to be 'smoking, overeating and unprotected sex' through a lack of concern about the future consequences of one's actions, though I haven't read that those great spiritual masters who commend living in the present were tempted by such indulgences. I don't smoke.

When St Augustine says 'Love God and do what you will' he obviously believes that, as DT Suzuki has it, 'To love God is to have no self, to be of no-mind, to become a "dead man".' The Zen master Bunan wrote:

> While alive
> Be a dead man,
> Thoroughly dead;
> And act as you will,
> And all is good.

'Living this day as though my last' is not easy. It gets swamped by a queue of tasks and the distractions of trivia. Yet it is the only way to fully appreciate all that is around me, the sights smells and music that tell us that we are alive in a beautiful world that we have no excuse for taking for granted. Alexander McCall Smith either reports or invents a development of this injunction: treat everyone you meet as if it is their last day, and while you know that, they don't. It might be worth a try.

Back to Rome! A sunny morning on the Palatine, tramping puddled paths that wind between stunted walls faced with quality brick, a site to stimulate the imagination, for without imagination there is only rubble, weeds and a scattering of trees. That is, until one descends to the house of Augustus. The frescoes, in vivid shades of blue, red and ochre, are among the best surviving examples of Roman wall paintings, the equal of those found in Pompeii and Herculaneum. Until recently they were buried and forgotten.

We descend to discover beauty. As I excavate my life will I unearth some hidden jewel like this or just a sack of fleshless bones ripe for reburial?

The Palatine Hill offers a more attractive model for this book than the catacombs. The most recent ruins sit on earlier ruins. The archaeologist begins with the present and digs down into the past. Modern archaeological excavation techniques are stratigraphic, each level assigned to a historical period. I can appreciate my life as a series of levels, distinct periods, usually related to the job I was doing.

I ventured into the Vatican museums for the first time. On previous visits I had avoided them, but the absence of queues in early February, combined with a Pope zealous for reform, encouraged me to explore treasures purchased with the offerings of the poor and tributes of the rich: 'Peter's Pence' in England. A growth in grandeur as successive popes commissioned new quarters for themselves, as well as the acquisition of paintings, frescoes and sculptures from the leading artists of the time, stimulated the puritan in me. 'Thank God for Henry VIII and Thomas Cromwell' I cried (*sotto voce*). But then I had to have a firm word with myself. Weren't/aren't many of my spiritual heroes Roman Catholics?

This gave rise to another line of thought: influences. There was Father Damien, who ministered to lepers; Father Borelli who worked with *scugnizzi*, the street urchins of Naples; Dorothy Day and the Catholic Worker movement in the US; Jean Vanier, the founder of the L'Arche communities; Mother Teresa of Calcutta who worked with the nearly dead and the newly born; the theologians Hans Küng and Matthew Fox, both slapped on the wrist by the Vatican: the latter has now become an Episcopalian; Thomas Merton, hermit and spiritual explorer. There is, of course, Francis of Assisi, everyone's favourite saint, but he lived centuries before the Reformation so can be claimed by both parties.

On the reform side I can line up Albert Schweitzer, a hero since my teenage years; Toyohiko Kagawa, the Japanese Christian leader and social reformer; Dick Shepherd, founder of the Peace Pledge Union; Dietrich Bonhoeffer, the German pastor who died for his involvement in a plot to kill Hitler; Brother Roger Schutz, the founder of the Protestant Taizé Community; and Martin Luther King. To complete this roll of the elect there are the mavericks Tolstoy and George Eliot; the Hindus Gandhi and Vinoba Bhave; and Tich Nhat Hanh, the Vietnamese Buddhist, and the philosophers Wittgenstein and Simone Weil, the latter a young woman of gravity and grace. Between Protestants and Catholics the scales are pretty evenly balanced, a blow to prejudice.

Formulating this list has suggested another possible treatment: thematic. The themes might be: youth work, radical social work, refugees, nonviolence, education, theatre, music, religion and spirituality, and building a house. I have been a curate in Hackney, run a youth centre on Loch Awe, Scotland, been employed as Peace Officer of the Martin Luther King Foundation and Director of Christian Action. I founded Tent City, Refugee Action and the Third Sector Schools Alliance; co-founded with Satish Kumar the London School of Nonviolence and Human Scale Education; I have been chaplain/warden, and am now Chair, of the Othona Community. I was Head of the Small School,

Hartland; Area Dean of Gambella, Ethiopia and project director there; co-founder and conductor of the Hartland Chamber Orchestra; bass player in the folk group the Common Round and a published composer, a somewhat heterogeneous list. Not to be forgotten is 'Vicar of Hartland'. My conversion record, however, rests solely in the transformation of a cowshed and a barn into a house and a holiday let. I have planted a lot of trees.

Looking at the list I wonder how I managed to cram it all in. Certainly here is no clear career path, no progression, merely a series of quick sidesteps. In fact, I have only once been given a job as the result of a formal interview. For most of the rest I have been head-hunted. (Can it have been my head they wanted? Some, I feel, would have treasured my scalp.) So I never planned in advance what I would do but have felt free to respond to whatever came up. As a result I have been presented with some interesting and exciting challenges that I would most certainly have missed had I been pursuing a career plan.

This list does not say an awful lot about who I am, just what I've done.

The Author in the 70s

'Concerned of Hartland' tendered sympathy because I had had to officiate at two cremations and a memorial service 'when you are supposed to be retired.' I don't know where this 'retirement' malarkey has come from. Perhaps a spy has been poking around in our post: my brother-in-law gave me a subscription to *The Oldie* one Christmas, which I thought rather pointed: that might have done it.

The author in his seventies

Then there seems to be the rather odd implication that retirement is a full-time occupation. Colin Hodgetts is a retirement executive. He is so busy developing retirement that he has little time for anything else.

My poor publicity machine has been leaking the message that I have not retired from the race but changed horses, and now my major activity is writing music and my memoirs. Perhaps the composition of music comes across as a pleasurable indulgence earned by a life devoted to teaching and various other activities. Instead of worrying at a Sudoku grid with a glass of claret at my elbow and a log fire at my feet, I have had to venture along twenty-five miles of icy road to take my place in the crematorium queue. Real work!

There is the further implication that being a priest is a job. I, a long-time believer in worker-priests, that is, priests who earn their living in an ordinary job such as labouring in a factory or classroom, or sewing tents, resent this. I have had so many different jobs that my occupation cannot define me. So who am I?

This mirror-gazing brings me to a favourite story told by my friend Keith Walker in school assembly. For eight years he worked on primary health care projects in India. In order to return home for a family gathering he arranged for money to be transferred to the State Bank of India. There was one small problem. The money order was made out to the Bombay, not the nearby Madurai, branch. A thousand miles separates them. The Madurai bank manager had to authorize payment. He examined Keith's passport and the money order: 'How do I know that you are the same Keith Walker as named on the money order?' The passport photo was not enough. Keith explained that he had been working with leprosy sufferers and needed to buy a plane ticket, but to no avail. 'Is there anyone here in Madurai who knows you and who could come to the bank and identify you?' Keith was sure he could find someone to vouch for him. Brother James Kimpton, with whom he was working, had also set up a project called *Boys' Town* where orphan boys trained in metal and woodwork. They had a shop in Madurai. Brother John, the shop manager, agreed to go with Keith to the bank. He introduced himself to the manager and said, 'This is Mr. Keith Walker. He has been doing valuable health care work in India for many years and I can vouch for him.'

An exasperated bank manager exclaimed to Keith, 'You don't seem to understand my problem. I don't know this man either!' He indicated that they should leave. Keith was at a complete loss as to what to do next. He might have to abandon thoughts of returning home. Then, as they walked through the main hall of the bank, one of the tellers, a friend of Brother John, called him over. They chatted and he explained why they were there. 'Give the money order to me. I'll cash it.' And within five minutes Keith was leaving the bank with the wherewithal to fly home.

Such experiences have a long history. Keith reminded me that Nasruddhin Hodja had been similarly challenged. The Hodja went into a bank to draw out some money. 'Can you identify yourself?' demanded the manager. The Hodja pulled a mirror out of his pocket and examined the image carefully. 'That's me alright!' he said.

I wonder when I wake up in the morning, whether I really am the same person who woke up in this bed yesterday morning. And often it is hard to believe that I am. It is not just that a vast number of cells have disappeared, and those of nails and hair have multiplied, but that my body aches in different places and my mind is in another region, whereas the chair, the dressing table and the rug are the same yesterday, today and possibly forever.

The painters Rembrandt and Van Gogh each left a series of self-portraits made over the whole of their working lives. The record is there, and not to be argued with: each painting shows the sameness and the difference. I am both the same and not the same.

I would like to lay out for you some of my values and will do this by exploring one of Van Gogh's works of art. On the wall by the side of my computer is a reproduction of *The Sower with Setting Sun*, which challenges and inspires. (*See the cover image.*) It is my ikon. It tells a story, a significant story, a sacred story, my story. Each element in the picture is a symbol: each stands for something other than itself. We are not faced with just a sun, or just a tree, or just a man sowing but with something much more profound. These symbols take meaning from each other, so the picture is greater than the sum of its parts. Vincent made a number of variations on the theme of a sower scattering seed in front of a setting sun. Especially striking in this version are the bright colours and the unusual composition, in which the tree in the foreground divides the canvas diagonally. There might possibly have been a Japanese influence.

The Sower with Setting Sun works on many levels. It is a reminder of the importance of being in touch with the soil, with sowing seed, tending shoots and harvesting the fruit; in touch with the weather, with natural light, with water. Do I need that reminder? I have just come in from fetching a carton of milk. There is a half moon in a clear sky. Frost crusts the top of the car and dusts the slates of the roof. It is 6 am. We look out on an acre of grassland and an acre of willow, a pond with four white Aylesbury ducks, an escallonia hedge in which a brace of pheasants seem to be setting up home.

Now, with my mug of tea, I may ignore all that and sit for hours glued to the screen. I often need reminding that it is interaction with the natural world, not the worldwide web, which feeds the soul. In a way, the painting feeds it, too, which is why it is an ikon, a visual prayer. But it also reminds me that too often I am an observer, and that I cannot really perceive until I recognize that I am part of what I perceive. I cannot know myself in isolation from that of which I am a part, as a drop in a wave in a sea in an ocean.

The elements that make up the picture: sun, sky, earth, river, tree and sower are strong presences. All except the last have at various times and in various places been worshipped as gods or goddesses. St. Francis of Assisi wrote a song, the Canticle of the Sun, in which Earth is 'mother', the Moon, Stars and Water, 'sister', and the Sun, 'brother'. He did not worship them, or ascribe to them divinity, but he did describe a relationship. They are his family, his mother, brother and sister.

The sun has in many cultures been regarded as a god. His light dispels the darkness; his rays give plants life; he is circular, a symbol of perfection, and hence the halo; he is fire. If we say that the sun is not a god, but suggests God, then we have turned it into a symbol. It is this ability to stand for something else that makes a symbol what it is. The circular mirror is a symbol of the sun; the sun is a symbol of God. In the same way we might say that 'God' is similarly a symbol, for our concept of God is not God but suggests God.

The earth, almost universally regarded as a mother, has also been worshipped as a goddess, one revived and, as Gaia, much called on in these ecological and feminist times. She has two aspects: as mother she is womb and fruitfulness. She is also death, tomb, decay. The seed dies in this tomb, which then becomes a womb to bear the new plant. For Francis, earth is a mother but no goddess, and death is a final end to life and not a preparation for return to life in another form.

The river is a well-accepted symbol of life. In many cultures rivers are holy, the Ganges in India, for instance. She purifies those who bathe in her and she carries away their trash, and their ashes when they die. She brings life to the fields along her banks.

The Jews had to cross a river to find freedom from their oppressors in Egypt. It came to symbolize a hurdle that had to be overcome before entering a new way of living based on a fundamental change in values and attitude. John baptised in the river Jordan as a sign that those who had responded to his preaching were entering a new life. The Jews and Francis did not, however, unlike the Hindus, worship their rivers.

There are German, Austrian and Swiss villages that have a tree at their centre in the leaves of which are the souls of unborn children. Traditionally the tree is the mother of life; and of death, because coffins are made out of her. The tree is also phallic and can therefore be father. Francis worshipped no tree; for him it was the cross to which Christ was affixed.

These symbols make rich resonances for Vincent's picture. And if we follow Francis they will not lead us to worship creation but to worship the divine through creation, a small change in wording leading to a big change in meaning. Francis would have understood that nature – creation – is not God but God's handiwork. It reflects its creator in the way that a pot reflects the potter who made it. That is a traditional position: panentheism. The theologian Sally McFague takes us on from there:

> If the world, the cosmos, is our point of contact with God, the place where we join God to work on a project of mutual importance – the well-being of the body for which we have been given special responsibility – then it is here that we find God, become aware of God. This means that we look at the world...differently: it is the body of God, and hence we revere it, find it special and precious, not as God but as the way God has chosen to be visible, available to us...It is not, then, mere earth or dead matter. (*Models of God*, Fortress Press 1987.)

This is somewhat different from the attitude of the Shinto practitioner who, through sacred rituals, calls on the power of the divinity within tree and wind, sun and river.

Vincent wrote to his brother Theo, 'Paintings have a life of their own that derives entirely from the painter's soul'. Paintings therefore reveal that soul. Vincent was the son of a clergyman and had undertaken some training to become a clergyman himself. For a period he lived like Francis on bread and water among the poorest of the poor to whom he gave his clothes. To Van Gogh, Jesus was the personification par excellence of his own view of the world, it has been said. Surely it was the other way round? Vincent derived his view of the world from the teaching of Jesus. Though he later rejected formal religion he remained in spirit a Christian.

Vincent writes that walking by the sea can do one a lot of good,

> But if one should have a need for something great, something infinite, something one can perceive God in, there is no need to

go far in the quest; it seems to me that I have seen something deeper, more infinite, more eternal than the ocean in the expression in a small child's eyes when it awakens early in the morning and yells or laughs on finding the dear sun shining upon its cradle. (Letter 242.)

Yes, the eyes of a child. For Vincent, nature may reflect God but it does not reveal God; only other human beings can do that. For Christians the one man who has revealed God more fully than any other is Jesus. The key to Vincent's soul is to be found in Christianity. We start with the sower himself – he is, after all, the subject of the work – and for enlightenment turn to a parable, that of the sower.

Is Vincent referring to the parable? There is no sign of the stones, birds or nettles that, we are told, impede the seed's growth. The sower seems to be casting his seed on well ploughed soil. This could be because the story has been translated to the artist's own landscape and time, where the Palestinian practice of sowing first, then ploughing after, is reversed. Casting seed is interpreted as preaching the Word of God. The seed is thrown, the Word is spoken. Vincent felt that the seed he sowed, both as a preacher and as an artist, fell on stony ground. This did not stop him from painting at a furious rate. He, like the sower, scattered generously, an open and a trusting act. The sower/preacher can have no control over what happens to the seed once he has let go of it. It has, however, to be a real letting go. A marvellous crop is hinted at in the young plant that the sower holds in his left hand.

Is Vincent presenting us with an ordinary peasant or is he showing us Christ in everyman? Is he asking us to identify with the sower? He once complained that 'the figures in the pictures of the old masters do not work' (that is, do not do physical labour). Here he paints a man labouring in the fields. The next step is to note his own identification with the peasants. He frequently referred to himself as a worker, as a peasant painter (and not just a painter of peasants). He sent a self-portrait to his mother with a letter in which he described himself as a peasant from Zundert:

...and sometimes I even take to supposing I feel and think like one, except the peasants are of greater use in this world. It is only when they have everything else that people acquire a feeling for pictures, books, and so forth and a need for them. In my own estimation I rank distinctly lower than the peasants. Well, I plough my pictures as they plough their fields.

14

Vincent the artist had to trust that the works that he was creating at such high speed – his seeds – would find an audience: fertile soil. He had to trust the future because he had no buyers and no public during his lifetime. (He did sell one painting.) He had to believe that his paintings were an adequate substitute for the sermons he had given up preaching.

In our picture the right hand that scatters the seed draws attention to itself by being too large for the body. It is open and generous. The bag that holds the seed is like a second heart, open and giving. The sower's stride is purposeful. The sower has no identity: the face is featureless. His dress is not picturesque, as in Millet's treatment of the same subject, which Vincent copied in other drawings and paintings. Perhaps the sower is the painter and perhaps he is everyman. Perhaps he is Jesus. After Jesus' death Mary Magdalene encountered him near the tomb and thought he was the gardener. The sower with no recognisable face, may he not also be Mary's gardener, the one she did not recognize?

There is no reason why the figure shouldn't be Christ and Vincent and Everyman, that is you and me, all at the same time. To understand this is firstly, to be a child of the imagination and secondly, to be a mystic. The outer eye sees a thistle, the inner eye sees a grey old man, said Blake. This is not merely a flight of fancy, the thistle suggesting the grey old man, for he himself is the grey old man. Blake's double vision is about finding a unity. Thistle and poet are one. We do not really see until we recognize that we are part of what we see. The painting reminds us of this unity.

As we build up several layers of meaning so, like a bell, it rings with a thousand overtones. In this picture the fundamental, the basic 'note', is the human figure. All the other objects and their interpretations are overtones or harmonics.

The lower rim of the yellow, life-giving sun, which touches the horizon, overlaps the sower's head and becomes for him a halo. That transforms the figure. Vincent wanted to

> say something comforting, as music is comforting. I want to paint men and women with that something of the eternal which the halo used to symbolize, and which we seek to convey by the actual radiance and vibration of our colouring.

Alongside the field runs a wide blue river and overhead a green sky, both promising fertility and a rich harvest. How can we be so sure, then, that the message is not of annual renewal? Well, across the picture, almost from comer to corner, is a tree, mostly trunk, and within Christianity the tree means the cross. The cross is a dead tree. This is a living tree, with leaf and blossom showing. In medieval imagery Christ was sometimes called the Apple Tree and was painted hanging on a living tree, the tree of knowledge from the Garden of Eden. The tree, alive, speaks not just of death but of resurrection, of a new life.

The progress of the human being is from birth to death. That is our journey through time. After death time ceases, and in Judaism, Christianity and Islam, there is no return into time. Alongside our time-dominated world, is another, that of eternity. For the Christian, 'resurrection' is the path or gateway between this world, in which death holds sway, to another which is eternity.

This beggars the imagination. Vincent wrote to his sister that we cannot suppose that white salad grubs that change into cockchafers have any tenable ideas about the nature of their future life as cockchafers. Similarly, 'I have little confidence in the correctness of our human concepts of a future life.' The task for the salad grub is 'to eat salad roots in the very interest of their higher development. In the same way I think that a painter ought to paint pictures; possibly something else may come after that...'

Vincent's belief that we cannot live with one eye on heaven is correct. We have to concentrate on the task in hand, on life itself. We can have no idea of what is in store for us, either after death or even before it.

Resurrection is not renewal, rebirth, revival or restoration because these words all mean a new cycle of time, 'and are in the last analysis the opposite of resurrection' (Frye). 'Next' is also a time word, and the next life would logically be the life that follows this one. But we are told that we can begin to live the resurrection life now, so it is in fact a life that lies alongside our ordinary, everyday life. Most talk about eternity is time bound. In the phrase 'life after death' the word 'after' is a time word. The phrase 'you can't take it with you' implies space. But eternity is beyond time and space. Sometimes it is described as a state of continuous peace and rest, metaphors drawn from death, hardly suitable for defining a state genuinely beyond life. These difficulties with language show how hard we have to work to get a proper appreciation of the concept of eternity. The paradox of eternity is precisely expressed by the philosopher Wittgenstein: 'If we take eternity to mean not infinite temporal duration but timelessness, then eternal life belongs to those who live in the present.' (Proposition 6.4311).

Let us return to our painting. The tree, I have said, represents the cross, death, and because it is alive, also resurrection, the movement from the world of time to the state of eternity. It also crosses out any cyclical suggestion we might get from other features of the painting. The strength of the tree statement is in its size. It covers between a fifth and a quarter of the surface area of the canvas, and nothing could be more discouraging of any pagan meaning.

Vincent wrote that, in a picture, he wanted to say something comforting, as music is comforting. For him the enormous sun – like his sunflowers – is not the god Helios but fire, such a fire as Pascal described in his account of his transforming mystical experience. It symbolized the need to transcend the self, to transcend the drabness of reality. And he went to great and costly lengths to do this. 'Instead of eating sufficiently and regularly I kept myself going (they said) with coffee and alcohol. I admit it; but in order to achieve that noble shade of yellow I achieved last summer I simply had to give myself quite a boost.'

The paintings produced at such cost are, as he hoped, a source of inspiration and comfort to those who view them. This painting suggests words that the prophet Isaiah spoke to the people in Jerusalem:

You shall weep no more.
For he will be gracious to you when he hears your cry;
and when he hears he will answer you.
Then he will send rain for the seed which you will sow in the ground,
and the wheat, fruit of the soil, will be rich and plentiful…

And on every lofty mountain and on every high hill
there will be streams running with water.
The moonlight will be as bright as sunshine,
and the sun will shine seven times more brightly,
giving seven days' light in one, on the day when
the Lord binds up the bruises of his people
and heals the wounds which his blows have inflicted.

(Isaiah 30: 19 20, 23, 25 26; JB Phillips)

As Isaiah comforts his listeners, including the wounded artist, so the artist, too, comforts us. Vincent manages to be both exhilarating and comforting because he presents us with a vision. It is a vision drawn from nature. Vincent could not paint from the imagination. The few times he wanted to paint a Biblical scene he reworked a picture of Rembrandt or Delacroix. He needed a landscape or a sitter. What he paints is a product of his communion with his subject.

Magnificent though this achievement of Vincent's is, art can never be a substitute for life itself. He acknowledged this when he described Christ living serenely as 'a greater artist than all other artists, despising marble and clay as well as colour, working in living flesh.' In the same letter to Emile Bernard he wrote, 'Christ alone of all the philosophers, Magi, etc. has affirmed, as a principal certainty, eternal life, the infinity of time, the nothingness of death, the necessity and the raison d'être of serenity and devotion.' We should therefore not be surprised to find references to these things in *The Sower* which challenges us to transcend our limitations and to live according to the teachings of the Gospel – work is love made visible – and to look for God in other people's eyes.

> Life is greater than all art. I would go even further and declare that the man whose life comes nearest to perfection is the greatest artist; for what is art without the sure foundation and framework of a noble life? …Jesus was, to my mind, a supreme artist because he saw and expressed Truth. (Gandhi)

In this consideration of Vincent's painting I have set out my inner story and indicated the source of my values, values that make me seem a stranger in a foreign land, for one who rates compassion above self-interest, who believes that small is beautiful and that land belongs to the Lord only, possession being nine-tenths theft, can never feel comfortably at home in today's world. I am also uncomfortable with Christianity in its official, creedal and institutional forms. That is why I have such sympathy for Rembrandt and Van Gogh, both of whom were greatly inspired by the Bible and yet at odds with Dutch Calvinism and the society in which they lived.

If I wanted a second icon it would be *The Return of the Prodigal Son* by Rembrandt, which I have had the good fortune to contemplate in the Hermitage, St Petersburg, and which, according to Kenneth Clark, could be the greatest picture ever painted. (*Cf. wiki*) The Father clasps his son, who has wasted his inheritance on wild living, to his breast. All is forgiven. 'Forgiveness' is the theme of many of Rembrandt's drawings, etchings and oils, evidence of 'his all-embracing, all-forgiving love of his fellow men.'

Jesus Preaching Forgiveness is also the subject of one of Rembrandt's most popular prints. Implicit in this scene is a denial that in his Crucifixion Jesus 'paid the price for sin', for he tells this story of a father's forgiveness, and assures the sick and sinners that they are forgiven as part of his ministry. I'll expand on this later.

These artists, writers, musicians, and others with a spiritual take on life, feed and encourage me. Science, on the other hand, hits a road block. It has been said that, even though every human being before us has died, it cannot be proved scientifically that I will die. Nevertheless, I know that I will die, a certainty that comes from an understanding that goes beyond the limits of science. We are not machines. 'We feel that even when all possible scientific questions have been answered, the problems of life remain completely untouched. Of course there are then no questions left, and this itself is the answer.' (Wittgenstein)

In a BBC interview near the end of his life the conductor Sir Colin Davies was asked if he was a believer. He replied that he didn't go to church but that he was fully 'into' the great religious opuses that he conducted. He added that their composers – Mozart, Beethoven, Berlioz, and Verdi – were not conventional Christians. He himself was not afraid of death, had no idea what came after, and he read the Bible regularly.

I reported with approval Van Gogh's belief that God is to be found in the eyes of a child. Here is another take on the Almighty: 'God never appears to you in person, always in action.'

Wittgenstein quotes words that JS Bach wrote on the title page of his *Orgelbüchlein:* 'To the glory of the most high God, and that my neighbour may be benefited thereby'. 'That is what I would have liked to say about my work' added Wittgenstein. Who can better that?

Chapter Two

Growing up in Guernsey

IF THERE IS ONE THEME running through my growing-up days it is the sea. Water surrounded us. The sea I relish in all its modes: seamless and relaxed, like float glass under an empty sky, or reflecting the grey stratus that looms over us, dimpled and lustrous like pummelled pewter. Victor Hugo, of a walk along the shore, writes: 'Here everything cradles, reassures and caresses. No more shadows in my heart; no more bitter cares. An ineffable peace unceasingly rises and descends from the deep azure of my soul to the deep azure of the sea.' Verses from Psalm 42 picture the sea changing our mood:

> I am sunk in such deep despair
> I will call you to mind,
> so I walk by the storm-rent shore
> and remember your might;
> in the water's roar deep calls deep
> and on me you waves break.

This destructive energy, a reminder that we are frail and vulnerable, I also enjoy. There are two sides to water: it is gentle enough to clean the delicate skin of a baby; powerful enough to reduce granite to gravel, sandstone to sand. Tranquil, it can reflect a face; whipped up, it can bring down cliffs. I stand above Hartland Quay and lean into a winter wind that whips waves into a cataclysmic frenzy and hurls them against the rocks, flinging spray high up the cliff face and shrouding its spectacular *chevron*-shaped folds.

Rambling along the North Devon coastal path or the peninsula lanes, my stomping ground for over thirty years now, I travel each day hand-in-glove with nature which, as Francis Bacon pointed out, 'cannot be commanded except by being obeyed'. It lures us outdoors; it confines us within.

For me, to sit on a shingle shore and listen to the waves as they gently break, running a little way up the beach, then turning tail and retreating, is to listen to a breathing of the natural world and by no means a reminder of 'the turbid ebb and flow of human misery', as Matthew Arnold would have it. To breathe with breaking waves is a rewarding form of meditation.

From the window of my teenager's bedroom in Cambridge Park, Guernsey – four floors up – I could enjoy a view of ships and boats docked or anchored in St Peter Port harbour. Beyond Castle Cornet and the lighthouse lie the sea lanes to Herm, Jethou Sark and Jersey, horizon islands firmly anchored in shifting waters. These routes I frequently travelled in my teenage years.

These are Channel Islands, les Îles de la Manche or les Îles Anglo-Normandes, the latter a reminder that we proud Channel Islanders were the last people to conquer England, as in our forebears' time we were part of the Duchy of Normandy. That is why the law is written in a form of French that is closer to that of Quebec than to that of present day Paris. Victor Hugo noted that 'the peasant of Sark speaks the language of Louis XIV.'

Jo di e dirai ke jo sui
Hodgetts de l'isle de Gersui

(I say and will say that I am / Hodgetts from the island of Jersey.)

Jersey is the largest of the islands, and there my father and I were born, I on April 15th 1940, and he some thirty-one years earlier. I was a late birthday present for my mother, and I sometimes wonder whether they had a plan that missed her anniversary by two days. There is no one now to ask.

Early years were lived out in a Jersey that led a dim half-life under German occupation for, on July 2nd 1940, when I was only ten weeks old, we were invaded. I remember little of that time, just a scattering of events with high emotional content.

One hot and humid summer's day Father led the Hodgetts family to St Clement's Bay, not far from Montrose, our house, to a beach that, being rocky, was unsuitable as a landing place for the

British enemy and so had not been mined – there were 67,000 mines peppering other parts of the island's coast. Bathing was *verboten*, and as we towelled ourselves down a squad of German soldiers descended, confiscating my parents' identity cards. There was consternation that evening over the possible penalty that might have to be paid, but next morning my parents were able to reclaim their cards with no more than a warning of 'dire consequences' should there be a repeat performance. No more sand and sea for a good while.

I have a chit from the *Standortkommandanturin*, St Helier, permitting my father to be out after curfew in order to telephone for medical aid for his wife valid from March 12th to the 22nd, 1942. That would be for the birth of my sister, Vivien Rosemary, who lustily announced her arrival on the St Patrick's Day.

There was the night we were awoken by the roar of an aero-engine as a German plane, trailing flames, passed just yards over our house and crashed in a field opposite. The following morning my father took me, hand-in-hand, to gloat quietly over the wreckage, relieved that we still had a roof over our four heads. We did not know at the time what had happened to the pilot and crew. That I have since discovered.

> At about 3:30 am on 21st June, 1944, a low-flying German bomber was hit and set on fire by flak from a German ship off the harbour. It sped over the south coast and crashed in a field opposite Brig-y-don, Samarès, the blazing machine lighting up the whole island. For a long time after the crash ammunition exploded, but some bombs were flung clear and were disposed of during the day. Fortunately no-one was injured among the civil population, but the whole crew of five perished – four on the spot and the fifth later in hospital. One house was slightly damaged and the engine of the bomber bounced and came to rest between two houses only 12 feet apart. During the day the wreckage was visited by scores of people but they were chased off by sentries who fired warning shots where verbal warnings were not effective. (The German Occupation of Jersey, *The Evening Post*, 1945)

My father, christened Percy Osmont, names his offspring revealed rather reluctantly, worked for Barclays Bank, or half-worked as the branch was open for only three days a week, business being rather scarce. The Manager, like many of those who had been born in England, fled from an undefended island before the Germans invaded. My father was given charge of the bank keys (but not the

Bank). In the flat above the office the Germans housed French prostitutes from whom he had to collect the rent. When Vivien learnt of this, many years later, she teased him mercilessly about his running a whorehouse.

Those living in Jersey of English birth who had not fled before the invasion, my Grandpa and Grandma Langley among them, were ordered to appear at the harbour for deportation to concentration camps in France. Grandpa knew that they always called more people than the boat could carry, so each day he and Grandma would appear a little late and thus, at the rear of the queue, they avoided deportation. They suffered no ill-consequences because they had turned up. The time came when the operation had to be abandoned, the journey having become too dangerous. So G'pa continued to run Donaldson's, his music shop, with German soldiers his main customers.

Grandpa Hodgetts, also a Percy, who had been born in Birmingham, spent three weeks hidden in a farm loft to avoid deportation.

G'ma & G'pa Hodgetts

My mother's brother John, then still a teenager, stole a fishing boat and escaped to England where, lying about his age, he joined the army. The downside of his departure was that he had deprived a fisherman of his livelihood. As a consequence, such daring deeds were not lauded by all.

Food was an all-consuming obsession. There were calamities. Some joints of pig, which we had put in salt to preserve them, became disgustingly slimy. Cousin Reggie's uncle lost sixty pigs, hidden from the Germans in a sound-proofed barn, in a fire. (Shades of Lamb's *Essays of Elia*, the 'Dissertation on Roast Pig'.) A crop of our potatoes was another disaster for they turned to mush when they were destined to become flour.

In the early years of the Occupation food was brought by ship from France but it was always severely rationed. Red wine, though, was often freely available, probably because there were hectolitres more than the French themselves could consume.

Fuel was in short supply and bakeries acted as communal bakehouses. The day Father went to collect one of our precious dishes only to find that it had been stolen ended in anger, despair and tears. He jotted down eight-course menus, like those in Mrs Beeton, on the backs of envelopes, a consoling dream.

German soldiers were no better off than us food-wise. Caught raiding gardens they could be severely punished. Towards the end of the war, with France cut off, starvation hit. The Red Cross offered food parcels which, in September 1944, Churchill refused to authorise as he was not going to feed enemy troops and thought they might be induced to surrender if they were unable to feed the general population. Eventually he gave in to growing pressure and we received boxes of Commonwealth delights which arrived from Lisbon on the most excellent ship the *Vega* on the last day of 1944. Churchill underestimated the enemy. The Germans supervised distribution of the parcels without laying hands on one. In all, the *Vega* brought to the islands 456,264 standard food parcels in five shipments.

Ours came from Canada and contained 6oz chocolate, 20 biscuits, 4oz tea, 20oz butter, 6oz sugar, 2oz milk powder, 16oz marmalade, 14oz corned beef, 13oz ham or pork, 10oz salmon, 5oz sardines, 8oz raisins, 6oz prunes, 4oz cheese, 3oz soap, salt and pepper. I have a vague memory of cheese and chocolate in tins.

There is surprise today that parcels sent to meet health needs should also contain cigarettes. Priorities were rather different then. Grandpa Hodgetts cultivated a thirty perch plot (about 1,350 sq. metres) of which five perch were planted with potatoes and twenty-five with tobacco which he cured for use in his pipe. There were no matches and no lighter fuel. A friend of his in the motor trade came up with the idea of using a four-cylinder impulse magneto which, by joining all the leads, produced a long spark that could ignite a wick. Through a hole in the lid of a tin a wick of window sash cord protruded. The fuel in the tin was oil: engine oil, or fish oil, or chicken fat, and sometimes all three. The noxious odours that emerged from pipe and tin stirred up in Grandma a degree of righteous wrath.

'Liberation' for me meant loaves anaemic in appearance and taste. Bread made with the newly imported bleached flour had the texture of cotton wool. Tantrums failed to bring back the grey loaves.

Comfort food in post-war years was milk-soaked bread sprinkled with sugar. Better yet was cream skimmed from the rich yellow milk that was delivered daily into the can at the door, and then scalded to prevent it turning sour. Less relished by Viv and me was our dessert spoon of 'strengthening medicine', the daily dose of cod liver oil and malt.. But the frequently recounted food story was that, at one Sunday lunch at the Langley house, with numerous aunts and uncles at table, I had asked for 'more meat bampa', he being a master of the very thin slice, and I, one who could not be fooled. For once my argumentative relatives fell silent. In the war just past there was never enough, and certainly never 'more'.

We grew fruit. We probably grew vegetables but I can discover no trace of them in the memory bank. Montrose, our house in Jersey, was detached with a veranda along the front and a conservatory against the side wall to the left. I remember the apple trees, my favourite bearing large, yellow and orange striped fruit. With the aid of a ladder we harvested black cherries from a tree in front of the house. Their juice stained tongue, lips and fingers – I really was red in tooth and claw. Our neighbours on the St Helier side, the Bowns, grew golden cherries in even greater abundance. 'Cherry Ripe' became a favourite song. Some years later I won a prize singing it at a Saturday afternoon talent competition in the great 'monstrous and unsightly' glass theatre in Candie Gardens, Guernsey. I greatly surprised my mother, who could hear the song from our house. 'I'm sure that's Colin!' she exclaimed to my father. The Beatles performed there on August 8th 1963 so I was in classy company.

Before the war my mother had had a maid, but that could no longer be afforded. After the war housework was full-on and full-time for her. She could well have been the model for the 'Darling' of 'Dashing Away with the Smoothing Iron'. Monday morning spent boiling clothes in the copper, putting them through the wringer – I tried to assist but even on tiptoe had to let go of the handle before it reached the apex of its revolution – hanging the clothes out on the line. Ironing lasted most of Tuesday, that is, if Monday had been a good drying day, Mother sitting on her nursing chair with a heavy, cloth-covered board supported on the seats of two dining chairs. I loved the sweet smell of freshly laundered sheets, still warm from the iron.

Then there was the sweeping of floors and carpets with the Ewbank, the sewing of dresses for herself and Vivien, by hand in preference to pedalling the sewing machine, a treadle Singer inherited from her mother that I used for perforating paper in the manufacture of stamps; the knitting of jumpers for the whole family – in later years she would knit a guernsey for each of us in turn – the darning of socks and stockings, and the cooking of three meals a day for four, and then five of us. For much of my youth we had no fridge and no washing machine. We did eventually acquire a Goblin, predecessor of the Hoover.

I was ever willing to give a helping hand but my efforts were not always appreciated. When I was about five or six I overheard my parents discussing the painting of a small greenhouse. I sought out a brush and, with a tin of tar, began the work. My efforts were not welcome and I was locked in my room. Outside my window there was a small ledge, part of the veranda that ran along the front of the house. That night I shuffled along the ledge and peered in at my parents' window, tapping on it. Agitation and concern! I was never locked in my room again.

Toys held little attraction and, because of the Occupation, there were few. (It can be quite comforting to paint a picture of deprivation!) Real hammers and saws were a different matter, tools of invention and experiment. I invented a pulley. I was about to test it by lowering Vivien from a first floor window when my mother intervened and halted the trial. She was not of a scientific bent. She did not appreciate that as much can be learnt from an experiment that fails as from one that succeeds.

Viv, two years my junior, had long golden hair in which our mother took great delight. But the morning ritual of weaving it into two plaits was resisted with ferocious energy. We were at my grandparents' house, 40 David Place, St Helier, the adults inhabiting a world of their own and ignorant of the third generation's boredom. It was decided between Viv and me that we could use the time profitably and relieve her of her morning misery. So, hidden behind the upright piano, and with a pair of kitchen scissors, I hacked off her plaits. Adult reaction was quite disproportionate. After all, hair grows again.

My sister's turn at hair styling came many years later. My father, like many baldies, used to sweep a few strands of hair from left ear to right ear as an alternative to painting rabbits on his bald patch – from a distance they might be mistaken for hares – one of his feeble jokes. These strands were difficult to keep in place, but that was not the reason Viv scorned them. He was 'cheating'. She would make an honest man of him. So as he napped after lunch she snipped off the offending hairs. He was furious. Did he fear not being recognized when he returned to the office? He soon found the new style to be far less troublesome, especially when the wind blew.

When I was six, and before we moved to Guernsey, I was sent to school: Victoria College. Fortunately I was there for only a year.

Two punishments marked both that short period and me. I, dawdling and dreaming, was beaten on the backside with a gym shoe for failing to get to my Grandma's house for lunch. Secondly, a psychological bruise: I was told off in front of the whole school for skipping down the hill. I had merely been expressing happiness, like the small boy in *Jour de Fête* following the trailer that has the heads of merry-go-round horses peering over the back. 'Only girls skip!' barked the Headmaster in front of an assembly that included ten-year-old cousin Reggie. I thus acquired the nickname 'Hoppy'. Hoppy Hodgetts. I would have preferred the sobriquet 'Skipper' as more in keeping with my self-image. What seems rather odd is that we left Jersey for Guernsey when I was seven but did not leave the nickname behind.

SARNIA CHERIE

'Sarnia', Guernsey's Latin name, was beautiful when my father and I first went there in 1947. Now, more than fifty years later, it has been uglified by money and the internal combustion engine. My brother David, born that year, returned to the island and is a person of some consequence. I have no desire to return. To walk up the Grange is to risk death by colourless, odourless, and tasteless, but highly toxic, carbon monoxide and other exhaust fumes.

Father and I flew to the island leaving three Hodgetts behind. We took up digs with a family called Le Page, around the corner from Elizabeth College, until Father found a house to rent, 'Greenways' in Collins Road, just off the Rohais. Then Mother, Vivien and David joined us.

'Greenways' had a large garden. We kept chickens and destroyed weeds with a flame-thrower. There was a proper greenhouse, not unusual in an island half-covered by glass, which leant against a high garden wall. With the help of another Le Page, who lived opposite and was the father and grandfather of those with whom we had boarded, we grew tomatoes for export to supplement the miserly remuneration Father received from Barclays. Guernsey needed glasshouses for growing tomatoes and flowers as it slopes to the North and is cooler than Jersey, which faces South in deference to its Maker who is, of course, a Jerseyman.

Most of the greenhouses were heated through cast iron pipes, though ours was not, and at the end of the growing season, to combat verticillium wilt, the soil was sterilised with steam from great boilers that were lugged from vinery to vinery. ('Vineries' because, before the tomatoes, there had been grapes.)

There were three factors in the decline of the industry: an increase in the price of oil, more expensive train transport and Dutch government subsidies to Dutch growers. Now the island's main crop is Money, creating a corrosive dependency on fickle international banks and providing lucrative employment for a legion of lawyers.

'Greenways' was detached and grey. There was a modest stone building, too small for a car, on the road. In it Dad garaged his autocycle, a James if I remember rightly. The building had a small dusty loft in which I tried to curry favour with the local lads by feeding them fags lifted from jacket pockets. It lasted only a few weeks because my crime was discovered and precautions taken. I fell out of favour with this loose gang one Christmas. The lads were carol singing in an unmusical way. The bathroom window was immediately above the front door. Through it I, as a joke, poured water on them. For some time I emerged from the house with trepidation, keeping off the streets as much as possible to avoid being beaten up. Some jokes have a rather short lifespan.

The time came when, with the Bank's help, Father could afford to buy a house. We moved into the terrace at Cambridge Park, in front of us a large expanse of grass, with a kids play area and sports facilities. Next door to the right of us lived Colonel Forte. He was married to a Siamese princess whom he had left behind in her native land. At the mere hint of sun the colonel would take to his chair in the garden in the shortest of shorts to acquire the darkest of tans. He had a grown-up son who was 'charming and useless', as the neighbourhood expressed it. To the left was a Baptist minister who made jokes by enumerating chapter and verse. I never got the reference but I laughed just the same.

Further down the road towards Castle Carey, in two of the large detached houses, lived Professor Callander, a Canadian pacifist and author of *The Athenian Empire and the British*, and Mrs Mitchell who had spent most of her life in India as an army wife, surviving two husbands. I frequently visited her for interesting reminiscences of an age of Empire that, much to Prof Callander's delight, had passed, taking tea poured into fine china cups from a silver pot set on a silver tray, or occasionally a sherry and a biscuit, both brought to us by Florence, her fearsome French maid. Learning from the school chaplain, Fred Pike, of my interest in music Mrs Mitchell presented me with a stereo gramophone and a top-rate clarinet despite not being at all musical herself.

Our garden at the rear of the house was on two levels. Across the road from the back gate was the rear entrance to Candie Gardens. I wandered through the flower beds on my way to school, intrigued by the Ginkgo biloba tree, a living fossil, studiously ignoring a statue of Queen Victoria in Imperial regalia but giving a friendly nod to Jean Boucher's statue of Victor Hugo, the stone author leaning into the wind, coat and scarf flying. He wrote *Les Miserables* and *Les Travailleurs de la mer* while in exile in Guernsey. He dedicated the latter work to

> the Rock of hospitality and Liberty,
> to that portion of old Norman ground
> inhabited by
> that Noble Little Nation of the Sea,
> to the island of Guernsey,
> Severe yet Kind, my Present Asylum,
> Perhaps my Tomb.

There certainly was some 'severity' on the part of his hosts. Now he has a celebratory statue but on his arrival he, having been thrown out of Jersey, received a rather cool reception. According to Henri Boland (*Les Iles de la Manche*, 1904) 'Their new guest was a great poet, it went without saying, but he was a revolutionary as well, and what is more, a freethinker, a terrible crime in the minds of a population of religious near-fanatics, severe and Presbyterian.' A few extended the hand of friendship. Relations were getting more positive, a little Guernsey circle was even forming around the poet when, one night at the theatre, he had the unfortunate idea of refusing to get up for the National Anthem. That did it. At the time of his funeral an Anglican minister proclaimed in a sermon that he was astonished that such homage should be paid to a man who could not even write French!

SEASCAPE

Growing up in Guernsey, the second largest of the Channel Islands, the church and music competed with the sea for my attention. Let us return to the sea; church and music can come later.

Guernsey was visited regularly by ships of the Royal Navy. The occasional aircraft carrier lay at anchor in the roadstead outside St Peter Port harbour. Smaller RN vessels tied up at the jetty. Visits were encouraged and I explored many a warship. I read CS Forester. Movies about ships in wartime were on the radar: *The Cruel Sea* and *Above Us the Waves*, and I imagined myself clad in duffel coat on the bridge of a corvette such as the *Compass Rose* getting drenched as we ploughed into two-storey high waves.

Pennies were saved for the purchase of a chart of local waters. The call of the sea was full-throated, and I would have had the Royal Naval College at Dartmouth in my sights had I not been by nature a pacifist. The merchant service might have been an option but the uniforms were drab and the red ensign, often grimed, no match for the sparkling white one. Was the uniform really the attraction?

There was a trace of navy in our blood. My grandfather's middle name was Le Hardy, and the Captain Hardy who kissed Nelson as the latter lay dying had a place somewhere in our ancestry. The good captain was a descendent of Clément Le Hardy, one-time Bailiff and Lieut.-Governor of Jersey.

Hours were frittered away hanging around St Peter Port harbour. Mail boats arrived, breaking their passage to or from Jersey. Smart yachts dropped anchor in the lee of Castle Cornet, there not being sufficient demand yet for a marina, and visitors pottered around in hired rowing boats. From time to time a fishing trawler would land its catch, but the most regular activity was generated by the harbour launches that plied between Guernsey and Herm, a small island just three miles to the West. The Gulf Stream washes up exotic shells on one of Herm's beaches and its waters are the warmest in the islands. Hundreds are ferried to it daily in packets of about sixty. They return the colour of boiled lobster.

The largest of the vessels making this journey was the *Martha Gunn*, owned by Captain Bonnie Newton. It was painted a reddish-purple and flew the Jolly Roger, quite attractive to a thirteen-year-old boy. The buccaneering, ginger-bearded mariner was physically quite short and well-known as a sailor, fisherman and small-time smuggler, with an unsurpassed knowledge of the waters around Guernsey and Alderney. Piracy was in Bonnie's blood though, as German and Italian ships had been fair game during the war, he was decorated for attacking them by the British, French and Italian governments.

Bonnie, standing at the top of the pier steps on which passengers for Herm were queuing to board the *Martha Gunn*, was bellowing obscenities to his son, John, skipper of the boat below. Some of the queue smiled, others cringed. I screwed up enough courage to ask if I could be taken on as an unpaid member of the crew. I was surprised at how gently and positively he responded.

31

During the twenty-minute voyage I entertained small groups of passengers with a potted history of the islands, such as a royalist Castle Cornet training its cannons on a parliamentarian island, a stand-off that lasted nine years. The tips I received kept me in soft drinks, cakes and the occasional book. For one leg of the journey we would usually be empty so there was plenty of opportunity to read, if, that is, I had not had bestowed on me the coveted honour of steering the vessel.

I moved on to other Herm boats. They rode on their anchors in the middle of the harbour. First thing in the morning I would haul in the dinghy and scull out to the launch – to scull is to describe a figure-of-eight pattern over the stern with a single oar – tie the dinghy to the buoy, start the engine, cast off and make for the quay. There I would sluice down the benches and deck, polish the brass and neatly coil the ropes. If we were early in the roster we might make two morning trips to Herm. Otherwise it was a single return journey before lunch and usually two in the afternoon, not a strenuous life.

Until I left full-time education my main holiday job was on the boats. That was as near to heaven as I could get. I worked with Herbie Renouf on the *Maywood.* He decided I should gain an engineer's certificate, which meant that I could be paid as the official second crew member. If a diesel engine fails at sea there is little that can be done, unless it is merely a matter of bleeding the fuel system. Nevertheless, I'm sure Herbie doubted my ability to master the beast and suspect that he gave the inspector who tested me a backhander. It didn't matter anyway as we never had to deal with engine failure in my time on the boats. A fouled propeller was the most common challenge we faced, and that could usually be sorted with the boat hook. Even today the smell of diesel is as potent as Chanel No. 5.

Two fishmonger brothers, the Taylors, owned the *Highland Laddie* which was skippered by Reuben Martell. Like most of the Herm boat owners they had their fingers in several profitable pies other than fish. They took me on.

We were one of the few boats to have Sark as a regular run. We went there each Monday in the tourist season to unload the *Brittany*, a British Rail ferry boat from Jersey that was too big to dock in Sark's small harbour. As we were also available for private hire, a market pretty well cornered by the Taylor brothers, we went much more frequently. For Herm we could carry about 70 passengers but on the Sark run our licence restricted us to twelve.

Sark was a feudal jewel. To prevent it from becoming a haven for pirates Queen Elizabeth I granted the island to Helier de Carteret in 1565 on condition that forty families occupy it. Government was, and until the millennium, remained feudal. Then the Barclay brothers, bullies extraordinaire, set about dismantling this system of government. Even the doctor moved away from the island as a consequence of their machinations.

A fading and probably unrepeatable memory is of the friendly hospitality that Reuben and I enjoyed on an island that moved at a feudal pace.

> Glens that know the dove and fells that hear the lark
> Fill with joy the rapturous island, as an ark
> Full of spicery wrought from herb and flower and tree.
> None would dream that grief even here may disembark
> On the wrathful woeful marge of earth and sea.

(Swinburne, from *A Ballad of Sark*)

Reuben was fun to work with. He gave the appearance, with his grey, knitted pullover under a drooping and stained navy blue jacket and his baggy grey trousers, of being a staid Guernsey grower or fisherman. That was deceptive for ours was the only harbour launch to have a two-way radio. Reuben's ears were attuned to SOS messages. He possessed a professional cine camera with which he recorded newsworthy events. As soon as there was trouble – news of fresh disasters – we would land our passengers with all due haste and he would race to the scene of action to film it. If it was at sea he would take his place as a member of the lifeboat crew. Reels were rushed to the airport to be despatched to the BBC.

The *Highland Laddie* was often out in bad weather while the crews of other harbour launches were relaxing in the Quay Café. Only the most severe of storms kept us in port. One Sark trip was through dense fog: I had to lean over the bow rock-spotting as we approached the island.

To be at sea nearly every day for hours at a time may well have had an effect on my character. There can be no rushing. These were not speed boats, for we made about eight knots and wind and waves could hinder progress. Impatience would have been a waste of energy. Activity was determined by weather over

33

which we had no control. I do not get as exasperated as some contemporaries do when well-laid plans are driven off course by the unpredictable. Wind and water kept the complexion fresh and the sun bleached my hair, already fair.

To supplement my income from the boats I spent my evenings as a waiter at *Le Nautique*, an upmarket restaurant overlooking the harbour that specialised in 'surf and turf', opened by a pharmacist. Two Italian waiters cooked at table, mostly steaks in a variety of sauces, and crêpes suzette. These were flambéed – brandy for the steaks, Grand Marnier for the crêpes– with great panache. They also conjured the skins off oranges and pears.

The kitchen was ruled by a Dutch chef whom these Italian prima donnas held in low regard, shouting abuse at him and denigrating his dishes to the clientèle, though many punters ignored these put-downs and ordered his lobster thermidor or some crab concoction. The pair could also be rude to customers: 'I will not cook for you. I am not happy with your face' was said to one unfortunate young lady. I was merely the hand that fed them their ingredients and removed the dirty dishes, though the time did come when I was allowed to prepare simple desserts such as banana split. The really sore point was the extremely meagre portion of pooled tips that I was given.

As a boy scout I had taken my cook's badge, consequent on a short course with a home economics teacher. She supervised our making, among other things, of éclairs and Cornish pasties. My experience at *Le Nautique* enabled me to add gourmet dishes to my growing repertoire. This was important compensation for the sharp rebuke I once received from the scout master, Mr Cooper, when away at camp for maintaining too energetic a fire under the dixie and burning the stew, treat of the week, which established me as varmint of the month. It never made a verse in 'The Quartermaster's Stores', probably because budding librettists failed to find a suitable rhyme for 'Hodgetts'.

Scouting was enjoyable. We met every Saturday evening in an underground bunker from which the Germans had given radio cover to the North Atlantic. It was somewhat damp, and every week one patrol was put on ventilation duty, for the premises were equipped with an enormous wind machine that had two pairs of handles. We built up quite a sweat keeping the air sweet.

There was plenty of space. Each patrol had its own room and storage was more than adequate for the heavy khaki tents, their cumbersome poles, sacks of pegs, blackened dixies and the field stove that we carted with us when we went camping, once near Southampton and once in Normandy. In France we were given wine with our cheese and baguette even though we were well under-age by Guernsey standards. It was our first experience of a schoolmaster stretching the rules, a precedent that I have religiously followed.

Advert for bob-a-job week

When we arrived at our Brittany camp site a local man, gesticulating wildly, shouted '*Vipres! Vipres!*' We armed ourselves with sticks in case we met with a snake. No one did. Afterwards Grandma Hodgetts chuckled. In the local lingo 'vipres' means 'wasps', not 'vipers'. There were plenty of those.

We went as a family on a camping holiday to Herm in 1948, the only away holiday we enjoyed together. Otherwise we spent summer afternoons on sandy beaches, Grandes Rocques and Vazon being the favourites, though not the latter when cars raced on it. Viv absented herself whenever she could, in part because it was uncool to be seen out with parents, especially if they had varicose veins, and in part because she wanted to be out with the pack hunting down boys.

In those pre-teenage days I wandered happily among rock pools, squatting to admire delicate, miniature universes, or practising goat-like bounds from boulder to boulder that would stand me in good stead when jumping from a boat with a rope in a desperate leap aimed at impressing the fair sex. I sprinkled salt on keyholes in the sand to tempt razor fish to reveal themselves; I popped bladder wrack, or searched with Dad for ormers among the rocks at low spring tide. In Australia ormers are known as abalone, but there they are bigger. Ours are the size and shape of a large ear. The shells have a mother-of-pearl interior. When nearly everyone smoked they did service as ashtrays and were sometimes used to decorate garden walls. We prised them from the rocks with a hook and, when we got them home, beat the hell out of them with a rolling pin. They were fried and then stewed for hours in onions and parsley to a palatable rubberiness.

I was a bit of a loner, perhaps because my main interests were not shared by any of my school fellows, until girls entered the picture in my upper teens, that is. Fine days would find me taking off on my bike. On one of these outings I cycled to the bathing pools – there are three in a row south of the harbour – and turned round at the end, where the tunnel, constructed by the Germans and which now houses an aquarium, lies. I cannot remember exactly how old I was: ten or eleven I believe. A man with light skin, sandy hair and freckles approached me and asked if I would like to earn half-a-crown, a prospect I could not ignore (my pocket money was a penny for each year of my age). He led me up to the plantation of trees, shrubs and flowers that lies between the road and the cliff. We sat on the ground. He took from his pocket a small bottle of oil, unbuttoned his flies and began to anoint his penis which tumesced in a way I had not seen before. I was innocent of his intentions and sat calmly by. Perhaps it was my trust that saved me, for he could not continue. I got my half-a-crown. I told no one. It was only later, when the organist at St Stephen's church, who also played the organ at the Odeon cinema, was convicted of homosexual acts with twins who were my contemporaries at College, that his intentions dawned on me and my good fortune became clear.

The Revd. Fred Pike, Welshman, college chaplain and Vicar of St James-the-Less, was gay, though not in any obvious way. When I decided to become a clergyman he helped me with my Latin, and later, my Greek. Our sessions took place on Sundays after Evensong. There was nothing improper about his behaviour. Nevertheless the rumour mills ground away juicily, like the large granite wheels called 'runners' that had once crushed apples for cider making. I was not particularly concerned.

My parents liked Fred. The four of us used to play tennis together in the holidays. Fred taught me to drive in his Daimler, its pre-selector gears a bonus. The critical confrontation came when he took me on a European tour in the summer of 1956. At the hotel in Chartres we were given a room with a double bed. There the law had to be laid down. If he touched me I would go straight home and tell. The threat was effective. We took in a clutch of cathedrals and a medley of concerts. We saw the Passion Play at Oberammergau, Orff's *Trionfi*, which includes *Carmina Burana*, at the Bayerische Staatsoper, and the *Magic Flute* at the Salzburg Festival.

I had read Fred the riot act before I knew what his intentions were. The fact that he continued to support and tutor me as though nothing had changed in our relationship leads me to think that his intentions were platonic. That has encouraged me in the belief that Benjamin Britten probably had an equally innocent relationship with the boys whose company he enjoyed.

It also meant that I was more sympathetic than most of my straight fellow students to the coterie of gays in college and to the uneasy situation of homosexuals in the church.

In my later teens, and in the winter months when I was not at sea, a group of us gathered in the loft of an outbuilding at Caroline Mauger's house. We mostly messed about at weekends, listening to records or taking advantage of John de Putron's jeep to race about the island. John was the only member of the group with a motorised vehicle.

Four years after my trip with Fred there was a rather different excursion to the Continent. Veronica, a Jersey girl, was living on her uncle's yacht moored in St Peter Port harbour. We went out together in a semi-serious way and enjoyed each other's company. Then I received a request from her parents in Jersey: would I be prepared to escort her and her sister on a tour of Europe? As they were providing a car and meeting all expenses I saw no reason to pass up the opportunity.

On the eve of our departure I was informed that the sister would not now be travelling, it would be just the two of us. When we reached our hotel in France all became clear. My companion had fallen for a man her parents considered to be a quite unsuitable match. They had despatched us together in the expectation that either I would seduce her or vice versa, from which an engagement would naturally follow. As my companion had no intention of giving up her inamorato I was in no danger, but I did feel used. Or unused.

We saw the operetta *Wiener Blut* on the lake at Bregenz. Nothing else of this trip remains in the memory, but as a counterpoint to the previous European tour it now amuses me, an amusement tempered somewhat by regret that she had received from me an expensive Ronson cigarette lighter at an expensive dinner in an expensive Jersey hotel.

Guernsey in summer was awash with young foreigners, most gaining experience in the tourist industry. Jütta was one. She was succeeded by a French girlfriend, Babette, whose pianistic abilities were to be envied.

Over the Christmas holidays the social diary became overloaded. Hotels were booked, bands hired, buffets planned by one, two or more friends who had persuaded parents that they, the friends, would face pariah-hood if they did not do their duty by the rest of us and host the event of the festive season. There were occasions when three invitations might be received for the same evening. Who was to be favoured, who ignored? Sometimes we put in an appearance at all three dances. If we timed it right we could benefit from three buffets. Tolstoy's description of Iogel's balls in *War and Peace* seems to fit: '...only those came to these balls who wanted to be merry...who put on long gowns for the first time...All of them, with rare exceptions, were or seemed pretty: so rapturously they smiled, so lit up were their eyes.'

Vivien insisted that before I attended any of these functions I had to have lessons in ballroom dancing. I received individual tuition in the basic foxtrot, quickstep and waltz moves, and learnt to tackle a corner with a spin, a figure that put me ahead of most of the competition. The Old Government House Hotel and the Royal Hotel were considered the top venues. Their bands could just about stretch to rock 'n roll. Viv and I developed a routine the highlight of which was my passing her over my shoulder and pulling her back through my legs. On the night we launched this on an unsuspecting public at the Royal Hotel we were gyrating brilliantly until the through-my-legs bit. I trod on the hem of her dress. There was a great ripping sound as she came up for air, her suspender belt exposed to dozens of eyes. Did she ever dance with me again? I can't remember, but probably not.

Barbara, my second German girlfriend – always anxious to do my bit for reconciliation – whom I had met on the Herm boat, was sweet. I stayed with her family in Hamburg. As they were Roman Catholics there was no possibility of the relationship developing. We had great fun, though, and she introduced me to a disgustingly pungent German cheese. By this time I was a student at Ripon Hall, Oxford, a theological college. I suggested a brilliant wheeze. We students collected our post on the way to breakfast. If she sent me a parcel of this cheese I would seat myself next to the Principal and cause a stir by opening it at table.

Well, the day came, and the parcel came, and I sat next to the Principal, not a sought-after spot. As we munched our toast and supped our tea I slit open the cardboard box. Instead of an overpowering smell, there jumped out of the carton a wind-up mechanical toy which kangarooed all over the table. The other ordinands delighted in my discomposure. For, although the Principal was full of bonhomie and joie de vivre, his humour glands were somewhat underdeveloped. He surely thought that my female acquaintance would never make a parson's wife, gravitas being in such short supply. Under his uncomprehending gaze my creative juices evaporated and I lost the power of speech. I never found a way to repay Barbara. Marriage might have done it.

Two other extra-curricular Ripon Hall events stand out. We were having a Quiet Day, led by some especially spiritual guest. A friend and I thought we could liven things up a little with a gentle joke. We purchased heads of celery which we put out on the lunch table. It is hard to keep a straight face when, at a meal taken in silence, forty people are crunching celery. Retribution came shortly afterwards. My room, rather dark, was at the base of the tower. Sitting in postprandial quietude at my desk I was disturbed by unusual bumps and scrapes coming from the room above. A quick crescendo, a loud thump and the ceiling landed on top of me, four inches of powdery plaster, together with shreds of lathes and strands of horse hair.

With head sore and hair gritty, as if powdered for a renaissance farce, I rushed upstairs to discover that one of my colleagues, usually a rather reserved fellow, had been demonstrating the correct way to conduct a Quiet Day, a turn that brought part of the house down!

My room was uninhabitable, my clothes had all to be cleaned, my books to be dusted, but there was a delightful reward. The following term I was given the best room in the place, at the top of the tower, with windows on three sides overlooking the Oxfordshire countryside. My sole neighbour was the one beneath me, a friend who shared my taste in music.

The second event was of a completely different nature. In chapel, which was a large, unprepossessing square room with plain windows that kept us in touch with the natural world, we were seated as in choir with two groups facing each other. It was announced that the chapel was to be renovated, and the plans were placed for inspection on the Common Room table. On these plans the seats faced the altar.

My friends and I felt this to be a retrograde step: theologically unsound. We preferred to look across at our fellow students than stare at the altar but we were assured that there was no other way to get more people in. I did not believe it. Here was an opportunity to exercise my criminal skills for the benefit of the community. So, late at night, I sneaked into the Principal's study and borrowed the architect's plans. Having carefully traced them they were replaced. I set out the seats as we wanted them, for there was indeed enough room, thus emphasising the community nature of the college. The plans were accurate, as well-drawn as the architect's and, as the staff had no answer to them, were adopted. A real triumph! But this was not the end of our scheming. Puffed up by this success we pushed on.

My friend Ken Bartlett and I were both organists who tried to make the best of a bad box of wheezing whistles. We saw an opportunity to dispose of this asthmatic heap. We persuaded the Principal that it was inadvisable to leave the precious instrument in situ during the refurbishment because it was in danger of being damaged by dust. We got him really worried. Then we offered him a way out. We would dismantle the organ ourselves and place the bits carefully in the basement. He was so relieved he gave us the go-ahead. We started work immediately, before he had a chance to change his mind. The organ was laid to rest with due care and ceremony. A piano was installed in the chapel 'for the time being'. The singing improved. The organ never went back. Motto for part 1: never believe what they tell you. Motto for part 2: never believe what we tell them.

While at Ripon Hall I was persuaded to join a fellow-student on an IVS project (International Voluntary Service). We arrived at the house of the old lady whose garden we were to get into some sort of order. My companion and I were on time. The project leader from LMH (Lady Margaret Hall) was late. We got out forks and spades from the shed and set to work. When she finally arrived Liz Shaw, the leader herself, was mightily impressed, and I was invited to take tea in her room at LMH. There I first heard the voice of Joan Baez on a record brought back by a friend from the US, novel and haunting.

More IVS projects followed, the worst being to clean a front room in which six cats had been imprisoned. Gluttons for do-gooding, Liz and I signed up for a UN work camp in Igoumenitsa, Greece. We had to hitch to Brindisi in Italy to catch the ferry.

One lift was in a furniture van which transported us most of the length of Italy. In the late afternoon the two-man crew stopped for the night. We were nowhere near a camp site. They weren't bothered. From the back of the van they extracted two single beds which they set up on the grass verge for us. Roll up! Roll up! Watch how foreigners sleep!

In Brindisi we enjoyed an excellent lunch and approached the ferry arm-in-arm and singing. The other passengers seemed delighted to welcome aboard two young people obviously in love. We basked in their friendliness and refreshed ourselves on the juice of real lemons.

The British consular official in Igoumenitsa was not so welcoming. We were not happy anyway with the project because volunteers lived in comparative luxury with fridges and air conditioning. After two days he told us to leave. We had no idea what to do next when a small French car drove into the compound. Liz recognised the General Secretary of Service Civil International (French for IVS): He had a project in a village in the hills above Igoumenitsa which we were welcome to join. We lived with the villagers and assisted with an irrigation scheme. When that came to an end we hitched a lift in a melon lorry to Athens. There we found accommodation in the Bertrand Russell Peace Foundation office. In return we helped prepare banners for an upcoming demonstration, not terribly worried by the warning that the office might be raided and we arrested. Like many young tourists we sold blood to pay for food.

When I moved from Oxford to Hackney, East London, Liz remained behind for her final degree year before coming to the capital to receive the remainder of her medical training at the London Hospital. Her father objected to our relationship: a clergyman was not good enough for her. As this was having a strong negative effect on her mother the Bishop of Stepney gave us permission to marry, which we did on January 16th 1965. Liz's parents came to the wedding but sat at the back. The reception was organised by parishioners and held in the parish rooms.

Life was busy for us both. We tried unsuccessfully for children, and then endured a series of embarrassing tests with a Harley Street consultant only to discover that I was infertile. We opted to adopt, and applied to Oxford as they were one of the most enlightened local authority services in the country. They arranged for us to receive the baby from the hands of the mother in hospital. Catherine has been a delight ever since. She has recently visited her birth mother in Africa for the second time. She sent us a photo of the two of them in a boat. They look like sisters.

After ten years Liz and I were divorced. How much this was a response to the free-wheeling spirit of the times and how much to our separate busy lives I am not sure. I am certain that I bear responsibility for it, and could, and should, have done more to save the marriage. I wrote several poems at the time. Looking at them now I wonder whether I was going through some sort of breakdown, so full are they of disturbing images.

At the court appearance I was in two minds about going ahead. Had Liz not turned up supported by a young man I mistakenly assumed to be her new boy friend there would have been no decree. That I was not bolder has been a regret with which I have had to live.

I then married Kate Skinner, daughter of the poet Martyn Skinner. She was a social worker at Christian Action's hostel for single homeless women in Soho. We joined the commune that ran the Student Christian Movement from Wick Court near Bath. Shortly after that I became chaplain/warden of the Othona Community in Essex but community life put an enormous strain on our relationship, as did our inability to have children. For although Kate accepted the fact at the beginning of our relationship, as time went on she got broodier. She also suspected that I was having affairs with women visiting the community, which I wasn't. The Othona Community Leader, Canon Norman Motley, said publicly that the relationship was damaging and should be ended. To do that I left the Community and spent six months living with Sally Martin in Birmingham, where she was taking a social work course. I worked on a book about worship commissioned by the publisher, Mowbrays.

In 1979 Save the Children appointed me to run their Vietnamese resettlement programme. Julia Meiklejohn I hired as my deputy. We got hitched two years later, three days before Christmas, at Islington Registry Office. This marital relationship, in which working together has been a key ingredient, has lasted for over thirty-five years.

Let me finish this chapter with my parents. My father was cautious, a caution that served him well when advising bank customers about their investments. It deserted him when considering his own financial dealings, and though he never risked huge sums, he lost most of what he did risk. His garden received a lot of attention.

Father had a dream of building his own house, and in the hours when he could not sleep he made sketches around a Georgian-style facade. Mother went hunting and found the ideal site, a field with outline planning permission and wonderful views. He got cold feet. She pleaded and cajoled. She knew that, even if in the end they could not afford to build, the field was bound to appreciate in value. He would not be moved; there was no guarantee. In fact, within a couple of years, they would have made a significant profit on the field had they had to sell it.

Father

Mother's passport photo 1946

Mother had a good business head. In a later age she could have become a successful estate agent or property developer. She shared with her father that natural instinct that can spot an opportunity and a bargain.

Dad was a churchwarden of St James-the-Less, our parish church. The decision to close it as a place of worship was taken by those higher up the chain of command. Nevertheless, he felt he had failed, that he would be blamed, and he talked seriously of leaving the island.

One of the things he was good at, apart from his job, was making after-dinner speeches. He would spend hours writing them. He told me that his secret was never to tell dirty jokes. The offerings of other speakers usually contained varying degrees of smut. And though the audience laughed, there was a certain unease about the laughter. So when he came along with his corny stories there was a sense of relief, and his jokes got a much better response than they deserved.

He died in my mother's arms of a ruptured aorta in 1980.

Father had never been Mother's first choice. Max was, but he had a rather wild reputation – he later managed a greyhound stadium – and Grandpa banished him from her sight. Father, on the other hand, was so cool a dresser that Grandpa assumed he had money, a great mistake – his money went on clothes. The crunch came when, in the Depression, she lost her job in the music department of Harrods. She needed help to return to Jersey and appealed to the two rivals. It was Father who responded.

A couple of years after Father died she received a call from her sister Joan in Jersey. Max was now a widower. Why didn't they meet? They did, and Mother said they took up where they had left off. She moved to Jersey to be spoilt by Max for a few happy years.

I was content to oversee an informal hitching ceremony: a formal marriage would have affected their pensions. If Mother was happy, my brother was exactly the opposite. He felt she was betraying our father. I felt she deserved to be spoilt after a hard life of washing, scrubbing and knitting.

When Max died Mother took it hard. She had lost two husbands and now was back in Guernsey living on her own. David and Christina were next door, fed her and kept an eye on her, but nevertheless she complained of loneliness. I visited whenever I could. Her first question would be, 'When are you leaving? Can't you stay longer?' Bidding goodnight she would add, 'and I hope I don't wake up in the morning'.

The Hodgetts family at Cambridge Park

Chapter Three

Learning and teaching

'IT IS TIRESOME TO HEAR EDUCATION DISCUSSED, tiresome to educate, and tiresome to be educated' (Charles Lamb). Too bad! I was a student for twenty years of my earlier life, and a teacher for about fifteen years of my later life. This does not tell the whole story for I have always learnt as I taught and, as an adult, taught as I learnt. WEA music evening classes, weeks run for the Othona Community and courses taught in the church rooms in Hartland came out of current study.

When I was Head of the Small School, Hartland, an alternative secondary school (1983-95), and for several years after that, I ran workshops on behalf of Human Scale Education for parents and teachers interested in setting up small schools. We began by exploring the participants' own schooling, because a vision of what is possible is usually limited to a tinkering with what they themselves experienced, their chief desire being to avoid the nasty bits.

When their parents take Darren or Trudy to see round a prospective school they rarely know what to look for or the questions to ask. They compare what they see with the school to which they went, plus other schools they might be visiting. If the difference is a bank of computers, smart blazers and orderly seating, and perhaps what the school says about itself, they may well be satisfied!

An account of my own educational experience was an exercise required by my tutor at the Institute of Education in London.

At six I was packed off to the Prep school of Victoria College, Jersey. The only thing I remember learning was:

James James
Morrison Morrison
Weatherby George Dupree
Took great
Care of his Mother,
Though he was only three.

Propaganda?

How at this school I earned a gym shoe beating, and how I acquired the nickname 'Hoppy', I have described in the previous chapter.

I wasn't sorry when, in 1947, we moved to Guernsey and I was enrolled in the Lower School of Elizabeth College. Our teacher was Miss Spillman, later to become Mrs Vaughan, a bewildering change of status for one so old. The Principal lived on the premises. Our classroom shared a wall with his hallway. Her great fear was of order progressing from boisterousness to riot. One afternoon, when affairs were on the verge of anarchy, she lined us up to dish out with her two-foot ruler a sharp rap over our knuckles. All was going to plan when one cowardly sniveller withdrew his mitt, which had been hovering above the back of a chair. A gleeful chortle rose from the yet unpunished as the ruler, hitting the chair back, broke in two, an indication of the force she was applying.

'Squad' was the mainstream punishment for behavioural offences, which meant picking up litter and, supervised by a sadistic prefect, circumnavigating the playground like a horse in a circus. I received plenty of those. The third in a term warranted the cane. Of 'detentions', which were work-related punishments, I received few.

Each pupil, like a jail inmate or hospital patient, was given a number. (Michel Foucault has explained the rationale behind this act of de-humanisation.) Mine I hesitated to reveal: it was 4711, the original Eau de Cologne, named after a house in that city which had been allocated that number in 1794. I feared it might lead to a nickname worse than 'Hoppy'. The fact that the scent was an *aqua mirabilis* concocted by a Carthusian monk was of little comfort. Fortunately the '4' was dropped in daily use as I and my contemporaries were all 'fours'. It was a relief that no one made the connection. Unless they had tried drinking it, my classmates´ knowledge of perfume was probably minimal.

While I was in the Lower School it moved three times. For the first year we were in the main building. Then we moved to the grounds of Sausmarez Park four miles from St Peter Port. The Park had trees to climb and large areas of grass around which to chase each other. The form rooms were dull. They had not been decorated since before the war.

Each day we undertook a trek to lunch at the Rockmount Hotel, about a mile each way. On one occasion I noticed an ignition key in a parked car. Why, I cannot recall, but I removed it. On our return we were confronted by an apoplectic driver. I owned up to the theft but without any great sense of guilt: drivers shouldn't leave keys in their cars should they? Nevertheless, Major Caldwell administered his cane medicine with grim determination.

Finally we moved into Beechwood, a former nursing home that had been converted for us, quite close to Government House. We enjoyed new paint, new floors and lots of light. It was easy to stare out of the windows for hours. Mrs Elliot is the one teacher with a prominent place in my memory. Nature Study was her subject and she made it exciting. She also read us stories about an Irish tinker, and filled the form library with Arthur Ransome books. (Did the authorities know he was a Communist sympathiser?) My other memory of this time is of drawing plans of feudal fields, but then this seemed to be demanded of us for almost every year of my Lower School life. My sister went to a Froebel school. From the stories she told it seemed that break time was the dullest part of her day.

Although I did many things that masters probably labelled anti-social I always owned up to my misdeeds. This was not a conscious decision. It seems that for me honesty has never been a tactic, but that I have a natural disposition to be honest, 'by nature honest, by experience wise'. One hopes!

At eleven we moved up to the Junior School and returned to the central site, occupying a new hut a hundred yards from the main college building, that which 'stands on an elevated part of the town: it is not as a whole an inelegant structure, although, to a tasteful eye, it would not be found to possess any great architectural beauty.' (*A Guide to Guernsey and Jersey*, 1839.) The only changes to our routine came from having access to the gym and being required to travel further for sports. Both had downsides. In the gym we could be punished by being made to hang on the wall-bars where legs could be whacked with a plimsoll; the journey to games could be more tiring than the games themselves.

I enjoyed short-distance athletics, shrugged off football and disliked cricket, especially matches against other schools. I was one of the bounders on the boundary and never a player on the pitch. In the senior school I hacked away at hockey and tolerated tennis, the latter the game that made most sense to me because it was possible to get the greatest amount of exercise in the shortest possible time with the fewest number of people. I also took up boxing, which went well until, at the age of fifteen, the Gym master put me in the ring with a sixth former. We were roughly the same height and weight but unequal in muscle development and experience. It is something to be thoroughly thrashed in front of parents and schoolmates, but at least I lasted the three rounds.

I sought intellectual enlightenment outside the classroom, lying on the drawing room carpet reading the latest volume of Arthur Mee's *Children's Encyclopaedia* to arrive through the post, for instance. I like Ian Sansom's description of it as

> …a vast labyrinth of facts, fancies, niceties, delicacies and wonderful minutiae. There are stories, and diagrams, and illustrations, and articles about animals, and history, and biography, and biology, and 'Great Thoughts', and 'Things to Do and Make', and 'Plain Answers to the Questions of the Children of the World' (*The Guardian* 12/7/2007)

Was this collection of 'musings and ruminations' responsible for my rather undisciplined approach to study, for I can easily be lured from the straight and narrow to wander down side-alleys?

The *Eagle*, which was published the day before my tenth birthday in 1950, had a beneficial effect. The Revd Marcus Morris, its founder and editor, wanted a comic based on Christian values where foreigners would not be depicted as either enemies or villains and at least one child in any group would be from an ethnic minority, 'innovative but somewhat risky ideas'. Dan Dare, Pilot of the Future, struggled with the Mekon, the first science fiction comic strip. The back page contained St Paul's Journeys. In the centre was a cutaway illustration of a piece of machinery or vehicle à la Dorling Kindersley. Vivien had its sister comic, *Girl*, which was not nearly as exciting, though I did read it and developed a soft spot for Lettice Leefe, the greenest girl in the school. David's *Robin* was scorned.

WHG Milnes

used by permission of the College

Let us consider now the man whose shadow caused grown men to tremble and criminals to quake, the Revd William Henry Goodenough Milnes, OBE, MC, MA, a force with an even more formidable wife, Phyllis Spurling Clare. The Principal was an Oxford tennis half-blue whose forearm drive, a cane grasped in his hand, made deep impressions on me. He was a liberal theologian whose sermons few understood, least of all the Chaplain, and a historian whose school text book, *A Rational History of England*, was used by one creep of a master despite its inaccuracies and plodding style. His memorial is a magnificent lab.

He was appointed Principal in 1937. In 1939 he evacuated the whole school to Derbyshire and returned to Guernsey with it still in good heart at the War's end. Then he built it up from 150 to 450 pupils, doubled its accommodation and playing fields and persuaded the Island's government to foot most of the bill.

Discipline was everything. Each item of uniform was standardised. Both socks had to be wrinkleless, every head hair short and in place. He carried a metal comb, bought for his Alsatian, which he used on untidy boys. If they were too unkempt then, 'Boyee, come here!', and they were sent to put their heads under the tap in the corner of the playground so that he could make a just assessment of hair length. We had to have permits signed by him to go into town or to the cinema, even on Saturdays. Requests for permission to visit the hairdresser's were always granted.

Snow was rare in the Channel Islands. When it did fall we had only a short time to play with it before it melted. We were having a snowball fight in the playground at break time. I moulded a generous missile and launched it. My victim ducked just as the Principal rounded the corner. He must have known it was an accident because my punishment was not severe.

Parents feared the Principal as much as, if not more than, we did and would promise anything to avoid an interview. When he strode about the school it was through deserted corridors, corridors that had a smell unlike any other, of disinfectant, not polish, strongest at the beginning of term. He was himself a sort of human disinfectant. Even the other masters, like fearful bacteria, avoided him. The staff room went quiet on the few occasions he was seen to approach it.

Anxious for our health he instituted gym in break. For half of our twenty minutes of free time we had to jump up and down flapping legs and arms under the watchful eyes of a gym master and prefects, which gave us less than ten minutes to buy and consume Smiths crisps or a Wagon Wheel.

On Tuesday afternoons we donned scratchy khaki uniforms in which to play war games, usually on the Common at Lancresse. The Cadet Corps was compulsory. After school on Friday, in blancoed belts that scrunched up our jackets, we paraded in the playground and drilled with our ancient, Lee-Enfield, bolt-action, magazine-fed, repeating .303 rifles. We might as well have been given bows and arrows. They, at least, would have been lighter for the shouldering and presentation of arms, and for bearing on the march.

Why was this imposed on us? The island militia had been disbanded at the outbreak of WW II. Islanders benefitted from the ancient privilege of immunity from military service out of the Islands, 'unless it be to accompany the Sovereign their Duke in person for the recovery of England or that the person of the Sovereign should be taken prisoner by the enemy.'

Parents accepted the situation in which we found ourselves. They had been through a similar experience themselves and had not been damaged by it. Teachers were professionals who knew what they were doing and answered to no one. Those were the days!

There were two sides to the upper school, Arts and Science. No one questioned this stupid division at age fourteen. On the Arts side the clever ones took geography while the dunces studied history. On the Science side the dim did biology instead of physics and chemistry. I suffered, even though I was on the Arts side, from having to study for music and art 'O' levels in my own time. Since then the arts started to receive a lot more attention, with many schools offering individual musical instrument tuition. Now, however, increased emphasis on core subjects has resulted in the return of the arts to Cinderella status.

Four of us jockeyed for position in the form's top places, though Peter Cogman was never dislodged from first place. He won an open scholarship to Cambridge plus the Kilby prize, gaining a Ph.D. and becoming a senior lecturer in the French department of the University of Southampton. Ian McCave became Woodwardian Professor of Geology at Cambridge with over seventy scientific papers to his name. Brian Sarre studied malting and brewing. He was Corporate Quality Systems Manager for Heineken International in the Netherlands. And there was me, a cleric.

George Eliot's account of Daniel Deronda's education seems to reflect my experience.

> He had not been the hardest of workers at Eton. Though some kinds of study and reading came as easily as boating to him, he was not of the material that usually makes the first-rate Eton scholar. There had sprung up in him a meditative yearning after wide knowledge which is likely always to abate ardour in the fight for prize acquirement in narrow tracks. Happily he was modest, and took any second-ratedness in himself simply as a fact, not as a marvel necessarily to be accounted for by a superiority.

Drama consisted of one Shakespeare play a year and nothing by any other dramatist. Each holiday we read a novel, usually by Walter Scott or Dickens, not for pleasure but to keep us from mischief.

There was an annual concert and a carol service, for which the minimum rehearsal time was allocated. Most masters resented choir practice. Yet the Corps wasted four hours a week of our time and no one in authority complained. Two societies were allowed, the Music Club, which I attended regularly, and the Science Society whose special evenings dedicated to firework-making, wine-making and space travel were incredibly popular. How come the sixth formers who presented these subjects could be more interesting than the professionals?

We could be hard on the staff. One flabby specimen we drove to a nervous breakdown. Another master, Capt. Jerry Chambers, responding to a request to tell us about his wartime experiences, would moisten up at the thought of his erstwhile colleagues. We giggled into the crook of an arm rested on an abused desk lid. He had one decent story. With a couple of hours to spare between trains he thought he would spend half of it seeing the sights of Dublin in one of the carriages that were drawn up outside the station. The driver cracked his whip and they sped off at high speed. 'Why the hurry?' he asked. 'Ach! D'yer think I want to be all day driving yer tro' de streets of Dublin for an hour?'

WWM Cooper

Mr Cooper, wiry in limb, hair and moustache, taught Latin. He also ran the extremely successful scout troop – in the late 50s there were more Queen's Scouts at the College than in any other British school – and was an enthusiastic amateur photographer who could easily be diverted from ploughing through Virgil's *Aeneid* Book I, a song about arms and the man, or *Caesar's Gallic Wars* Book IV, in which Britain is invaded in Chapter 23, by being presented with a defective camera or an intelligent question concerning the chemicals employed in the arcane art of processing film. Why wasn't he teaching photography? It is a science as well as an art. He introduced philosophy to us in the Sixth form, thus satisfying in part my 'yearning after wide knowledge'. For my Latin exam I learnt the crib.

I left at seventeen before taking my 'A' levels. Because the Principal was retiring Fred Pike, the Chaplain, panicked. The new man was reputed to be a socialist and therefore unsound. (His son tells me he was not a socialist but an enlightened and committed Christian, a lay reader, which is almost the same radical thing.) I was hurried on to the University College of St David, Lampeter, in Wales. Like Oxford and Cambridge it had at that time a minimum entry requirement of five 'O' levels, one of them being Latin. St David's had been founded to educate Welsh clergy who could not afford English universities.

This move to university without 'A' levels was a mistake. Not only had I not mastered the art of essay writing, nor become an independent learner, but many of my fellow students were years older. They had done their National Service, experiencing a freedom that was now denied them. Because, in terms of my educational development, I was behind most of my contemporaries I had to repeat a year, which meant I had to take a year out. During the winter months I worked for the *Guernsey Evening Press* as a reporter and proof reader.

The job was a consequence of their publishing nine long articles I had written about a semi-official visit to the Soviet Union organized by the National Union of Students.

The worst part was reporting events such as funerals and tennis matches. One was required to collect the names of all who had been active in, or even present at, such functions. It is an operating principle of the local press that names on the page equal bigger sales. And names are a pain to the proof reader.

Reporting the local Eisteddfod, an enjoyably relaxing assignment, I discovered an ability to identify quality, useful when watching *Cardiff Singer of the World*, or *Young Musician of the Year*. Corine Singleton, the Ladies College music mistress, would sit with me in judgement of the adjudicator.

A recital by the great Chinese pianist Fou Ts'ong was mine to cover. His speciality was Chopin. His recital at the Little Theatre was not particularly brilliant, and I put this down to the quality of the piano. Interviewed afterwards he was severely critical of the ageing concert grand. My piece was given prominence in the *Guernsey Evening Press*. As a result the island's Arts Council was forced to invest in a much better instrument. I realised then how influential even the local rag could be.

My media career came to an abrupt end. John de Putron, a friend, was a rifle whizz kid recently returned from Bisley where he had hit the jackpot. He came to the office to pick up Bruce Parker and me for an evening out. (Bruce was also at Lampeter.) The office was pretty well deserted. The next day's paper, set in lead type, was on the bench in its frames. The leading article on the sports page was about John. It had the headline, 'Good Shot Needs Thorough Preparation'. John, being of a technical bent, managed to work out how to operate the type-setting machine, a tricky manipulation of molten lead. An *i* was substituted for the third *o*. Bruce and I lost our jobs. Bruce continued to take journalism seriously and ended up with the BBC. John had no job to lose. He later taught physics at the Ladies' College.

Kierkegaard would have breathed a sigh of relief at my come downance. He saw in the press an evil: it made the passing moment a thousand or ten thousand times more inflated and important than it really is.

> If Christianity is really to be proclaimed, it will become apparent that it is the daily press which will, if possible, make it impossible. There has never been a power so diametrically opposed to Christianity as the daily press. Day in and day out the daily press does nothing but delude men with the supreme axiom of this lie, that numbers are decisive. Christianity, on the other hand, is based on the thought that the truth lies in the single individual.

Today he would surely be saying something similar about all the newer news media.

At university I read General Arts, a course specifically designed for those intending to become clergy. It included History, English, Philosophy, Psychology, Sociology and classical Greek. All these subjects were approached from a historical perspective. Lectures were compulsory, dull, and delivered in badly lit, depressing rooms from deadly scripts. As time went on I

> ...felt a heightening discontent with the wearing futility and enfeebling strain of a demand for excessive retention and dexterity without any insight into the principles which inform the vital connections of knowledge. (*Daniel Deronda*)

Discipline was strict. My youth was not centuries away, but when I share with today's students stories of yesterday's student life they glance over my shoulder for a sighting of the Ark. You, my reader, perhaps understand that forty years can pass in the twinkling of an eye, in the squeak of a bat, with the scent of honeysuckle, and so we can feel that we still belong to the same world as twenty-year-olds, even if they do not return the compliment.

Though, in many aspects of university life, change has marched faster than progress, few would want to return to a time when, because independence did not come until one was twenty-one, the authorities were in *loco parentis* and exercised their care with a zeal and strictness that William Blake would have understood. My reaction to a control/punishment regime may have been unusual. Few eighteen-year-olds today would tolerate the limits imposed on us. But what form would their reaction take?

We were expected to live in college in our first and third years, a building described by the borough surveyor as 'not unlike an evacuated monastery'. It was not long before the rebellious and the rakish courted me. I soon appreciated why. College doors were locked at 11pm. Mine was a ground-floor room near the main gate. The bars on its window were of wood and could therefore be removed. Curfew breakers were frequent window tappers. I was happy to cooperate as long as they left no footprints in the flower bed.

It was many years before women were admitted to the college. In my day the Junior Common Room voted against their admittance, not surprising when Mr John Read, proposing that they be allowed entry and 'speaking with a Dimbleby-like eloquence' said 'he really would like someone at hand in the College to decorate his room with flowers and to darn his socks'. His seconder was only marginally better: 'a future vicar's wife was worth two curates'.

Female visitors could only be entertained on college premises at the weekend with written permission. Pubs were off-limits. Beer was available with meals but there was no bar. Gowns and ties had to be worn in town and hall, and to chapel and lectures. The standard fine for a breach of the rules was £5, two-and-a-half weeks of my spending money. The recidivist could be sent down.

Rules have always been a challenge to my creative instincts and subversive nature. There was some fun to be had from the odd practical joke, but what really began to fascinate me was the lack of imagination or subtlety in the responses of Authority, an Authority that puts great trust in the locked door whilst ignoring the unlatched window.

Though I preferred pranks that were not directed against particular individuals, there were occasional exceptions. One such victim was the Professor of English. As well as his teaching duties he had charge of the library. In the library were several near life-size statues. Prof. SC Boorman often disappeared at weekends to London, it was assumed for sleazy purposes. (I later discovered that he was editor and commentator on a Shakespeare play series so he was probably away on business.) His rooms were on the first floor of the Canterbury Building, now demolished, a distance from the library of the width of the quad plus about a hundred yards.

One Sunday I noticed that his bathroom window was not quite shut: a window of opportunity! Through it we gained access to his flat and unlocked the door. We tucked up in his bed one of the library statues. We locked both bathroom window and front door. The real giggle came not from his shouts of agonized surprise in the early hours of the next morn but in the assumption made by the Authorities that students had acquired a set of college keys. All the locks in the building were changed.

This reaction of the Authorities surprised and intrigued me. I did not expect a knee-jerk reaction from a body of intelligent men and one woman. It was obvious that no one had thought through what had happened. They had a hypothesis but they never tested it. The removal of the college bell provided me with more material over which to mull.

Chapel had to be attended three mornings and three evenings a week, plus Sundays: a recording angel on the door marked us down as we entered. Dinner was formal and taken every day. To summon us to meals, chapel and lectures the college bell was rung. It therefore symbolised the daily round and grind. Could we spike it? We could try.

So it was that one moonlit night a shadowy, hand-picked crew made their careful way across the roof to the bell-tower. There the bronze beast was liberated from its fastenings, shunted across the slates, lowered to the ground and hidden in the rhododendrons.

Early the next morning the chapel clerk collapsed in a heap when he hauled on the bell-less rope. The blood vessels of Authority began to pulsate. We spread a rumour that the bell had been pinched by students from another place: Aberystwyth. For a short while this explanation prevailed, until Authority realised that the thieves had not boasted of their trophy nor demanded a ransom. An appeal was made for the bell's return.

Nothing forthcoming, Authority upped the stakes and threatened to share the cost of a replacement between all the students. Panic spread among the monetarily challenged and a witch-hunt began. The comrades kept their cool. A hand-bell was substituted for its great grandparent. We recorded it and broadcast the tape at random intervals, causing a certain amount of confusion.

After a suspenseful forty-eight hours I pinned a scrappy map to the notice board, an X indicating that 'hear lyeth the treshoor'. Was it true or was it a lie? Authority hesitated: if they sent out an exploratory expedition on a wild bell hunt they would look foolish. It took half-a-day for them to risk it. And lo and behold, there rested the swag! Treasure maps may sometimes be trustworthy.

I was one of those who volunteered to manhandle the beast back to its lair, and thus I heard the Principal opine that it was one of the better pranks played during his time as either a student or a member of staff. Were all their threats a bluff, then? No, the anger had been real enough. This was the conviviality of relief. As he spoke I was running a different scenario through my mind: What if Authority had completely ignored the loss of the bell?

It was certainly a funnier episode than the locking of the academic staff in the Board Room, which I believe someone did only because the key was in the door. It was a lost opportunity as none of the demands that could have been made were made. Unfortunately one lecturer was late and he released his colleagues. The Censor, the Reverend Renowden, MA, rushed furious into the quad and fined the first five people he saw. This was a travesty of justice. I was on the organ for Evensong. As the staff left the chapel I played Handel's *Dead March in Saul.*

As the chapel emptied, the Precentor, the Revd Dickie Dai, elbowed back into it exuding purpose. Being somewhat short

he walked with chin raised to the stars. Now he lifted it to the organ loft. 'Mr 'Odgetts!', Welsh voice as high as his chin to make itself heard. Playing stops. 'Mr 'Odgetts, 'ave you heard that piece played other than at funerals?' 'Yes, sir. At home we have it on Good Friday!' Not a response designed to avert disaster.

The Revd. Dickie Dai

58

Yes, I lost my organ exhibition but it was soon restored to me because of my ability and willingness to accompany the Psalms in Welsh.

My diary was packed. There was much making of music; there were productions of the Drama Society, mentioned elsewhere, and the fashioning of cucumber sandwiches for the Conservative Association's croquet matches. It was not that the Socialists would not play. They could not as only two comrades declared their political allegiance. It became clear that I might be a fellow-traveller towards the end of my time at Lampeter when my pacifism and membership of Christian CND clearly divided me from the supporters of that OAP, Harold Macmillan, at the time occupying Number 10, and his college acolytes who could be discerned dripping obsequiousness whenever a prominent Tory came to address the Conservative Association. It was then that I discovered that one of our professors, Thomas Woods, by whom I had the misfortune never to have been taught, was the author of *Some Moral Problems* containing a chapter on the immorality of nuclear weapons. We could have sung duets!

There is more to be told of this period but it will be found under 'Theatre' and 'Music'.

At Ripon Hall theological college, where I was being prepared for ordination into the Church of England, I enjoyed most of the teaching, in particular the lectures given by Ian Ramsey, Oxford Professor of the Philosophy of Religion, whose exposition of 'disclosure' situations caught on, but more of that in Chapter Five. As, after breakfast, a group of us strolled around the lake in our grounds we might experience quite extravagant 'disclosures' so that we arrived at the first lecture or tutorial of the day in quite a merry mood.

The parish in which I served my curacy was St John-at-Hackney in East London. In it were three denominational schools, the one with which I had most to do being the Hackney Free and Parochial Church of England Secondary School, a rather Victorian-sounding enterprise whose name has now been changed to The Urswick School, it having gone through a period when it was dubbed by the *Daily Mail* 'Britain's worst school'. It now has a better reputation. At the time it had about 320 pupils in a building in Paragon Rd dating from 1952 that replaced war-damaged premises. It was founded in the 1580s.

I was required to pop into the school twice a week to give Religious Instruction, which for me was no hardship. What surprised me was that there was little to distinguish this church school from State secondary schools. Its disciplinary regime was the same: it had corporal punishment and the usual lesser chastening penalties for inappropriate behaviour or scholarly slackness. The only difference I could discern was that pupils had three, instead of two, RI lessons a week and had to attend Sung Eucharist in the parish church on the odd High Day. I challenged the Headmaster: Why is the school not run on Christian principles? The Head replied that, as I was not a trained teacher, I did not understand how schools had to operate. He claimed the cane was the kingpin of discipline.

Now our Rector, the Revd HAS Pink, had been Secretary of the National Society (for Promoting Religious Education) at the same time that the Bishop of London, the Rt Revd Robert Stopford, was its Chairman. It was agreed between them that I should take a year out to gain a PGCE from the Institute of Education in London.

It was a year I enjoyed though, as usual, it was not my time in the religious education department but workshops in my subsidiary subject, music, and extra-curricular lectures on the history of science that fired me up. I was astonished by the contradictions in the Institute between theory and practice. In our own classroom practice we were encouraged to use visual aids, to vary the presentation of material, to engage with our pupils. Yet every Friday morning the whole of the student body had to attend three lectures, given one after another in a large hall next to the Senate House in Malet Street, with latecomers housed separately and fed through a speaker system. Professor Peters would read a chapter from his latest book on the Philosophy of Education, Professor Vernon addressed Psychology by detailing experiments on dogs, rats and monkeys, all of which were adequately described in our text books, and the only novelty was feed-back from an experiment to discover whether language enrichment for mothers in the East End would have an effect on the educational achievement of their offspring.

It was also odd that, though I had been teaching in an ordinary secondary school, and had made it clear that I intended to work in the state system, I was sent to a public school for my teaching practice. That was a doddle, apart for being torn off a strip for sitting in a senior master's chair in the staff room, a room that was the setting for much petty squabbling. My suspicion that teachers of one gender who spend all their time with adolescents of the same gender revert to adolescent behaviour themselves was confirmed. The boys were a pleasure to teach, responding well to some lively innovations. The Headmaster of the Forest School offered me the chaplaincy and headship of the department, the only job offer I have ever declined.

Now qualified, I again approached the Head of Hackney Free and Parochial School and, like the hero in a fairy story, discovered that as each obstacle is overcome another is put in one's path. Training was still not enough. Experience was required before I could be considered adequate as a partner in dialogue.

My probationary year was spent at the Edith Cavell secondary school in neighbouring Dalston. There were a lot of West Indians in the school, which led to a change in the way I taught music. Standard practice was to accompany singing on the piano, but this meant either playing the piano seated with one's back to the class, an invitation to disorderly behaviour, or playing it standing up, peering over the piano lid, a practice no Alexander teacher would commend. So the guitar usurped the piano. With that strung round my neck I could stroll up and down the aisles bellowing down the necks of potential troublemakers.

Calypsos were a favourite – Cy Grant, Britain's Harry Belafonte, had been on the TV each night singing Bernard Levin's take on the news of the day – so it was a with-it form. Now, when youngsters sing lively music they like to move, and when the music is Afro-Caribbean then it is hard for the children of West Indian origin to remain stuck in their seats. As they were singing as well as moving I saw no harm in this. Other teachers, however, were disturbed by what they ignorantly described as 'noise'. One of the most vociferous was the Head of English who patronised me, perceiving me as inept, and probably, ideologically challenged. I had one music soul mate on the staff, the woodwork teacher Alan Cartwright. He played a Gibson twelve-string guitar. Together we rustled up a few lively numbers which we were able to introduce into the daily assembly.

Now there was in that school a Head Girl whose name was Hyacinth, lively and beautiful, who, among other subjects, was taking 'A' level English and 'A' level RE. Her results were a great boost to my self-esteem, and 'coals of fire' heaped on the pate of the opposition, for she achieved an A in RE and only a B in English. Teaching her was a real delight.

The school had its full quota of troublemakers. I came out of school one lunch time to find that the windscreen of my Thames minibus had been smashed. Later that afternoon a fourth-former approached me oozing sympathy. He could offer help. A friend of his had a second-hand windscreen that would do the job. This could not be condemned as mindless vandalism. Rather, it was evidence of an entrepreneurial spirit.

Before the summer term was out I was called to another quarter.

Crown Woods in Eltham, South London, was one of the new breed of comprehensive schools, built to accommodate up to 2,600 pupils, whose head, Malcolm Ross, a former fighter pilot, was a great innovator. He combined aristocratic charm with creative deviousness. I don't know another Head who could use the story of Cain and Abel, a classic example of fratricide, to take to task the boy who set off the fire alarm yesterday, achieving the transition in three smooth and easy steps! He allowed me to work with sixth formers, including a jazz group, to present assemblies on fairly radical themes, but he drew the line on one I had prepared about Jan Palach, the Czeck student who set himself on fire as a protest against the invasion of Czechoslovakia by the Warsaw Pact armies that ended the Prague Spring. He said he didn't want boys making bonfires of themselves in the playground.

The school had bought a Victorian shooting lodge in Scotland, Inverliever Lodge, as a place to which youngsters, preferably fourth-year leavers, could be taken for an experience of bracing outdoor life.

Development had been in the hands of Donald Naismith, a history teacher who had been given the additional responsibility of organizing extra-curricular activities. He had been immediately struck by two closely related difficulties. First, any attempt to provide constructive, intelligent leisure activity was inhibited by environment. 'We are cramped' he is quoted as saying, 'cramped by the paving stones and the 124 bus and the trains to Charing Cross and the TV Times. If we stay with these things all the time, then all leisure activity is bounded by them. We have to get away'.

He therefore determined to find a place far from Eltham where children could stay for relatively long periods and where competition would be replaced by freedom. Loch Awe in the Western Highlands was the site of the building bought for this purpose.

Unfortunately one party, returning to South London at the end of the summer, left the windows of the lodge open. By the following spring much of the wood was rotten, so the army was called in to demolish the place. The residents of Ford, the nearby village, made uncomplimentary comments concerning the expertise of the demolishers.

Money was raised to erect on the site two dormitory chalets and a kitchen/dining/recreation chalet manufactured by a Scandinavian firm. A deal was done with Scottish Hydro-Electric to get a cheap power supply, and underfloor heating was installed. When I took over, three concrete bases had been laid and two shells erected but building work had stalled, which is why they needed a teacher with more time to oversee the completion of the buildings and to undertake the marketing of it to other schools.

I was nominally a member of the music department of Crown Woods and paid by the ILEA, but I did little teaching as I spent long hours on the road between London and Loch Awe, often driving there overnight. The upside of this was having nearly clear roads and skirting three Scottish lakes, Lomond, Long and Fyne, as the sun rose over them. On the return it was driving at speed through empty London streets. Those were hitch-hiking days. I would leave Loch Awe on my own and often land up in London with a full quota of passengers in my minibus.

I arranged for interior decoration of the newly completed chalets to be undertaken by a group of boys, 4th-year leavers. They stayed on site for a fortnight. Two teachers supervised the painting party, each for a week. This was quite instructive. The first, a woodwork teacher, took a laissez-faire approach to discipline. Time-keeping was not of the best but a reasonable amount of work was achieved without too much grumbling.

For these 4th-year leavers the experience was not a bundle of joy for they were not much interested in roaming the hills and we were limited, through a lack of sufficient transport, in what we could offer by way of excursions. They were happy, however, not to be in school.

The second, a PE teacher, tackled the task as though training the group for participation in the Emulsion Olympics. Anyone who believes that William Golding exaggerates the  propensity of boys for primitive behaviour might have had a change of mind had they observed a strict regime following a laid-back one. The boys built a bonfire, adorned their near-naked bodies with war paint and, brandishing roughly crafted spears, charged round the fire chanting abuse. In his report to the Head this teacher attempted to blame me, but it did not wash. This, coming on top of my Edith Cavell experience, taught me an important lesson: as far as discipline is concerned you cannot run a mixed economy. Though I firmly believe in a light touch it seems more important that there is a united attempt by staff to croon from the same rule book. Mixed messages might lead to a group nervous breakdown.

I bought two minibuses and a large lorry, a former field operations centre, cheaply from a defunct Civil Defence Corps for local transportation. The real challenge was to get the cost of travel between London and Loch Awe reduced to an affordable level. Malcolm Ross took this one on.

The appropriate British Rail Regional Manager was invited to visit Crown Woods which had a small, smart dining room with silver service for the entertaining of important guests. Was it the food? Was it the wine? Who knows, but by the end of the meal we had been promised a £4.10s return fare on overnight trains, with a blanket for each thrown in for good measure.

One of the selling points of the Centre was that visiting parties were free to use it as they wished. Apart from a caretaker,

Sandy, the former gillie, there were no staff on site to dictate how life should be lived. Nor was there anyone to cook or clean. These were the responsibility of the visitors. To offer help and advice I had to become an expert in quantity catering. Meat off the bone: 4oz per person; meat on the bone: 8oz p.p. Cook the meat; cut it when cold; re-heat it in gravy. I could give you more but you might be about to consume your cornflakes and I wouldn't want to put you off. I bought a Scottish recipe book. It is amazing how many dishes can be concocted from a mere handful of ingredients: oats, herrings, cabbage, potatoes and neeps. Oh, and nettles!

I was present with the occasional group: I wouldn't have missed out on the school orchestra and purchased a reasonable grand piano from a youth hostel for it.

Many youngsters found sleep difficult because of the silence, which wasn't complete because a noisy stream rushed by, but seemed so to them. I went early one Sunday morning into Glasgow to meet the train and a teenage girl insisted on coming with me. While I was at the station she stood staring at the test card on the TV screen in a shop window. She was reassured by this, and the street noise, and returned to the countryside happier for the fix. Few of the youngsters who came up were ready to listen to the breeze or the stream, or to discover and enjoy silence in the hills. Would they today be prepared to leave phones and games at home?

When I came out of the station there was a policeman standing at each end of my vehicle. The nearest took my driving licence, looked at me, looked at the licence again, then looked me in the eye. 'You're very, very lucky. We never charge doctors, clergy or other policemen.'

We drove parties up the Loch to Oban, where the Caledonian MacBrayne ferry could take us to Mull with onward travel to Iona. We walked through heathered hills or pottered in a boat with an outboard engine on Loch Awe, the longest freshwater loch in Scotland.

One Christmas we received a party of Czech students. This was an exchange arrangement. They came at a time when their country was in turmoil. The group leaders, a couple called Holí, escorted their charges back to the Czech border and returned to the UK seeking refugee status, which they were given. Our return visit to Czechoslovakia was not an easy one. There were

Russian troops on the streets and no one prepared for our arrival. Half our time we spent in Prague and half in the mountains. I have to say that our youngsters, a mixed group, took it all in their stride.

The Good Life is ephemeral, as I soon discovered. There retired to the nearby village of Ford a former General Secretary of the YMCA who took it on himself to keep a watchful eye on proceedings. He had a Scottish name and so, for the first time in his life, sported a sporran and a kilt as normal day wear. Sandy the gillie was not impressed. 'He has nae the knees for it!' The ultimate revelation of his Sassenach soul was at Hogmanay. 'It is ordinary among some plebeians in the South of Scotland to go about from door to door upon New-Year's Eve, crying Hagmane.' (*Presbyterian Eloquence* 1692). And on New Year's Day, carrying with them a few wee drams of whisky. Our friend brought with him a 70cl bottle of the golden distillate. Then he took from his pocket an optic spirit measure and slid it into the bottle neck. 'A real Scot would ha' thrown away the cork' was Sandy's comment, confided to me in a stage whisper.

Our faux-Scot brewed trouble for me, pressing the committee with the need to have proper oversight of groups using the centre, and offering his services. I was already involved in a spat with the committee. Its members had early on appointed as a fund-raiser a retired Canadian Brigadier. Without his help I had raised from the Carnegie Trust £12,000 to build a field lab and dark room. He was claiming £1,200 of this as, according to his contract, he was entitled to 10% of money raised. It did not specify that he had to do the raising. I opposed his claim. I had done all the work and the full amount was required to purchase the building. It annoyed me that committee members were unwilling to challenge him.

While buildings were under construction, and custom being drummed up, I was given a free hand. Within eighteen months of my appointment we were in profit. That was when the rule-making started. The Trust had a resource that they now wanted to encase in swaddling bands. I would have none of it and resigned.

A SCHOOL FOR REFUGEES

It was not until 1979 that I again had direct dealings with schooling. I was running Save the Children's Vietnamese resettlement programme. Refugees were in our fourteen centres for three months during which time English language tuition was being provided by teachers employed by the LEA. Some of these teachers were following up youngsters who, in settlement, were in local schools, to see how they were getting on. The schools reported that they were doing well. However, in many cases they were doing well in remedial classes. This worried our teachers as they knew that many of their former charges were bright. It worried me because the Vietnamese community needed youngsters who could obtain professional qualifications.

Professor Alan Little and Dr Richard Willey of Goldsmith's College had been undertaking a study for the Schools' Council. Their report's main conclusion was that

> ...there has been a failure to implement policy statements on multi-ethnic education, and a consequent lack of progress in the schooling of ethnic minority children. Two remaining deficiencies are a lack of advanced English lessons, particularly in specialist subjects, and a continued neglect of the special needs of West Indian children.

We established a pilot project at Campion House, our reception centre at Osterley. Fourteen youngsters were selected to be taught at a special language unit established by the local authority in Hounslow. The scheme was monitored by the Institute of Education. We had four questions: How would the experimentees cope with absence from their families? Would they progress as rapidly in a longer-term project as they had in reception classes? How would they cope with formal, written and specialist English? How much of what they had learnt in Vietnam was transferable?

It soon became apparent that any fears were unfounded. Progress in learning and social adjustment were rapid, and I concluded that we needed to go ahead with a residential school project. There were objections. Boarding schools are elitist and destructive of family life. Such a school would prevent pupils from integrating. The expense would be too great.

We were not seeking to create a cadre of the elite but to compensate for disadvantage. The Chinese and Vietnamese attach great importance to education and it is within their culture for the family to make sacrifices so that a member can study. The health of the Vietnamese community in the UK depended on having an educated leadership. In fact the Vietnamese house-mother said the school we established was 'a source of pride and a mark of identity'. As far as the youngsters themselves were concerned, I was convinced that if they underachieved they would not settle happily. Finally, we knew we could provide boarding education cheaper than any public school.

The Childcare UK Committee agreed that Save the Children would fund the school. We already had a reception centre in two of the halls of residence of the former teacher training college at Bingley in Yorkshire. It was relatively easy to acquire a third hall of residence. A couple, the Butchers, were recruited to run the school: Headmaster and 'Headmattress', as their pupils referred to them. The curriculum was science-heavy: 'O' levels in Physics, Chemistry, Biology, Chinese and Vietnamese, plus Cambridge First Certificate in English. I knew that, to make good progress, subjects needed to be understood both in the pupils' second language, English, and their mother tongue, so where possible everything was translated.

The school opened in September 1980 with 46 pupils, seven teaching staff, a house-mother, a secretary and two Vietnamese domestic staff. One of the teachers was Vietnamese, another Chinese. Most had taught abroad. Four had a maths/science background. In the light of the national shortage of such teachers it demonstrates that, if you offer a challenge and give responsibility you can usually attract excellent staff. We were not paying above the odds.

The school ran for two years during which time I had moved on so was never involved in its assessment. The report now lies buried in an archive in Birmingham. However, early on the teachers reported that in trying to keep pace with the speed with which their charges were consuming the curriculum they had never worked so hard.

In 1983 I went to Hartland to run the Small School, the subject of another chapter. There I became aware of an important aspect of teaching and that is the non-verbal dimension of what is taught and what is learnt. It is more than just an attitude towards, or enthusiasm for, a subject, though these are important. Faced with a page of music the player may play all the right notes but nevertheless fail to realise the spirit of the piece. That can be learnt not by instruction but by demonstration. The spirit is passed from one to the other. It is similar with the creative dimension of other subjects like art, literature and theatre, and also in the acquisition of a foreign language. There are limits to what can be learnt online.

Nevertheless, at the practical level, we educators need to show people how to teach themselves: where to find information, how to assess it, how to use it and how to write. This last point I underline because I fear that digital tools are in danger of undermining 'good writing', that is, writing that is rich, complex, and valuable. I seek help from the w.w.w and this is what comes up:

> The direct 'effect with' word processors tend towards more easy production but less planning and less meaningful revisions. Instructionally guiding tools, such as Computerised Supported Intentional Learning Environment (CSILE) and Writing Partner, that provide scaffolding and stimulate writing related cognitions, improve self regulation and metacognitive monitoring of the writing activities. Collaborative based writing tools, synchronous and asynchronous, embedded in meaningful learning environments provide another dimension of knowledge construction. In these environments, writing becomes an important mediation channel together with additional supporting 'mindtools', such as outliners. These mind tools can produce not just sequential essays but hypertexts that provide additional means of constructing and presenting knowledge. (Salomon, G., Kosminsky, E, & Asaf, M. (2003). Computers and Writing. In T. Nunes & Bryant, P. (Eds.) (2003). *Handbook of children's literacy*. (pp. 409-442). London: Kluwer.)

It may already be too late! Some, it seems, are born to obfuscate whilst others, on their iPhones, truncate.

So, yes, I commit strongly to the idea of learning throughout one's life, and of using the internet for this purpose. But there will always be a need for flesh-and-blood teachers to add a third dimension to the two dimensions of the computer screen.

Chapter Four

Inventing a school

IN THE LATE SEVENTIES my friends Satish Kumar and June Mitchell, with their two children Mukti and Maya, moved from West Wales to the North Devon village of Hartland taking with them the magazine *Resurgence*. As with most parents, a major concern was the education of their children. The village primary school they found to be reasonably satisfactory. The comprehensive school in Bideford was not. To begin with, the journey took an hour each way on an unsupervised bus, a breeding ground for bad behaviour and bullying.

Teresa Thorne, a pupil, gave a reporter her reasons for preferring the Small School to Bideford comprehensive: 'The journey took so long and the boys used to smoke on the bus and mess about in the lessons.' There was violence in the school: I was told that one teacher had had an arm broken and another's car had been upended. The comprehensive's academic results were mediocre. In the light of this unease about Bideford, reinforced by criticisms of the school in the press, a small group of parents met to discuss their options.

Nothing concrete had emerged when Satish took his family on a visit to India. Shortly after his return in early 1982 he learnt that the Methodist Sunday School was up for auction. In India he had seen dedicated people engaged in village work, and especially in education, and was inspired to set up a school in the village. He called a meeting of those who might support a new school, but purchasing the buildings was a step too far too soon. Undaunted, and with nothing in his purse, he bought a large hall (until 1915 a church), the schoolroom, a kitchen, a garden, two outside toilets and a two-bedroom caretaker's cottage for £20,000.

The deposit he borrowed from *Resurgence*, in the next issue of which he appealed for ten shareholders who would each put up £2,000. Eleven responded. The shareholders became trustees of the buildings but were given no say in the running of the school.

Shortly afterwards the house next door was acquired. A field behind the school, with outline planning permission for two houses, plus a barn that became a forge and then, when neighbours on the new estate objected to the smoke, a pottery workshop, were purchased in 1987. For each of these acquisitions shares were issued. Shareholders could realize their investments at any time, with reasonable notice, and their shares sold on at the appropriate proportion of the current market value. No interest was to be, nor has been, paid on the investments.

first year

The school opened that September with nine pupils. Michael Nix was appointed because he was prepared to accept a one-year commitment and, being local, would not suffer greatly if the school folded. He had lived in the village for eleven years, taught at the primary school for eight and thus knew many of the children. He was also a respected local historian who had set up the Hartland Quay museum.

The first year was not without difficulties.

Problems were identified by Wendy Berliner in an article in *The Guardian*. Although fees were only £100 per term some parents could not afford this.

> Devon County Council can offer no help because the school is private. Its officials also consider that any secondary school of less than 350 pupils which offers a sufficiently wide and varied curriculum will be extremely expensive to run.

Satish decided to approach the DES with a request for financial support and asked me to write a suitable paper. At the Institute of Education in London I had read up on AS Neill's Summerhill and a similar Scottish venture, as well as Bertrand and Nora Russell's school, Beacon Hill, but these were residential, middle-class and left of trendy. Since that time I had been challenged by Fritz Schumacher who concludes a chapter on Education with:

> The problems of education are merely reflections of the deepest problems of our age. They cannot be solved by organisation, administration, or the expenditure of money, even though the importance of these is not denied. We are suffering from a metaphysical disease, and the cure must therefore be metaphysical. Education which fails to clarify our central convictions is mere training or indulgence. For it is our central convictions that are in disorder, and, as long as the present anti-metaphysical temper persists, the disorder will grow worse. (*Small is Beautiful*)

I thought the Small School might meet Schumacher's challenge, though I did not say so. I focussed on the strength of diversity in provision and cited the Danish system as offering a convincing model for the UK. The Small School would be a pilot project.

Private schools in Denmark include small independent schools in rural districts (*friskoler*), progressive free schools, Rudolf Steiner schools and immigrant schools. Private schools receive government financing regardless of the ideological, religious, political or ethnic motivation behind their establishment. Private schools are usually much smaller than the municipal schools, but that does not seem to make them too expensive.

North Devon is a poor area so we needed government funding, and because we wanted to be seen as a state school – a village comprehensive – we were asking for voluntary aided status. The condition was that we teach the national curriculum and apply the associated tests, just like any state secondary. We would do that and more. We would give proper attention to the arts and to acquiring practical skills.

Satish and I went with Dr Clark, who taught biology at the Small School, to see Dr Rhodes Boyson, a Minister at the DES. He, the first secondary school head to put his pupils in for 'O' levels, author of one of the *Black Papers*, successful head of Highbury Grove Comprehensive school and ardent promoter of a voucher scheme that would have been of help to us, had written an article for *The Guardian* praising the small schools of Denmark and Holland. We journeyed in the joyful expectation of a positive outcome. We met Dr Boyson and a civil servant after lunch, which must have been a particularly good repast because he quietly dozed off. When he awoke, towards the end of our allotted time, he expressed sympathy for our project but regretted that he could offer no help.

Back in Hartland there was another setback. Differences had arisen between Michael Nix and Satish Kumar. There were squabbles among the parents. Michael reduced his commitment to three days a week. Daphne Kent was appointed to cover the other two days.

A confusion of aims was identified by Cyril Selmes and Mary Tasker from the University of Bath's School of Education in a research report on the school. They confirmed the differences in educational philosophy between Satish Kumar and the two teachers, who appeared to be 'somewhat didactic and traditional' in their approach.

Devon Education Authority's Senior Adviser for Secondary Education and the Principal Educational Psychologist visited the Small School in March 1983. Compared with home education, standards were acceptable but they fell short of those in a normal secondary school.

Satish arrived at my Islington door on a charm offensive. Michael and Daphne had resigned. Half the children were being withdrawn. Would I take over the school? I had, after all, written the paper for the DES. Hesitation was slight. How could I resist the challenge to try out my theories and turn the school around? Nothing was keeping me in London as I was on the point of resigning from the British Refugee Council. Julia was running Refugee Action but was prepared to work herself out of a job. We would sell up in Islington and move to Hartland, the Devon village 'furthest from the railway', and far from other marks of civilization. It is fifteen miles to the supermarket; twenty-five to A & E.

Nothing comes without a shadow side. The hiccup in the ointment: Satish had not consulted the other parents about my appointment. They, very properly, insisted on a selection process and one other candidate was quickly called for interview. I felt sorry for her as it was clear that the outcome was pre-ordained.

Having committed myself to the task I had to address criticisms and reservations made by the professionals who, I believe, imagined small schools as big schools hit by dwarfism. I was certainly not going to reproduce a dinky version of my own school experience. As a boy I was fitted out with a grey uniform, given a number and sat at one of thirty desks set in rows. My brother went into the army. He wore a uniform, was given a number and made to stand in rows. When my mother became a nurse she was issued a uniform and tended numbered patients laid out in rows. (Mr Oakroyd, in JB Priesley's *Good Companions,* is shown to 'Number twenty-seven, Lister Ward'. Number twenty-seven is his wife.)

These similarities between school, army and hospital are no accident. Michel Foucault has shown how, with prisons and factories, they share a common organization in which it is possible to control the use of an individual's time and space hour by hour. The buildings are designed to serve this end. Discipline is imposed not only by punishment but also by observation and supervision. The staff oversees meals and play. The exam is a surveillance that makes it possible 'to qualify, to classify and to judge'.

Steiner and Montessori designed and demonstrated viable alternatives to this rigid regime. Lady Plowden's report on primary education (1967) promoted child-centred learning, and education through discovery and play. Why should her methods, I wondered, be restricted to primary schools? I was late in asking the question for, by the 1980s, with the exception of the Beatles, everything from the decadent Sixties was being ditched so, along with any extant copies of the schoolkids edition of OZ, the *Plowden Report* itself was trashed. Condemning some English materials published by LINC, the philosopher Roger Scruton declared that they 'show an indelible mark of the egalitarian nonsense that was being taught in the Sixties'. He also demanded that teacher training colleges be closed down because they were hotbeds of this nonsense. I still believed in the Sixties and dissed Scruton: an impressive handful of philosophers can be called to Plowden's defence.

Plato, Quintilian, Locke and Rousseau were on her side. Study as play, study as diversion. Surely that is better than dragging a lad through the processes of education, as DH Lawrence has described, to produce 'a profound contempt for education and for all educated people (which) has meant nothing to him but irritation and disgust'?

I determined to pursue a third way that fell between the army camp and the flower garden, to being either 'drilled' or 'watered'. I faced two questions. Were the critics right that we would need specialists to teach the main subjects? Would we find teachers prepared to teach for poor remuneration and without job security or the promise of a pension?

That was not all. Bell and Sigsworth itemised the disadvantages of *The Small Rural Primary School*:

1. Teachers may suffer professional isolation.
2. A wide age range in a single class may prove too difficult for some teachers.
3. The range of curriculum to be taught may be daunting for a small staff.
4. Small peer group size does not provide adequate stimulation and competition, particularly for the older children.
5. Small schools are costly.

(Falmer Press 1987, p.65)

I believed that I had an answer for each of these points. Professional isolation is not restricted to the staff of small schools. Heads of schools of all sizes felt, and still feel, isolated and report high levels of stress. They receive no proper support.

It is true that not every teacher can cope with a wide age range in a class. Nor might they cope with a wide range of ability. However, one can teach in a way that makes such considerations irrelevant. And teaching a group of eight is quite different from teaching a group of thirty.

Does each subject require its own specialist? We expect youngsters to command a clutch of GCSEs. Why, then, might we not expect to find teachers who are able to cover several areas of the curriculum? I would search out Renaissance men and women, surely not an extinct species.

We would have to see what the effect of having a small peer group would be.

On point four I am, like Dora Russell, more interested in cooperation than competition and do not embrace the latter as a suitable motivator.

We would appoint full-time teachers at the ratio of one to twelve pupils, and supplement these with local part-timers. We would not be paying salaries at the national rate. Instead we would be offering the opportunity to participate in an exciting educational project.

The challenge I faced in bringing together parents, teachers and pupils for the invention of the school was to tease out the commonalities and negotiate compromises. But also to remind them that we were committed to responding to individual need in appropriate ways.

A programme of work negotiated between teacher and pupil solves the curriculum problem once it is accepted that there does not have to be the same, uniform, programme for everyone. Surely, if our starting point was the needs of the children – children living in a rural environment – everything else would follow?

To start from the child's needs does not mean allowing the child to become a dictator but to put the interest of the child before any educational theory, teacher comfort or state interest. Education has to be conceived and organised 'as though children matter', and at its heart the human being in all her fullness, not the curriculum, the economy nor the school.

Satish had his own ideas of how to organize the school. He envisaged some sort of manual work that would earn the school money. That was what he had seen in India. Julia and I had seen it too when we toured schools there. One was Laxmi Ashram, a boarding school for girls in Kausani in the Himalayas, a beautiful spot dubbed by Gandhi the 'Switzerland of India'. It was founded by Sarala Ben, an English disciple of the Mahatma, in 1948.

The girls at the school come from poor families. They spend the morning doing physical work. I watched a group of them precariously perched in the dizzying heights of evergreen oak trees harvesting young leaves to feed to the cows, necessary as there was only a limited area, under the pines after the rains, for the grazing of their small herd. Others were balancing bowls of manure on their heads to feed to the biogas plant. Yet others were preparing the ground for the planting of capsicum seedlings in beds thirty feet long and ten feet wide. Beans, potatoes, coriander and radishes were developing nicely. In these ways the morning was spent, with formal lessons taking place in the afternoon.

This accords with ideas expressed by Satish's mentor, Vinoba Bhave:

> Teaching must take place in the context of real life. Set the children to work in the fields, and when a problem arises there give them whatever knowledge of cosmogony, or physics, or any other science, is needed to solve it. Set them to cook a meal, and as the need arises teach them chemistry. In one word, let them live...

With this I could not, in principle, disagree. But sums scribbled on the back of a postage stamp led to the conclusion that there was nothing in Hartland that we could produce for sale that would not smack of child slavery, so many hours being required to add value to the limited pool of available raw material. Nevertheless, we have done what we could, both practically and for income generation.

Pupils have had to take responsibility for their environment, the afternoon ending with Henrys and dusters. Lunch has been prepared daily by two pupils and a teacher, the latter teaching as they cooked. We baked our own bread. To begin with many boys questioned the propriety of having to cook. After a couple of years new boys were 'sorted' by the older boys and it became routine. In the early days up to eight pupils brought in sandwiches. Quite quickly all were enjoying school lunches. Once a week three older pupils cooked unsupervised. Catering could also generate some income.

On a number of occasions the main classroom has been transformed into a restaurant and themed meals served. We had delicious Italian, Indian, French and Gourmet Vegetarian evenings. The single failure was the Norwegian meal for, despite most of the ingredients being imported from the country itself, the attempt to make salt fish (*klippfisk*) and a kind of porridge (*rommegrot*) exciting failed dismally. Their names alone should have been warning enough. Our vegetarian cuisine was a lot more appetising than that. Outside catering became profitable. We have provided lunches for those attending the Schumacher Lectures and the Triodos Bank's

AGMs, usually in Bristol. The café at the monthly Farmers Market was run by the school.

These events, which bring together students, parents and teachers in a common endeavour, are real team builders that show parents that their teenage offspring are not really adolescent layabouts but that they can play a full part in grown-up work. Four hundred meals prepared, packed and transported to Bristol and then served is no slight challenge.

Parental contributions and local fund-raising produced about half of what was needed to run the school. The rest of the money has come from charitable trusts: the Calouste Gulbenkian Foundation, the Sainsbury Family Charitable Trust, the Ernest Cook Trust, the Tudor Trust, the Northgate Devon Foundation, the Wates Foundation, the Chasers Trust, the Howe Green Trust, the Elmgrant Trust, and the Cherry Tree Foundation. We were a campaigning project. They gave because we managed to persuade them of the benefits of small schools. Like us, they wanted to see a widening of government provision. That also meant that we had to court publicity and be up front with our monitored successes and failures.

TRANSMITTING VALUES

'A school is not merely a teaching shop, it must transmit values and attitudes', wrote Lady Plowden. Fritz Schumacher described education similarly as the 'transmission of ideas of value, of what to do with our lives.' These ideas of value do not come from within education. Education has its values brought to it from outside itself. There are three major influences on these values: the home, the peer group and the teachers. A divergent problem now rears its head. What values? Whose values?

Parents and teachers are unlikely to reach agreement on what those values are. A majority of people in the UK today seem to find their values in the store between the Sock Shop and the Tie Rack. Some buy club ties and others dispense with socks; some subscribe to the Moslem creed, a few to the Christian, but most seek street cred and go for Shopping. However, parents usually want their offspring to outperform them, value-wise, not replicate their shortcomings. They look to the school for this. One small example: parents who smoked telling us we had to discourage their children from inhaling various 'weeds', not just *nicotania tabacum* but also cannabis.

A concern with values and their transmission means that the teacher must engage with the whole child. Likewise, the child should meet the whole teacher, values and all. Not for me the professional mask. For me the struggle to live what I teach in the place where I teach. This is crucial if we are to address the whole person: intellect, will, feelings, imagination and aesthetic sensibility.

A teacher who has succumbed to nihilistic philosophy and who passes on what Viktor Frankl called the 'nothingbutness' of man, 'the theory that man is nothing but the result of biological, psychological and sociological conditions, or the product of heredity and environment', is of little help. We are more than that. We feel and respond to the challenges posed by what is going on in the world around us, by conflicts, by depleting resources, by pollution and by the widening gap between rich and poor, both in our own country and the world at large. The way a school is managed and the lifestyle of the teachers provide the model for appropriate responses. If I thought this was obvious I was brought up sharply by the heads of small primary schools in Dorset for whom I was running a workshop. Several of them were horrified at the idea of living where they taught. They would not be able to 'be themselves'. They declined what they described as 'a fishbowl existence'. In school they wore the mask of the professional.

Where social deprivation is the root cause of disaffection, where farmers' sons are forced from the land, where rights and benefits are eroded and lives deprived of purpose and meaning the teacher, through understanding and insight, shares the pain and suffering. That is, a teacher who has a vision of a more just society and already lives those values. We also have a responsibility to encourage access to a wider range of avenues that might lead to gainful employment.

Formal qualifications – certificated – are never enough. The youngster whose sense of worth has been brought out, who knows his or her strengths and weaknesses and is confident, honest and has a sense of humour, is an asset to any society and attractive to most employers. And we have already seen that, in the minds of politicians, preparing pupils for gainful employment is a primary goal for schools. Of course, these attributes are more difficult to develop and test than literacy and numeracy, and those who employ teachers and pay for schools are reluctant to subscribe to goals that cannot be tested.

The centrality of the pupil to our enterprise began with the interview. Peter Dollimore wrote of his experience:

> I came to the school straight from primary school. It was my own decision. My parents had given me a choice between the comprehensive, twelve miles away, or the Small School, six miles from home... On visiting the comprehensive my parents and I were shown around by the head of the first year. He paid hardly any attention to me ... When I visited the Small School I was immediately accepted, and just joined in with what was happening... I actually felt that my contributions to the conversation were as important as anyone else's. After half-an-hour I already felt part of the school, and it seemed the obvious choice... If I were allowed to retake that decision at 11 years of age I would do exactly the same as I did, without a doubt. (SMALLTALK)

SETTING THE AGENDA

My arrival at the school for its second year was a new beginning. Half the pupils had left, as well as the two main teachers. Within months of my becoming Head Selmes and Tasker (Bath University) reported:

> This confusion of aims [see above] now seems to have been resolved. With the appointment in September 1983 of a new head teacher, Colin Hodgetts, a philosophy of participatory pupil learning, grounded in the community, has emerged. The feeling of the school is now purposeful and optimistic. ...His contribution to the fourfold organism – children, parents, teachers, community – is, however, to bring to it a conviction that all four elements are crucial and that in the dynamic interaction between the four elements there must be the opportunity for all to have their say.

Mary Tasker put her finger on what it is that I do. I establish and nurture a positive environment for our work together. Then, whether we are creating a school, a play, a concert or a building, I encourage those involved to believe that we can pull it off. Leadership is not a matter of knowing the 'right' answers, of being able to present a detailed plan which everyone can follow. It is a matter of convincing people that we can reach a common goal and that all things will work together for good. Sometimes individuals are not convinced and they drop out, for not everyone is a risk-taker or believes that 'all things are possible for those who have faith'. Occasionally some adult wants a change of course – it has happened twice at the school – which they argued for as a 'democratic' development but in reality was a leadership challenge. One just has to be more patient than them and remain 'a still centre'.

second year

For *Inventing a School* (*Resurgence*, 1991), my account of the first years, something on aims had to be written. I boiled it down to two simple statements: 'The school exists for its students' and 'our model is the family and not the factory'. This may seem too obvious to need stating until one realises that in many, if not most, schools decisions are made for the convenience of the teachers or to implement a government policy or to meet some parental requirement, governors' interest or society goal. One has to keep reminding staff, parents, and trustees, gently of course, that the students always come first.

We committed ourselves to the development of the whole person, body, mind and spirit, in all its aspects, creative, practical, intellectual, ethical and emotional. This, again, may seem unexceptional were it not that most schools have downgraded the arts and creativity, and don't take seriously what it means to address the spirit. 'Spirituality' is not something that can be taught.

It is something that is 'caught', and that has led to a fourth important statement: 'The person of the teacher is more important than the matter taught or the methods used.' Because no one can inspire others to be better than they are themselves, it is not possible to lay down a vision and expect others to follow it. It has to be shared, which can put us teachers on the spot!

Learning, whether to read or swim, has a great deal to do with motivation. Paolo Freire and others have shown that, when the printed word contains material essential to the improvement of life, people of any age will learn to read in a remarkably short time. In order to discover the motivational key I have chucked a lot of material around.

Poetry is the most challenging aspect of Eng. lit. One year students were fed bits of Ted Hughes' 'Crow'; Tony Harrison on TV returning to his home town and using a lot of swear words; an article in the *Observer* by a prisoner turned on by Eliot's 'Four Quartets'; odd verses and poems read at random from the books on the shelves. Then they had to choose either several poems by the same poet, or several poems on a theme, for their project. Most had no idea what to do. In their search, they read a lot of poetry. A choice was made but more often than not, abandoned when the real work had just started. Eventually something was found that held the attention. Most were now motivated to pursue their poetry project.

Andrew took one of the *Canterbury Tales* and compared the language to Devonshire. Sam responded to some poems by Rosalind Brackenbury, who had run a writing week for us, Naomi studied Eliot's 'Four Quartets', Peter took those 'Crow' poems in which God speaks to Crow, Ruth chose Wendell Berry's 'A Part', and Hannah, George Mackay Brown's two versions of the 'Stations of the Cross' with reference to 'The Wreck of the Deutschland' by Gerard Manley Hopkins.

Katy, one of the previous year's candidates, explored Eliot's 'Preludes'. She noted that all but two lines begin with a weak word.

> 'I experimented with messing up the position of words in this poem and discovered that a strong word at the beginning of a line gives the other words in that line less weight... Eliot put weak words to start the lines, making all the words equally stressed. In doing so he made every image equal.'

She concluded her essay:

> 'Preludes' describes, in general, through its images, the effects city
> life and poverty have on people. 'Preludes' is not written by a
> neutral observer. T.S. Eliot hates the state of the place he is living
> in. The writer's attitudes are shown in what he writes. It is not
> only the picture created by his words which is depressing but the
> underlying assumption that, if everything is broken, sordid and
> decaying, happiness is impossible.

Pupils also had the freedom to choose their wider-reading project.
Claire could not decide on the subject and came to me to discuss it.
She had been reading Thomas Hardy. Asked for her reaction to his
writing she said that she had the impression that the novels got
gloomier and gloomier and that the public would not have
accepted one darker than *Jude the Obscure*. Could she test this thesis?
She read the final six novels in chronological order, quite an
achievement for a 15-year-old. Her A-grade essay was very
perceptive.

Sometimes one has to discover and remove a block.
Simon Rodway was a bright pupil of ours who was advised that he
would need maths and a foreign language to get to university. He
was turned off maths and he had not been studying French. He
cracked the latter in a matter of months but he had a real block
about maths. At primary school his text books were illustrated with
silly cartoons so in his mind maths was a silly subject. With the
help of his mother the block was removed and he passed his exam.
Now he is a lecturer in Celtic studies at Aberystwyth University.

The national curriculum makes the approach just
described exceptionally difficult, as does the frequent change in
policy. A minister is in his or her seat for a far shorter period than
a child is at secondary (or primary) school, yet with each change of
minister there is a change of direction and sometimes two.

A quick look at current educational research reveals three
problems that tend to perpetuate the present system in all its
banality. The first is technical: there are too many variables that
cannot be isolated. This has led to a greater use of direct
observation, which is fine, except that in the effort to keep it
rigorous its focus has tended towards the marginal and the trivial.

The second is statistics, 'damned statistics'. Most research
deals with what may be true in general in a population. But in the
classroom I am dealing with Tracy, and Tracy may be an exception

to the general rule. How am I to know? It is the individual with whom we have to reckon. To know that 80% of the group are honest is unhelpful. We need to know that Jill tells the truth and Jack is a liar. Anything less precise is useless.

How the success of the school was to be assessed was a big problem for us, being too small for the methods of most researchers. In any case, the critical question, how far has this school helped this child to realise his or her full potential, is impossible to answer. You cannot test potential.

SILENCE

Each day began with Circle and I accompanied a song on the guitar. There would be a talk by one of the staff, often of a personal nature, or a reading, followed by a silence. Pupils still remember some of those talks and the words of the songs.

Silence has always been important. I discouraged other teachers from hushing the group so that the Circle could begin. We would wait until all had come down to silence. That meant I had to hold the silence.

I was invited to give the Sunday evening address to pupils at Christ's Hospital where Ruth, a former pupil, was taking her 'A' levels. As the staff were lining up to process into Chapel the Head told me that it was quite usual for some of the boys to chat quietly. They were not being disrespectful. I was not going to have that. So standing statue-like at the lectern I brought them down to silence. Then I spoke. I have to admit to not knowing whether it would work, and was relieved that it did. Yes, silence is something that we carry with us.

We do not need to be loud to be listened to. It is in the still small voice that the truth is to be heard. An interview with a member of the Modern Jazz Quartet was a reminder of this. When they started they were playing to audiences that were noisy and rude. Instead of turning up their own volume, as most other groups did, they turned it down: people had to make an effort to hear. It worked. They also bucked the trend with their appearance: they wore dinner jackets.

We had no punishments. An individual who disrupts a lesson can have either positive or negative reasons for doing so. On the positive side it may be an excessive exuberance that can be the fallout from what has been going on before the lesson, or it can be a lack of engagement with the material, or a personal problem. So we bring the group down to silence and explore what is going on.

The individual who is not participating would probably be sent to the kitchen where practical activity, coupled with Caroline's sympathetic ear, met the situation. We had some youngsters with serious problems. It was a constant challenge to find ways of meeting their needs whilst allowing the main activity of teaching and learning to plough on.

STAFF

We have been lucky with our teachers. For my first year Peter and Kirsty Rosser lived in the cottage. Peter had a degree in psychology and was a trained probation officer. He was responsible for rural studies/conservation projects and games. Kirsty was a qualified French teacher who took charge of the kitchen and taught basket weaving.

Peter teaching biology

Peter also chaired the Small School meetings. His Quaker commitment meant that we always sought consensus. What is important is that the meeting decides when and how a particular issue will be resolved. I was impressed by this process and have adopted it when chairing meetings of other organisations.

Peter and I worked well together. One morning there was a strange atmosphere in the school. It was clear from the buzz that something had happened, but we weren't sure what. Several of the boys were more hyper than usual. Nigel (not his real name), something of a troublemaker, was one and we asked to see him. 'We know what has been going on', we said, 'and it will be best for you if you tell us about it'. Nigel fell for it and admitted that he and some others had been shoplifting. We told the offenders that they would have to take back the items that they had stolen to the shopkeepers. They were not happy about this, fearing retribution. We informed the parents, some of whom wanted us to call in the police. We stuck with our recommendation and promised that if the same thing happened again then we would follow their advice and call in the police. With grumbles they agreed to our proposal.

Peter offered to go with the boys and sit outside in the car. Reluctantly they set off. Nigel returned radiant. The shopkeeper had been quite taken aback and did not know how to respond. It had never happened to her before. She told him to keep the things that he had pinched. What disappointed me most was the lack of taste. They had lifted a lot of tatty junk.

There was no more shoplifting, but it was not the end of Nigel's misdemeanours. A parent who lived near Nigel requested an urgent appointment. Nigel had stolen about £500-worth of his goods. The nature of these goods was not clear. Once again Nigel was up for interview. Again he was honest. This parent had been growing cannabis alongside the edge of the road. Nigel and a friend had harvested it. I phoned the parent and said I thought the case was too tricky for me to deal with and the police would need to be called. He withdrew the complaint.

On the impending arrival of their first child in December 1983 Pete and Kirsty moved to a smallholding in Welcombe and were replaced by Chris and Becky Howe who, with their twin daughters, moved into the cottage.

With numbers increasing we converted the kitchen in the house into a small lab and sought a science teacher. Maggie Agg had read zoology at Durham and been a research assistant in Bristol. She and her husband Mike, a design engineer with Rolls-Royce, moved into the village. Interviewed by Susanna Kirkman of the *Times Educational Supplement* Maggie said that she was convinced that though the school was small the curriculum was not hampered by lack of facilities.

> As well as chemistry and biology, the pupils are doing a general ecology course covering coastal, heathland, rocky shore and wetland areas. Hartland is only three miles from the dramatic North Devon coast and within striking distance of Dartmoor and Exmoor. Physics and craft, design and technology are taught by a former design engineer, Tim Neville, who now runs a smallholding and works as an electrician. We think it's important that children are taught by people who can actually earn a living from the skills they teach. It gives them more authority.

Kirkman noted that the school is based on the belief that learning how to make a living and to get on with others is more important than passing exams. She cited the examples of Billy Jewell, taking extra maths and animal biology to help with his farm work; of Stephen Partridge, learning bookkeeping through doing the school's books so that he could help his father, a farmer and agricultural contractor; of Patrick Clark who developed his interests in forestry and conservation, as well as learning how to re-tile roofs. His mother said: 'the school transformed my son from a self-conscious young man to someone who can cope with life.' Patrick had been exceedingly unhappy at his previous school and begun to truant. These were pupils who came to us partway through their secondary schooling. Those who were with us for the full five years took exams.

As Chris and Becky's twins outgrew the cottage they moved on, to be replaced by Philip and Annabel Toogood. Philip had been headmaster of Madeley Court comprehensive school where his experiment with mini-schools offended many and he was forced to leave. Having taken early retirement he came to Hartland to edit the journal he had founded, *Dialogue in Education*, to coordinate the Human Scale Education Movement, which Satish and I had founded with the help of the Gulbenkian Trust, and to support Annabel by acting as caretaker. Annabel had charge of the kitchen and taught typing and French.

Their daughter Sarah was beginning her 'O' levels and he undertook to tutor her. He also taught some English and assisted with humanities and games. This was a difficult time for us. Philip wanted to have charge of all those who were preparing for exams, and at each staff meeting argued for more responsibility, including having his own group for assembly. Many hours were spent turning down his requests, for he repeated them at every staff meeting. I managed not to lose my cool. Fortunately he was lured away by a party of parents from Derby.

Julia Meiklejohn arrived at the same time to teach maths. Her degree is in economics and she worried that, as she was not a trained teacher, she might have some difficulty. However, we signed up in its early days to GAIM, the Graded Assessment in Maths project, which enabled us to undertake GCSEs with 100% coursework. Julia participated in workshops and training. She had no difficulties in the classroom. As this system is based on individuals progressing at their own speed it was ideally suited to the Small School, particularly as at age eleven there can be a six-year age spread of ability in maths.

Caroline and Keith Walker took over from the Toogoods. They had been in India since 1979 where they were involved in community development and primary health care. My colleagues had to be persuaded to accept them on the basis of the experiences and values outlined in their letter because there was no way we could ask them to come from India for an interview.

Their reasons for applying fitted exactly with our philosophy:

> We want to tackle at the source the problems of underdevelopment, the effects of which in terms of poverty, illness, ignorance and exploitation we have been dealing with in our daily life for the past seven years. This means that we want to be part of the growing movement for change, not only in the outward structures of society, but on a personal level. Everything we have read about the Small School convinces us that you are making a really important contribution to this movement.

Caroline ran the kitchen and taught French and humanities. Keith helped with games and humanities, as well as doing the caretaking. Caroline wrote in *Inventing a School*:

> In the course of our work and our studies connected with it, we began to discern a global perspective to the problems around us. We were convinced that change was necessary, but it became more obvious as time went on that housing the homeless, treating the sick, and other activities directly involved in the relief of suffering, although personally satisfying, were only partial solutions to the problem. We saw that without change in national and global political and economic structures, poverty and

inequality continue to exist, and yet as foreigners we had no part to play in political activity in India. The underlying ambivalence of our situation became apparent and we realised that only in our own country did we have a chance of being effective workers for change; and it was at this point that we saw the vacancy at the Small School.

So we have arrived at another principle: 'Think global, act local', an idea whose paternity is variously ascribed to the town planner Patrick Geddes (1915), to Jacques Ellul, *Penser globalement, agir localement*, (1968), and to David Brower, founder of FOE (1969). It is a concept that has informed most of the projects described in this book. Governments may think globally but they cannot act locally, not because their decisions do not result in change at a local level but because they cannot envisage and plan for all the variations that may arise there.

Considering the national shortage of trained science teachers there were a surprising number of applicants for Maggie Agg's job when she left to have a baby. We appointed Sue Clark, a biologist, to replace her. In response to a journalist who asked why she had taken such a large cut in salary Sue replied: 'I just thought there must be more to life than this. It was a lot of pressure for little reward. I taught eleven different classes, that's 300 kids. The hardest thing was trying to get to know them.' (*The Teacher*)

Sue came with a wide experience and training in mountaineering, rock climbing and other outdoor pursuits, including the preparation of youngsters for the Duke of Edinburgh award. She was also a member of a group organising Amnesty International's national training programme. In addition she taught sewing.

At this time we also gained the services of Antoinette Moat who once a week worked with individual children using the Alexander technique. It is usually music and drama students who get this attention but Antoinette was concerned that our students, too, were not using their bodies properly. 'The joy of seeing a child's shoulders open out and widen and their bodies emerging free is a great gift to me.'

The fact that we could do 100% coursework for our GCSEs was a great boon. We had made a decision that everyone would sit five subjects: English, maths, science, humanities, and art, for those are all that are required for University entrance – a balanced handful.

We had some spectacular successes. Mukti's science project for which, having sought advice from our tame Rolls-Royce engineer, he designed and built a wind generator, was commended by the moderator and later published by the examination board as an example of work deserving 100% marks. Our artwork always received high praise, the best of it up to 'A' level standard. When later Paul Wilkinson added photography the examiner said the standard was first-year university.

Our package soon became six subjects because I taught English and English literature together: two for the price of one, and in the time allotted to one. An element of the course regarded as tricky was, and remains, the Shakespeare play. Participating in the English teachers' training-for-marking GCSE sessions I discovered that many schools were taking just a few scenes from their chosen Shakespeare play, sometimes as little as the Witches scenes in *Macbeth*. It seemed that this was short-selling the Bard. We studied whole texts, and where possible, produced the play, the first being *The Tempest* which we put on at Bideford College. How can you tell if a play script is any good if you don't see it in production? We were quite geared up to Shakespeare as you will discover in the chapter on theatre.

Humanities was shared between members of staff and is intended to cover History, Geography, Social Studies and RE. There were eight modules a year. In 1991 these were The Community, Health, Beliefs, Education, The Family, The Mass Media, Persecution & Prejudice, and Pollution & Conservation.

The teaching of building skills was a relief from book work. To begin with my group undertook repairs and decorating on a Friday afternoon. This was not completely satisfactory. Preparation and cleaning up took too much time. To discover the proper rhythm for a building project would require a whole day. We had a real project: to add a woodwork shop to our buildings. This involved reinforcing the garden wall, erecting block and stone walls, slating the roof, fitting a wooden floor and laying on water and electricity. All this was done without outside help. There was no scaffolding or hardhats. Messing about, however, was never an option. The building did not remain a woodwork shop for long. It was snaffled by Sue the science teacher and equipped as a lab.

the building group

Two of HM's inspectors visited in the third year. They were particularly impressed with the unity and commitment of the staff, and with the quality of the school building and its resources. They were less happy with pupils' written work. I replied that, thanks to radio and TV we are living in a post-literate society, and thanks to the pocket calculator, in a post-numerate one, too. Shouldn't we rather spend our energies in developing powers of discrimination, vis a vis TV, and oral skills, than in pushing book after book under disdainful noses in the slender hope that one will kindle a spark? (Have you spotted the bulge where my tongue was putting pressure on my cheek?)

Fun was to be had with Her Majesty's Inspectors. To begin with, I could not supply them with a lesson plan. I like to work with whatever comes up in class, because that is at the forefront of pupil's minds. Knowing the curriculum and knowing what each pupil knows and does not know is sufficient. (And what happens if you get run over by a bus?) At the right time the pupil's need can be met with the appropriate response. It seems pointless to spend a lesson teaching the difference between 'their' and 'there' if half the class knows it already. What I really enjoyed was getting the inspector, who was supposed to be observing, involved in the lesson itself, maybe by asking direct questions of him. As in subatomic physics, the observer changes the thing being observed. By joining in the Inspector becomes less visible.

One difficulty we had with HMI was that not all activities were undertaken every week or even every term. With music and drama we coxed and boxed, term and term about. Fortunately the inspector concerned, having experienced music, accepted a video of one of our play productions as evidence of quality drama. Another thing they could not examine was our six Special Weeks, and to these I shall come back.

VISITORS

We have had some interesting visitors, including Jhampa Wangdu Lama, head of Tibetan refugee education in Nepal, who stayed for two weeks. He had become disillusioned with the education system inherited from the British. It did not meet the needs of his Tibetan refugee children; it was too narrow and lacked creativity. It emphasised the intellectual at the expense of everything else. He wanted to establish a new school and had a clear idea of what this would be like. His difficulty was in persuading the education authorities to approve it. He therefore needed a new British model with which to challenge the old, so he came to the Small School. Julia and I later visited the school that he established in Kathmandu. It had a vibrant character of its own.

Beaford Arts sponsored a week of workshops on Ghanaian culture, history, geography, arts and religion by four members of the Lanzel African Arts group, ending with a Yam Festival of food, music and dance on the Saturday night attended by many people from the village.

The three members of the Omelette Broadcasting Company provided an afternoon of hilarious improvisation and mime which stimulated new departures in school drama and led to a request for them to lead a workshop.

One visitor, a PGCE student from Kings College, London, spent a week in the school and wrote:

> The children are really delightful. Most of them have a very distinct quality, a mixture of independence and openness... They are completely unselfconscious, with a few exceptions of course, and treat you very much as an equal, without any false airs, a real contrast to many of the children of their age at my teaching practice school who had a veneer of hostility while actually being much more emotionally dependent.

Inventing a school

These are just three examples of visitors and their inputs.

SPECIAL WEEKS

The second half of the summer term can be a fairly unproductive period. It was therefore decided that we would have six special weeks, each one devoted to a particular subject. Every year we had a Writing Week, and most years during my time we went cycling in Brittany. There might also be a Craft Week, and perhaps a Drama or a Music Week. We have had a Science Week in which groups were given the task of designing an experiment or piece of equipment that would accomplish a particular task.

Caroline supervising clothes week

We went camping in Guernsey. Pete Rosser took a group to Exmoor to explore the flora and fauna. In another week we hiked down the Cornish coastal path as far as Falmouth, staying at youth hostels on the way. In 1989 we took 19 pupils to Denmark to participate in an international fortnight working on a project to raise money for a school for street children in Mozambique. There were also trips to Poland, Germany, Italy and Japan. I will come to Japan later.

A journalist observed an Italian week.

Everything is Italian – language, lessons, lunch. There is a tantalising aroma of *tagliatelle col pesto* curling up from the kitchen below, where two children, as usual, are helping to prepare the

93

midday meal. Others are discovering Marconi in the cramped laboratory and have managed to pick up Radio One on a crystal set. Even the organiser of this particular week, teacher and parent Pam Rodway, usually delicate and softly spoken, appears to have turned herself into a formidable Neapolitan fishwife. (Diana Winsor, *The Sunday Times*)

Writing Weeks were led by a poet or novelist. The teachers joined in. Writing or composing is a sweaty business. During one of these I wrote a poem in public: six drafts on the blackboard with a description of the process: the choices, the frustrations.

By the end of the week we saw some exciting writing, but the first two or three days could be a difficult time. Many students were not used to concentrating on a piece of work for longer than the duration of a lesson. On the first day of one of these weeks I wrote a Frog & Toad story to address this, and read it at Tuesday morning's Circle. (People of all ages seem to like children's stories.) It was about the difficulties they were facing.

For several years we spent one of our Special Weeks in London, taking advantage of Tent City which had been established when I was Director of Christian Action. In return for our labour Tent City paid for our outings. Keith Walker wrote:

... In exchange for bunk beds and board we helped erect fourteen marquees, brightened up some of the permanent buildings with paint, and cooked meals for ourselves and the rest of the staff. The quality of the cooking was praised by several people. We visited three major museums: Science, Natural History and the Museum for the Moving Image...We saw three exceptional theatre productions, a musical by Stephen Sondheim, *Sunday in the Park with George*, about the painter Seurat, Ibsen's *The Wild Duck* (Peter Hall) and the RSC's *As You Like It*. Not only was this an opportunity to see some outstanding acting but for many it was their first experience of the glamour and excitement of big London theatres. A group visited Centrepoint, the shelter for young homeless near Piccadilly, and heard about the problems faced by young incomers to London. There were also visits to Chinatown, Covent Garden, the Tate and an exhibition of the history of rock 'n' roll. Some went on a boat trip on the Thames to Greenwich.

Youngsters were encouraged to explore on their own, learning how to use the tube and find their way around, just as long as they stuck to the rule of three: no fewer than three in a group. I sigh when I see school crocodiles processing from site to site.

By 1988 we were offering German, Italian and Latin, as well as French. The Italian group went to Umbria where they worked on a lovely old Italian farm and in the olive groves, with trips to local towns like Assisi and Gubbio, as well as to Florence. They witnessed a spectacular local festival involving the procession of large wooden structures representing saints around the town. The young men bearing them were startled when some of the girls tried to assist.

At Easter 1990 the German learners went with Sue, Stephanie and Agee to Berlin, returning with bits of the wall. Abi, Ruth, Claire and Bis wrote of their experience:

> On Sunday we visited *Sachsenhausen KZ*, one of the concentration camps in Germany. We felt that we had to go in to find out what really happened and to honour those who were murdered there. As we walked through the gates we saw the cryptic words, *Arbeit Macht Frei*, 'work makes free'. This was an illustration to us of the perverted nature of Nazi thinking. There was a large track which stretched around the main square of the camp. The prisoners were made to march, wearing badly-fitting boots and carrying a 20 kg sack of sand, round this track fifty times a day: about 40 km. In this way the old and the sick were killed off quickly… The day was cold and the wind raw, to match the gloomy atmosphere… Inside the museum we were sickened to see on display a clump of hair and a collection of teeth with gold fillings. These were two of the gains mass murder gave to the Nazis. We went over to the shooting galleries and the gas chambers, where prisoners were told they were going to have a shower and were gassed instead. Luckily, there was no more to see and we were all relieved to be out of that hellhole.

A trip like this combines so many elements: history, geography, ethics and, of course, German.

That year, 1989/90, we had our full complement of pupils, thirty-six. Simon won a scholarship to the sixth form of a local independent school. Katie moved to a sixth form college for her A-levels. Andrew gained a place on a two-year course at Bicton Agricultural College. Brendan began work on his father's farm with short courses at Bicton. He learnt how to weld at the school and has become much in demand among local farmers. In 2015 his engineering firm sponsored two floats in the local carnival. Jeanette was working with her family. Nick was doing building work. Becky moved away to start a family.

Of the five criticisms of small schools by Bell and Sigsworth listed earlier, it can be shown that the first four do not apply to the Hartland Small School. Teachers have not 'suffered from professional isolation' because they were working with others in a cross-curricular way. The age range was not as wide as the ability range.

The make-up of the school was interesting because we had a higher proportion of clever girls to boys. My assumption was that parents were prepared to take more chances with daughters than with sons. On the whole the boys who came were worried by the size of the comprehensives, some having had a bad experience there. There was also the matter of sport. Although we took games seriously we were unable to offer team sports, a restricting factor.

The limited size of the peer group had two positive outcomes: friendships developed between youngsters who would not normally have sought each other out and the relationship between boys and girls was more mature than is usual. Also many pupils had friends outside the school. What they had in addition was a wider and richer range of experiences than those in bigger schools.

It is true that, with a maximum of thirty-six children on the books, and if we were paying teachers proper salaries, we would have cost more per place than an LEA school. With sixty places, however, we could be competitive.

Michael Young – Lord Young of Dartington, the inventor of the Open University – spent a day at the school. He reckoned that up to about 80 would be the maximum size for an institution such as ours. More than that and the nature of the institution would change. Sixty seemed to me to be a good number for us. A staff/pupil ratio of one to twelve would give us five teachers to cover the major curriculum areas.

Even if this were more expensive per pupil than a large comprehensive, should this be the determining factor? If it is giving a better education then we should be prepared to pay more, as long as it is not a lot more. Money must not rule!

We as a society face a problem in some deprived areas where there can be three generations of the unemployed in the same family. Smaller schools might make an impact on this. Schools of eighty pupils aged 11-16 would mean a class size of sixteen. The size of the institution and the size of its classes would give teachers the opportunity to equip their charges for the world of meaningful employment. The extra cost would be marginal compared with the cost of being on benefits, on probation or in prison.

Campaigning for change is an uphill struggle. Together with Lord Grimond and Baroness Cox, Lord Young started the Centre for Educational Choice which offered to help us in our efforts to get voluntary aided status. The Centre organised a public meeting in Westminster Cathedral Hall at which I spoke. Afterwards a small delegation met Kenneth Baker, the Education Minister. He sat on a 'throne' flanked by his fellow education ministers, who stood. There was no real discussion. We were told what we were to think, which was that we should support current government policy, and what was going to happen, which was nothing.

This chapter cannot be concluded on that depressing note so let me go back to something that Caroline wrote.

> We were particularly attracted to a school where all are on first-name terms. This convention reminds us of the shared nature of teaching and learning: our experiences in grass-roots training of community workers had showed us the truth of the saying 'How can I teach, but to a friend?'

That is the key to how Caroline and Keith, Sue, and Julia and I, as well as our other teachers, operated. Our homes were always open and pupils were – are – our friends. During the time I was Head I did few things outside the school. When we went to the theatre, the opera, a concert or even on holiday, there were usually students with us. Students had first call on our time. Because they were friends we were happy to share with them.

Chapter Five

Clergydom

HOW DID I COME TO BE ORDAINED? I don't mean the ceremony, the hands-on-head ritual, for which the chief instruction, as for confirmation, was to 'forego the Brylcreem!' Obedient, we sacrificed vanity and paraded without pomade. No, not the service. I mean the life choice/commitment thing. *De temps en temps* I try to puzzle it out but get lost in a labyrinth of influences, both conscious and, I suppose, unconscious.

Family background proves sterile territory. My maternal grandfather carted with him his eight children to whichever Congregationalist, Methodist or Baptist church he was serving as organist and they, being musical, provided it with the core of a choir. The values he tried to impart to me in our time together, when he took me to meet members of his extended family and revisit his roots in Leicestershire, concerned the making of money.

My paternal grandfather's affiliation was to a handful of Masonic Lodges– he was a Grand Master – a commitment mocked by Grandma who joked about rolled up trousers, exposed calves and the riding of goats. Despite its smart regalia and its charitable work freemasonry has never attracted me. Single gender organisations are only half-human.

My parents referred occasionally to a Baptist youth group where they played tennis and badminton. That was all we knew of their shared courtship interests and religious background. In Guernsey Viv and I were sent to Brock Road Methodist Church Sunday school. There we swallowed Old Testament stories in digestible dollops and went on a picnic in a charabanc. I'm not sure that juicy accounts of David's slaying of Goliath, Cain's murder of Abel, Joseph's cheating of Esau, Moses' slaughtering of idol worshippers and God's drowning of Egyptians made an appropriate formation for a minister, though they might be appreciated as a sure foundation for financiers and politicians.

It was a love of music and a decent treble voice that had me snapped up by the Anglican Church. Then my parents abandoned their nonconformist background and they, too, were confirmed, my father later becoming a churchwarden.

The church we belonged to was the extra-parochial one of St James-the-Less. Its seating capacity of 1,300 made it the largest of the thirteen Anglican churches on the island. For many years it was known familiarly as the Garrison Church. From 1950 it also served as the chapel of Elizabeth College. There was no salary attached to incumbency: pew rents and the Easter offering were the Vicar's remuneration. Now it is a concert hall, its acoustical properties praised by Yehudi Menuhin.

Most Sundays I attended three services, serving at the 8am Holy Communion and singing at Matins and Evensong. I loved, as much as any other chorister, being in the public eye and jumped at the opportunity to sing a vesper verse or to propel the pulpit. Yes, the pulpit was on rails and we pushed it to the centre for the sermon. I fancied it fitted with a motor, the preacher racing it up and down the aisles like a dodgem car. We hardly ever had holy thoughts. Was being in the public eye a motivating factor in my quest for ordination? Was it a quest for status?

Or was it the message? We received Religious Instruction twice a week, and each day's assembly contained a Bible reading. With attendance at two or three services each Sunday, and a daily assembly through a dozen or so years of schooling, the Good Book dripped into our psyche.

Such exposure to the exhortations of prophets, the parables of Jesus and the cogitations of Paul is not enjoyed by many today. References in the works of successive poets, novelists and playwrights must be missed by ignorance of the source.

It was people active in the world's poor places who really stirred my imagination. The greatest living example was Albert Schweitzer who achieved doctorates in theology, philosophy and music, an inspiration on three fronts that preoccupied me: music, theology, and social action.

His ethics were the fire-lighting spark. He lived what he believed – 'reverence for life' – taking responsibility for improving the lot of those less fortunate and living this out in the challenging conditions of an African primeval rain forest. It is hard to understand why he attracted so much criticism: not among theologians, because he was challenging deeply-held convictions; not among musicians, because modern baroque practice has Bach's works played faster than Schweitzer played them, but by those who resented his moral superiority, not that he claimed it, and by members of the medical profession. A year spent running a project in Ethiopia helped me to appreciate precisely the importance of his approach to development. We will return to this when we look at that experience.

There were two poles to my ethical and moral thinking: the destruction of Dresden, Hiroshima and Nagasaki were the negative pole. These horrific war crimes speak chillingly of man's inhumanity to man. The positive pole is the hospital at Lambarene, Schweitzer's 'Reverence for Life' made concrete or, more accurately, made tin and wood. Response to the latter was straightforward: my choir of fellow teenagers raised money for lepers in Africa. Response to the former was confirmation of my pacifism. Schweitzer was awarded the Nobel Peace Prize in 1952. His acceptance lecture, 'The Problem of Peace', is considered one of the best ever given.

By comparison Sunday sermons in Chapel at Lampeter were a pale shade of grey. The *Cymanfa Ganu*, held in the town's Victoria Hall, Bryn Road, led by a conductor and a pianist imported for the occasion, was a more impressive event. Welsh hymns in glorious four-part harmony raised the roof. At the other end of the spectrum was High Mass in St David's Cathedral on St David's Day, executed by the College's society of the same name. I participated as organist. There was so much bitching in the sanctuary during the rehearsal that I had to bellow instructions from the organ loft: I was the only one, it seemed, who had studied *Ritual Notes*.

Riding the waves between Guernsey and Herm I read Søren Kierkegaard and Karl Barth. Kierkegaard asks, 'Are the means as important to you as the end, wholly as important?' For him the end does not justify the means. 'There is only one end: the genuine Good; and only one means: this, to be willing only to use those means which genuinely are good – but the genuine Good is

100

precisely the end.' (*Purity of Heart*, Fontana.) That is another powerful argument for pacifism.

Barth asks, 'In what does the Gospel differ from Jewish and pagan morals, so that we could not compare it to them?' He answers, '…precisely in this that all this new law, all this new "commandment" of the Gospel rests on the forgiveness of sins.' 'Christianity is also a lifting up of the soul and a renewal of society. But each of these to the extent in which it is inspired, borne, created, by the forgiveness of sins.' (*The Faith of the Church*, Fontana.)

In *Middlemarch*, our greatest English novel, George Eliot puts into the mouth of Dorothea two speeches which I am sure express her own position and anticipated mine.

> That by desiring what is perfectly good, even when we don't know what it is and cannot do what we would, we are part of the divine power against evil – widening the skirts of light and making the struggle with darkness narrower.

> I have always been thinking of the different ways in which Christianity is taught, and whenever I find one that makes it a wider blessing than any other, I cling to that as the truest. I mean that which takes in the good of all kinds and brings in the most people as sharers in it. It is surely better to pardon too much, than to condemn too much.

Having pleased the old ladies of St James-the-Less by signing up for ordination the choice for university of Lampeter, an Oxbridge-type college in the Welsh countryside, seemed sensible. It offered a General Arts degree designed for gentlemen of the cloth. Although the lectures themselves were uninspiring I at least got a grounding in disciplines that would later be of use.

For my theological training I applied to two theological colleges, Mirfield and Ripon Hall, reflecting two disparate sides of my character. The attraction of Mirfield, run by the Community of the Resurrection, of which Trevor Huddlestone, whose book *Naught for your Comfort* records his anti-apartheid activities in Southern Africa, was a member, was its commitment to a simple, even austere, life. The downside was a catholic theology to which I only partially subscribed.

Ripon Hall, famous, or infamous, for its close connection with the Modern Churchmen's Union (founded as The Churchmen's Union for the Advancement of Liberal Religious

Thought and now called Modern Church) was theologically radical. I was tickled by the information that an attempt had been made to try a prior Principal, the New Zealander Henry Dewsbury Alves Major, for heresy. That the college was in Oxford, not way up in Yorkshire where it had originated, and where Mirfield lay, was a plus.

A choice did not have to be made. The two Principals consulted each other and decided that Ripon Hall would suit me best, or more probably, if they had picked up my willingness to question authority, that I would suit Ripon Hall better.

I never regretted their decision. Gordon Fallows was an open-minded and even innovative Principal. We were possibly the first theological college to have sociology lectures. Ordinand's wives (one each!) were given as sympathetic a welcome and support as was possible in an all-male college.

However, were some enterprising body to charge me with developing a new theological college, I would do away with the servants and insist that the students do the cooking, cleaning and gardening. They would also help to develop the programme and assist in running the place. I saw this as a possibility for the new theological college at Gambella Anglican Centre in Ethiopia.

Though we were mollycoddled we were a shrill and savage crew. As, after breakfast, we took our constitutional around the lake in the grounds the air would be filled with questioning cries, the dreadful sound of the ripping apart of dogmas and the ecstatic greetings of a Ramseyan 'disclosure'. Not for us the earthy certainty of Wycliffe Hall or the airy-fairiness of St Stephen's House. One for a joke and a joke for all, that was us!

Although Gordon Fallows became a bishop, first of Pontefract, then Sheffield, we were not generally considered, unlike the products of Westcott House, Cambridge, and Cuddesdon-in-the-countryside, to be ideal bishop material, though at least two of my contemporaries were elevated to the purple heights. The bishops' bench held no attraction because my attention had already been caught by the worker-priest movement that had developed in France during the Second World War.

In the 1930s Simone Weil, one of my heroines, had taken a break from teaching to work in fields, vineyards and factories. Despite her migraines and other health issues she lived the life of those with whom she laboured. She was in Marseilles at the same time that Father Jacques Loew started the worker-priest movement there, he labouring in the docks. His movement was an attempt to 'rediscover the masses' of industrial workers who had become disaffected with the church.

Worker-priests campaigned for improved pay and conditions for the workers, and the movement became prominent in the industrial unrest of 1952 and 1953. Factory owners complained to their Catholic bishops that the support by priests of the unions was divisive. By 1953 ten priests had married and about fifteen were working with the Communists. The French bishops instructed worker-priests to return to their parishes. Around fifty disobeyed.

Marriage and membership of the Communist party, downfall of the French worker-priest movement, was not likely to undermine a similar Anglican effort. After all, wasn't the Dean of Canterbury, Hewlett Johnson, a Christian Marxist? What harm did he do? He was the butt of a few shafts of Anglo-Saxon wit. An air-to-air missile system (abandoned in the 1950s) was named 'Red Dean'.

I liked to hark back to the days when the Revd. Conrad le Despenser Roden Noel was Vicar of Thaxted, Essex, put there in 1910 by the parish's patron, Lady Frances Warwick, a member of the Social Democratic Federation (Marxist). To a friend she wrote: 'Socialism is the one religion that unites the human race all over the world, in the common cause of Humanity, and it is very, very wonderful.' (Oliver Cromwell and Nell Gwynn had a place somewhere in her ancestry.) Noel shared her enthusiasm for left-wing politics.

The calling off of the miners' strike in 1921 was received in Thaxted with dismay. On the Sunday after St George's Day Noel preached about flags, objecting to the Union Flag because it incorporated, not the cross of St Patrick, but the arms of the Fitzgerald family. To bring balance he introduced into the church the Sinn Fein flag and the Red flag. There was a fierce reaction, and these were seized from the church by Cambridge undergraduates and sent to the Bishop of Chelmsford, who was not happy to be a receiver of stolen goods. The 'Battle of the Flags' which ensued hit the headlines. There were scuffles in the church and riots in the town. The raiders were outsiders, stirred up by

Thaxted Conservatives, and included many from a school for Army Officers at Chatham.

In his autobiography Conrad Noel wrote:

> We are often rebuked for mixing politics with religion. Well! the blind following of any political party, the politics of the party hack, these are certainly not the business of the pulpit; but politics, in the wider sense of social justice, are part and parcel of the gospel of Christ and to ignore them is to be false to His teaching. Worship and beauty are not to be despised, but worship divorced from social righteousness is an abomination to God.

Addressing the issue of passing from bourgeois democracy to an integrally human democracy, to a real democracy, Jaques Maritain asserted that he was not dealing with Christianity

> as a religious creed and road to eternal life, but rather with Christianity as leaven in the social and political life of nations and as a bearer of the temporal hope of mankind; it does not deal with Christianity as a treasure of divine truth sustained and propagated by the Church, but with Christianity as historical energy at work in the world.

'Social Action' was the battle cry that summoned me. It meant earning a living outside the church. St Paul supported himself by making tents, a fairly respectable precedent.

By the time I reached Ripon Hall I had begun to turn against wearing clerical dress in the street, though the black shirt and white tie adopted by Dr. Alec Vidler, Dean of King's College, Cambridge, was tempting. It is a style that has not become popular, probably because it replicates the dress code of Italian criminals in Hollywood films, the only way to distinguish between mobster and clergyman being to note the shoes and the quality of the cloth.

One reward for sporting a collar was to be treated with great deference, and even brought a cup of tea and a biscuit, by a crisp and fragrant nurse when making an out-of-hours visit to a patient in Barts' hospital.

In Hackney I found it embarrassing when shop assistants gave me preferential treatment, serving me before elderly ladies. No collar in the streets. Eventually I took to wearing jeans and sandals, a small step in the direction of the Franciscans. My sartorial come-downance happened at an event at which I was speaking. The organiser, an otherwise reasonable woman, scolded me for looking 'like a deck-chair attendant'.

Mary Douglas draws a 'connection between deliberately tatty bodily style and sectarian revolt against the dominant culture', a comforting thought. In *The Road to Wigan Pier* George Orwell coupled 'sandal-wearer' with 'sex-maniac', a creature who would naturally be a Quaker, a pacifist and a feminist. Whilst sympathetic to – even attracted by – the beliefs of the Society of Friends, and a committed pacifist and feminist, I fail as a sex-maniac.

I am getting ahead of myself. We haven't yet made the journey from Oxford to London, which came about after this manner. The preacher at Evensong in the university church of St Mary the Virgin was the Rt. Rev. Evered Lunt, the Bishop of Stepney who pleaded for clergy to serve in the East End of London. Having nowhere better to go I offered my services. He sent me to suss out St John on Bethnal Green, an early 19th-century church by the entrance to the tube station, opposite a shop that used to sell warm, well-filled salt beef sandwiches.

I popped into the church before seeking out the Vicar. It was splattered with pigeon droppings and encrusted with dust. Incense was indispensible in a church that was 'high' in both senses of the word. No wonder few people graced the pews on a Sunday.

I was dragged aside by the curate. 'Don't come here, whatever you do. The man is mad!' His six cats were named after characters in Wagner operas. A massive pair of loudspeakers poured out Wagner as he lay in bed. He toured the pubs on a Friday night singing light classics in a light tenor voice and passing round the hat, the main source of income.

We have not finished. He wore *lederhosen* under his cassock. When he cycled through the parish and the corridors of the Bethnal Green hospital his clericals trailed behind him revealing leather shorts and tanned knees and thighs. The bishop eventually persuaded him to join the staff of St Paul's, Covent Garden, the actors' church.

During my visit I received a call from the Revd HAS Pink, the Rector of Hackney. He had heard I was in the area and would I like to call in on him? He was but a short 253 bus ride up the Cambridge Heath Road. A cheese moment! I jumped on a bus, relieved to shake off the chalk dust.

The Revd HAS P was a small, self-contained man with a bit of a twinkle and a reserved laugh. He had two other curates and a woman worker on the books, a luxury which no incumbent with a single parish has today.

The church had a moderate level of ceremonial. As I and the three curates who followed me were products of Ripon Hall, and the Rector indulged us, the theology was liberal verging on radical.

The vestry doubled as the parish office, and it was there that couples booked their marriage slot. Saturday was the only day on which to get hitched. We could have up to five weddings in an afternoon. We were quite fierce about timing. Any couple more than ten minutes late would go to the back of the queue, sufficient a threat to ensure it happened only once in my time. There could be pile-ups in the porch, and one bevy of bridesmaids did get half-way down the aisle before they realised they were following the wrong bride.

The preparedness of couples for the nuptial state was a worry. I was given the task of arranging marriage courses. These took place one evening a week for five weeks and involved up to ten couples. At the heart of the course was a sex talk given by a woman doctor. Many of the couples had never spoken to each other about sex, and some women had odd ideas about how babies were conceived and born. Contraception was also a necessary topic. In the early 60s few of those who came to the church to be married would have had sex before marriage.

The renting and buying of accommodation, and financial management, were areas where accurate information was in short supply. Then there was a 'green card' style inquisition to discover just how much fiancés and fiancées knew about each other. A fourth session explored personal relationships with the accent on a Christian understanding of marriage, and the bringing up of children. Finally there were details of the ceremony itself: what is this 'troth' that the affianced are being asked to pledge, and does the female element really intend to be obedient?

For me the big gain was getting to know those I was marrying. It makes a huge difference to the quality of the twenty-minute ceremony if we are comfortable with each other.

Communication was high on our agenda. Russell Thompson, the senior curate, edited the widely-circulated parish newspaper the *Tower*, the tower being a landmark and all that remained of the old church. I contributed cartoons.

Clergydom

When Liz and I married in 1965 we moved into a flat above Russell and Ora in Sutton Place, a Georgian terrace just off the churchyard. One churchwarden, Stan Piesse, lived next door. The other, Bill Turney, lived opposite, next to the Metal Box factory in which he worked. They kept a close eye on us during the interregnum. Stan was the bruiser, Bill the duster-down.

We had two youth clubs, a closed one for those who came to church, which Russell ran, and an open one, the J-club, to which I was attached that had its own premises in Hackney Grove, next to the Town Hall. I lived above them when I was single. There was a coffee bar, with snooker, table tennis, darts, badminton and a little jive on the menu. It operated on Tuesdays and Fridays and fielded three football teams that played on Hackney Marshes on Saturdays. A dance to a live band took place on Wednesday evenings in the secondary school hall. Attending this latter was, in part, a policing job and hard on the ears. On one occasion an alien gang attempted to close us down by threatening to beat up the first people to emerge. We called in the cops. The gang fled, leaving knives and other weapons scattered on the path and pavement.

I didn't seem to make much impact on members of the J-club. My relationship with the closed club was much more positive. We undertook a number of theatrical ventures together, details of which will be found in Chapter Six, 'bard & boards'.

Most members of the closed club attended grammar school. They found themselves immersed in a culture very different from that of their parents, putting a great strain on their relationship. We tried to respond to the challenge of bridging this cultural divide.

A great way for a teacher or youth leader to gain mastery or mistressy over their charges is to take them into an alien environment where the said charges become dependent on the adult for most of their basic needs. Foreign is best. For this a vehicle was needed. The Rector approached the manager of Barclays Bank and asked him to lend me the money to buy one. The manager complied without a murmur.

I found a second-hand grey Thames van kitted out with two bulky sofas. These were replaced with ten picnic-style chairs that the owner of a local garage, father of a girl in the group, bolted to the floor. They had armrests and, without padding, allowed more room. When those who are health & safety brainwashed hear of this improvisation they hold up their sanitized and sanitizing hands in horror.

The first real outing was to Yugoslavia. It set a pattern for subsequent trips to the continent: catch a ferry at 11pm, arrive in Belgium at around 5am and reach the German border at about 9am where bratwursts and coffee await. Not everything went smoothly on that first trip. A kettle caused a hiatus on the Autobahn by leaping off the roof rack. Within seconds of our stopping to pick it up two *polizei* were removing pistols from their holsters. We were able to reach Munich by nightfall.

On the second night we camped by Lake Bled in North Western Slovenia, feeding at the medieval castle that, encircled by forest and mountains, overlooked it. We then drove to Stinica in Croatia to catch the ferry to the island of Rab.

On the return drive, descending through the hairpins of an Austrian mountain, the brakes failed. Getting down to second gear I hoped we would not meet a truck or catch a coach taking the bend wide. Fortunately ours was a right-hand-drive vehicle, so we could keep close to the edge of the road. On our left, as we reached level ground, was an inn. Opposite, a field acted as a car park for it. The soggy surface brought us gradually to a halt.

The inn looked expensive but we needed time to recover. Worry quickly dissipated, helped by a log fire, reasonable prices and trout that was utterly delicious. It was one of those magical moments when, despite the odds, everything has resolved itself perfectly. The minibus brakes, having cooled, were working properly again. What struck me particularly forcefully was the trust the youngsters had in me. No one had panicked as we careered down the mountain.

At the time I took this trust for granted but, looking back, it surprises me that in many of the things I have done people have been prepared to be led by me.

With trust developed and group cohesion achieved, the leader has to be careful not to bind individuals to him or herself. We leaders will be moving away. So, whilst we are totally committed to the group's welfare, and the growth of the individuals in it, and whilst we are totally open and available ourselves and not wearing the mask of the professional, there is a life that we have in which they do not share.

The danger is that we cease to be the fertiliser that encourages growth and become the pot that restricts it. The warning signal is in the use of the word 'My': *my* class, *my* youth group, *my* school, *my* church. If we remember that they are not ours at all, we can perhaps avoid some serious pitfalls.

I recently sent a photograph to Geoff Coward, who helped with drama productions, and was so pleased that memories are still alive when he replied:

> Memories that the photograph stirs – climbing Sugar Loaf Mountain in the rain – getting blind Pam to the top – watching Jean (now Funnel) sliding on her arse back down the mountain in one of those terrible plastic macs we all owned at the time – Beacock getting it together with Lorraine – drying banana skins over an open fire in the house we were occupying hoping that they would get us 'high' – not sure of the year – either '67 or '68.

Although we had many West Indians living in the area few of them came to the parish church. If they had trouble with their children they took them to the Vicar of Dalston up the road. He would deliver the deserved beating on the parents' behalf, or parent's behalf, because I suspect it happened most frequently when the father was absent.

We needed to do something for the West Indian community so I organized the first West Indian festival in East London. It wasn't a big affair because there was no funding for it, but we had musicians, a storyteller, an artist, and a designer whose fabrics were being sold at Liberty and Heals. When the Rector moved on to become Archdeacon of Hampstead I commissioned a cope for him using some of this designer's colourful material.

The painter built up his pictures, perhaps a horse and cart being loaded in a field of sugar cane, with polyfilla on framed boards. This was sealed with white emulsion. Then a coat of red paint was applied. That was covered in gold, the valleys filled with dark brown varnish and the hills rubbed back to red. Never one to miss a trick, I employed the same technique one Christmas to create a life-size Joseph and Mary, using chicken wire and cement, as well as plaster. The figures stood by the old tower alongside the pavement. There was worry that they would be vandalized. They were not. Thirty-something years later I repeated the project for the church in Hartland.

The most challenging part of my job was as Anglican chaplain to St Joseph's Hospice for the Dying. Opposite, a scent factory emitted a sickly and sickening assault on the nostrils that bore no relation to the fragrant aroma of a flower and put me off from walking that road. The breath of many of the patients carried on it a somewhat similar sickly smell, which I labelled the smell of death. The latter I was gradually able to accept.

This was the early 60s and Cicely Saunders, who later founded St Christopher's Hospice, was trying out her ideas here, such as the appropriate use of morphine mixture and heroin to alleviate pain at a level that gave relief while allowing the patient to remain alert.

'An indefinable atmosphere which left one feeling that death was nothing to be worried about – a sort of home-coming' was noted by a group of social work students who visited the hospice. Cicely became for a short time my mentor.

The most difficult challenge was how to undermine the Great Lie. The patient knows that they are dying and talks about 'getting better', the lie they tell their families. Some families know that the patient is dying but play up to the pretence. Somehow this has to be overcome so that relationships can be open and based on the truth. There is such a sense of relief all round when that happens.

I tried to give support to a young woman suffering from motor neurone disease, marking the degeneration from week to week, trying to sop up some of the anger as mind and body writhed until, one week, there was just an empty wheelchair. Could it ever be possible to help a sufferer like this come to terms with her illness?

In Homerton the Eastern Hospital incorporated St John's Hospital for Diseases of the Skin, given over to geriatrics and 'Sub Normal Children Patients'. It had about 500 beds. I visited it only a few times. My concern was with the geriatric wards. Staffing was so tight that patients were confined to their beds as there was no one to help them dress.

I was admitted once to a locked ward, described as being 'for severely mentally handicapped children'. It seemed like a ward of deformed homunculi. These were babes and children born with phocomelia, resulting in shortened, absent, or flipper-like limbs, a consequence of their mothers taking thalidomide during pregnancy. No one knew what to do with them so they were locked up. These thalidomide children and the *hibakusha*, victims of the atom bomb, the outer and visible signs of the inner ugliness of our 'inventive' society: dis-grace.

In Hackney we focussed on ways in which the lives of both parishioners and the poor of the world could be improved but faced by these thalidomide children we felt powerless.

After a year spent teaching in Dalston, and part-time curacy, I became General Secretary of the Inverliever Lodge Trust. I was attached, in an honorary capacity, to St Mary's, Woolwich, a church with a radical reputation bestowed on it by the Revd. Nick Stacey, a man once described as 'a gimmick manqué'. He had turned the galleries and side aisles into offices, meeting rooms, and counselling rooms. The crypt became a discothèque and a folk venue.

Nick, a former naval officer and Olympic athlete, was a man with friends in high places, so the parish received plenty of media attention. I remember a televised sermon by one of the curates who preached from the pulpit in a white dinner jacket. The point of it passed me by. Nick deemed the whole experiment a failure and left to become Kent's Director of Social Services.

When I signed off with the Trust and became Christian Action's first Director there was no point in my remaining on the Woolwich books. In any case, that was only a nominal attachment as I never preached there. I had no hesitation in accepting

Prebendary Austen Williams' invitation to join his team as an honorary curate at St Martin-in-the-Fields.

St Martin's was a church I held in high esteem. David Shepherd, the founder of the Peace Pledge Union, had been its incumbent. For many years a monthly Sunday evening service has been broadcast by the BBC to the world, and many people working in Commonwealth countries thought of the church as their spiritual home. More important to me, however, was its work with down-and-outs through its soup kitchen and its Social Service Unit.

There was another connection with Austen. While in Hackney Liz and I had taken in Norman, well-known to St Martin's Social Service Unit, who had mental problems. He was reasonably fine when taking his medicine, but resented it when we both went out to work. Austen gave us a TV set to occupy him during our absences. This was not sufficient to mollify him or hold his attention. One morning he tried to heave an armchair over the banisters onto a departing Liz, at which point we knew we had taken on more than we could cope with, and he had to move on. To help people like Norman would be a full-time commitment.

My time at St Martin's was enlightening and enjoyable. Of my four clerical mentors: the Venerable HAS Pink, Canon L John Collins, Canon Norman Motley and Austen himself, he was the one who most influenced me and for whom I had the most respect. He never got flustered; he never lost his temper or even raised his voice. If a baglady walked from one side of the chancel to the other, or a disturbed character shouted abuse during a service, perhaps even during a sermon, his reaction would be no more than a wry smile. No one was ever escorted from the church as far as I knew. One of the regular congregation would engage the offending abuser in a quiet conversation. Austen's pet phrase of comfort was 'underneath are the everlasting arms'. He wore the scarlet cassock of a Queen's Chaplain. He resisted attempts to make him exchange it for the purple one of a bishop.

Austen was not one for show. We were asked not to wear academic hoods in church as they are not relevant to our work. My ermine hood went into the dressing-up box and there it has remained. The Sunday after Enoch Powell's 'Rivers of Blood' speech it was my turn to preach. As Director of Christian Action I felt obliged to reply to this inflammatory propaganda from the pulpit. Christian Action announced this in a press release, and a TV crew turned up to record my sermon. However, as I refrained from descending into personal abuse and couched my response in measured and moderate language, nothing appeared on the news. This, in all probability, pleased Austen as he was not happy with this sort of publicity stunt. He himself operated quietly, never drawing attention to himself or his actions. As a consequence it is little realised that he made a major contribution to the nature of the plans for the regeneration of Covent Garden, the market having moved to Nine Elms, preventing a crass commercial development that could have turned the area into a city officescape.

Reverend Austen Williams, known familiarly as 'Austen'... was a major figure in the community backlash against Greater London Council development plans for Covent Garden. Invited by an upstart architectural student to a protest meeting on 1 April 1971, Austen felt he could hardly stay out of the conflict. He immediately joined the cause with charisma and passion, becoming the first chairman of the Covent Garden Community Association (CGCA), which was created on that day. At the Inquiry of the GLC Plan, he testified to the deeply entrenched social ties of the community and the sad and utter lack of interest in public participation demonstrated by the planners.

Austen Williams protests

After his evidence was dismissed as irrelevant by the Inquiry officials, Austen appeared to grow more radical in his efforts to help save Covent Garden. He boldly led group demonstrations and protests, the largest of which took place in Trafalgar Square in 1973. Other members of the clergy and local authorities were shocked by his involvement in the quarrel and tried to get him to come to a compromise. Fortunately for Covent Garden, Reverend Williams wouldn't budge. Eventually the GLC Plan was dropped, but the necessity of redevelopment remained. The Covent Garden Forum was set up to allow the GLC and the CGCA to negotiate; Austen remained the CGCA chairman during this tough period. (Anne Bransford, http://coventgardenmemories.org.uk)

Every Monday morning the clergy enjoyed a boiled-egg breakfast on the first floor of the vicarage that overlooks Trafalgar Square. These were lively affairs particularly as the Revd. Trevor Beeson, the editor of *New Christian*, the Christian equivalent of *Private Eye*, was one of us. He was always good for a bit of ecclesiastical gossip and scandal.

One such morning I was handed an envelope which held a stalls ticket for *Godspell*, on in a theatre just up the road. My fellow breakfasters seemed rather amused. I thought this was probably a clergy hair-letting-down outing, but when I took my seat in the theatre I found myself sitting next to a member of the Buckingham Palace staff who fancied me. How do you respond to that? My recorded response to the show was that it was more true to the Gospel than *Jesus Christ, Superstar*, on further up the road.

Another incident that gave great amusement resulted from a service I took at St Margaret's, Westminster, attended by Lord Hailsham. I am not sure whether it was my sandals or a scandalous sermon that caused the offence, but the noble lord wrote to Austen instructing him never to send me there again. Trevor Beeson, on the other hand, became responsible for the church when on the staff of Westminster Abbey. Perhaps the noble lord had gone to another place by then.

My Christianity is not about preserving an organisation, a creed or a liturgy but attempting to live out the Golden Rule. As Karen Armstrong has pointed out, that attempt can inspire overt hostility. The vitriol of some of her critics not only reveals an uncompassionate tendency in modern discourse – are we not all flawed beings? – but also a visceral distaste for the compassionate ethos and a principled determination to expose any manifestation of it as 'lying, pretence and deceit'.

It is not only the chattering class that spreads this negativity. It is also rampant among citizens of cyberspace. The communities to which cybernauts give allegiance are ersatz communities. Communicating in one-liners they, with others on social networking sites, create for themselves a feeling of self-worth: 'I've shared therefore I am.' Looking at the world through electronic devices they lose any capacity for solitude. Facebook, Twitter and Amazon define them. Google knows them better than their parents, who have outsourced them to the internet. There is an overlap between 'real life' and 'virtual life' and sometimes a mix-up between them. Sitting on a train an individual can have a real conversation with the person next to her and a virtual one through her smartphone or iPad at the same time. Which is the real world?

Anonymity has lead to online harassment and to cyber bullying. These are difficult to stop because of a belief that everyone has a right to be heard. It is almost impossible for members of an online community to arrive at a code of conduct and how it should be policed. Value systems are hidden, though one value is easy to discern: social media try to monetize everything. The founders of Google, Amazon and Facebook are worth more than twenty billion dollars each.

Social media are believed to give everyone an equal voice. Anyone can go online and air their opinions. What is not sufficiently appreciated is that, because of this libertarian ideology, political technocrats can also manipulate social media for their own ends. Half-truths and lies can be promulgated by agents masked or disguised and there is no one to hold them to account. Beware! Be very aware.

These downsides of cyberspace are a significant addition to the negative factors enumerated by Philip Cushman in his account of the tragedy of our times.

> Instead of having vibrant, authoritative communities and moral traditions to guide us, we are faced with a multiplicity of scientific theories, a cacophony of voices, one more dogmatic and self-righteous than the rest. Each promises a universal truth, a magical technology, and some type of certain deliverance from the vicissitudes of twentieth-century living. A society-wide consensus, a shared sense of right and good and true simply does not exist in our time. It has been shattered by historical forces, military events,

and intellectual trends. (*Constructing the Self, Constructing America* p.9, Da Capo Press.)

There is currently no moral consensus but a smörgåsbord of value systems. My commitment to the Golden Rule and the Sermon on the Mount is intuitive, not rational. It is not related to the pursuit of pleasure, the motivating factor in other offerings, because it accepts that some situations may involve sacrifice ('the Cross' in theological terms). The problem of conflicting values is insoluble in principle, and those who subscribe to an anti-faith set of beliefs dominate by shouting the loudest and focusing on extremes, not by being right. The faithful should not be too quick to respond with an equal shouting.

Tich Nhat Hanh has written that for him 'the life of Jesus is his most basic teaching, more important than even faith in the resurrection or faith in eternity.' (*Living Buddha, Living Christ* p. 36) That, too, is my position.

There are many of my generation who rejected Christianity when they reached years of discretion in favour of a worldly, scientific materialism, tempered by an idealistic commitment to making the world a better place, only to discover that the ground on which they were basing their lives was shifting. The scientific certainties have become less sure, the technological 'fixes', bodge jobs. For me the Social Gospel is surer ground.

In the face of a 'scientific' materialism those with a religious faith should continue to make common cause, following in the footsteps of the like of Thomas Merton. The teachings of faiths other than Christianity can offer us a way of testing our own position. Gandhi's exposure to Christianity helped him to redefine Hinduism. Our exposure to Buddhism, Hinduism and Islam can add insight and spiritual resources to those of Christianity. I set to music my versions of a Buddhist, a Hindu and a Moslem text for inclusion in the *Othona Psalms*:

To forsake the foolish and follow the wise;
    to honour those worthy of honour:
       this is the greatest blessing.

To live rightly, helping one's neighbours and friends,
    pursuing a peaceful vocation:
       this is the greatest blessing.

Clergydom

To be meek, long-suffering, hating all wrong,
     untiring in works of compassion:
      this is the greatest blessing.

To be patient under correction, and meek,
     to act in full love with true virtue:
      this is the greatest blessing.
  (from the *Kuddada-Patha* and *Sutta Nipta*)

The pilgrim on the path to God
walks fearlessly, is pure in heart,
for wisdom searches ceaselessly;

controls all passion, freely gives,
explores the scriptures tirelessly
and sets their sense to daily life;

is humble, truthful, even-tempered,
harming neither man nor beast,
renouncing things that others prize;

is tranquil-minded, tender-tongued,
compassionate to those who suffer,
gentle, modest, free from greed;

is free from false activity,
committed to the higher self,
forgiving and enduring all;

is pure and free in mind and deed
from hate or pride. Such are the marks
of those who take the path to God.

(from the *Bhagavad Gita*)

Praise be to God the Lord of the Universe,
the Merciful, the Compassionate,
the one who tries us on Judgement Day.

It is you whom we worship, and you whom we ask for help;
Let us see the right pathway, the way of your favoured ones,
not of those who cause anger, and those who have gone astray.

 In the Lord of the sunrise I shelter from evil ways;
from the evil of envy which poisons the jealous heart.
In the Lord of the people I shelter from whispering lips,
he who furtively whispers and troubles the people's hearts.

117

By the white of the forenoon and black of the brooding night
know the Lord has not left you nor looks on your face with hate.
He, the Lord, will reward you and you shall be satisfied.
For he found you an orphan and see how he sheltered you!
for he found you were straying and see how he guided you!
for he found you were needy and see how your hands are full!

When you look on the orphan refrain from severity;
when you look on the beggar refrain from abusive words;
when you know the Lord's blessing declare it unceasingly.

(from the *Qur'an*)

Are not these a good supplement to the Christian diet?

The really serious challenge does not come from the East but from the 'empty self'. Philip Cushman, in his cultural history of psychotherapy, puts it thus:

Individualism in the post-war era, less and less leavened by communal commitments and moral traditions, was endlessly promoted by the advertising industry and implicitly elevated to an unquestioned social value. The public was increasingly driven by escalating wishes for personal recognition and sensual gratification and tantalized by the prizes of an economic boom and the promise of possible electronic fame. (op. cit. p.240)

The Othona Community, the place where these songs were written, has not been unaffected by Cushman's challenges, but it was and remains a place where we can learn how to serve each other.

I now took a break. The three years that followed my spell with the Othona Community were spent working for Vietnamese refugees, a more than full-time occupation and a period when I was not attached to any church or parish.

HARTLAND

When we moved to Hartland in 1983 my metaphorical dog collar was resurrected to help out at St Nectan's, the parish church. The most magnificent feature of this Grade I listed building is the mediaeval screen which runs from north to south, spanning the entire building. The most beautiful roof in the church is that of the Lady Chapel, considered by experts to be the finest of its kind in the country. The elaborately carved Norman font was probably brought to the church from Hartland Abbey.

The Vicar was the Revd. Louis Coulson, a shy and retiring character whose wife Elizabeth used to sit in the front pew and issue him instructions. Although his churchmanship was 'catholic' he was sensitive to the breadth of the congregation and so ritual was middle-of-the-road. He and I debated the ordination of women, which he opposed. The PCC and parish sided with me. When women were ordained he resigned and became a Roman Catholic.

The appointment of the Revd David Ford marked a move in an evangelical direction. After his wife reported to him a Christmas sermon of mine he stopped asking me to preach.

David left a deeply divided church and none of those who came to view the parish was prepared to become its incumbent. I had been holding the fort during the interregnum, as I had during the previous interregnum. I accepted an invitation from the churchwardens to take on the parish. My determination to tackle whatever challenge confronts one was stronger than the decision, made thirty years before, to avoid the life of a vicar. I was in post from 2003-2006 and continued, unpaid, for a further year.

The first task was to bring the parish together. On Ash Wednesday we all gathered in the church rooms for an act of reconciliation. Parishioners were asked to write down on a piece of paper the things that had hurt them and the things they may have done that would have hurt others. These, instead of palm crosses, we burnt. The ashes were used to mark each one's forehead. The air cleared over a cup of tea. A new start was now a possibility.

One of the reasons behind my original decision not to go in for parish work was the disproportionate time spent on fundraising. Now I was faced with the task of bringing about improvements to St Nectan's, the most urgent being the repainting of the interior. The churchwardens had frozen on receipt of an estimate of around £22,000. About £13,000 of this was for the hire of scaffolding. We bought two scaffolding towers and with voluntary labour limewashed the whole place for a total of £2,000.

We replaced the lighting. My attempt to improve the seating, pews made by local craftsmen in the days of James I, was thwarted by English Heritage who insisted they remain without alteration as they are one of the few examples of such basic work. When there are concerts some members of the audience set up camping chairs in the aisle.

On the edge of the parish, by the West Country Inn, was St Martin's, a little tin-roofed Mission Chapel. We had a monthly service there for about six people who were loyally keeping the place going. They agreed with me that there could be no long-term future for the building and it was decided to close and sell it

Because English Heritage would not allow us to make any alterations I proposed St Nectan's be made redundant. As it is a Grade I listed building it would have to be kept open, with its upkeep and insurance becoming the responsibility of the Churches Conservation Trust and not the parishioners. The parish would be allowed to use it for services six times a year, and it would be available for weddings, funerals and concerts. As there exists St John's, a chapel-of-ease in the centre of the village, presently in use as an arts centre, services on three or four Sundays a month could be held there. The PCC rejected this plan. In theological debate the rational is supposed to be queen. In practical matters, nostalgia and sentiment reign.

I apologize for presenting you with a rather boring account of the things that had to be done, none of them necessary steps on the way to establishing the kingdom, nor requiring a theological training. In the background a question to which I have not found an answer nagged and, like a loose tooth, could and cannot be ignored. It is, How do we establish a more just society based on spiritual, not materialist, values? And related to that, How do we interest and educate our young people in our Christian heritage?

I am at heart a teacher: my sermons contain more instruction than exhortation though, as Sydney Smith remarked, 'the object of preaching is to constantly remind mankind of what they keep forgetting; not to supply the intellect, but to fortify the feebleness of human resolutions'.

The intellect has not been ignored. I have offered reassurance to those who have problems with certain aspects of the creeds: the current service book offers alternatives to them. I have shared the findings of contemporary Jewish archaeologists who argue that the Exodus has more going for it as myth than as history. It would seem fairly obvious that 600,000 Israelites (Exodus 12:37) wandering about the Sinai desert for forty years would leave some 'footprints' but there is not a trace to be found, and Egyptian records are unusually silent about the drowning of an entire army. Nor is there any evidence of Joshua's conquest of Canaan. The first five books of the Bible – for Christians the Pentateuch, for Jews the Torah – are powerful mythic stories, and in synagogue worship are read right through each year in weekly chunks. There is evidence that the Synoptic Gospels and Acts are designed to follow the same pattern of weekly readings. All four Gospel writers adapted, and probably invented material to flesh out their version of the Jesus of Nazareth story.

There are the occasions when individuals have sought spiritual help and advice. This is not something that can be written about because it involves individuals whose stories I am not willing to tell. There has to be complete confidentiality for there to be trust and therefore complete honesty. What I will say is that most frequently 'forgiveness' is the key: helping others to forgive themselves or to accept that they are forgiven; helping them to forgive others. You have to take it from me that lives can be changed, sometimes dramatically, and the ability to assist this to happen is a precious and humbling gift. Change is always possible.

Viktor Frankl tells the story of Dr J., 'the mass murderer of Steinhof', a mental hospital in Vienna, where he helped the Nazis with their euthanasia programme. After the war he was imprisoned in Ljubljanka where he died. But according to an Austrian diplomat, before he died

> …he showed himself to be the best comrade you can imagine! He gave consolation to everybody. He lived up to the highest moral standard. He was the best friend I ever met during my long years in prison!' (*Man's Search for Meaning* p.133).

The individual can change. So can society.

Many in the church realise that we cannot continue as we are, but few can imagine a different future. It seems that nothing changes until there is a financial crisis. If that is really the case, then we have sold out to materialism. To promote change because we are strapped for cash is to genuflect to Mammon. One bishop has coined the sound-bite, 'money is the sacrament of seriousness'! What we should be exploring is how to be a poor church. We need to revisit Francis of Assisi: poverty is the real sacrament of seriousness.

Sometimes I have to go to other faiths for a sane perspective. I seek refuge in the Buddha.

Do not put faith in traditions,
even though they have been accepted for long generations
and in many countries.

Do not believe anything because many repeat it.

Do not accept a thing on the authority of one or other of the sages of
old, nor on the grounds that a statement is found in the books.

Never believe anything because probability is in its favour.

Do not believe in that which you yourselves have imagined,
thinking that God has inspired it.

Believe nothing merely on the authority of your teachers or of the
priests.

After examination, believe that which you have tested for yourselves
and found reasonable,
which is in conformity with your well-being and that of others.

(*Kâlâma Sutta*)

I spent a year in Ethiopia as Area Dean with responsibility for
Nuer, Anuak and Opo clergy, but that is the subject of another
chapter.

Chapter Six

Half a sabbatical

WHY HALF A SABBATICAL? Because it was a six-month break rather than a year's, though as there were two of us, Julia and me, I suppose it really could be said to amount to a whole year. 'Half a sabbatical' because, as it was to be devoted to travel, we were limited by our bank account. 'Half a sabbatical' so as not to put too great a strain on the Small School.

In Nepal we would be looking at schooling for Tibetans; in India, how Gandhian education was faring; in Malaysia we would be visiting refugee camps for the Vietnamese and in Japan, giving lectures on alternative schooling.

First stop Kathmandu. Jhampa, who, with his wife Dolker, stayed with us when they spent time at the Small School, greets us warmly. As we drive from the airport he tells of the two nurses who arrived to sort out his dispensary but had immediately fallen ill. With us he is taking no risks and we are delivered to the only smart hotel in the Tibetan quarter, which is to the east of the city. From a second-floor balcony we pick out the fluttering prayer flags of the stupa, and a monastery sited on a small hill under which sits Mount Kailash School, Jhampa's precious project.

We take a stroll along the herringbone-patterned brick pavement, passing meat stalls meanly stocked with portions of dismembered goats, their devilish heads a vivid red and possibly smoked. Plastic combs, ginger, and tiny potatoes are laid out on the ground. Four boys sit behind sewing machines waiting for business. The weight of passing feet has broken through the drains every thirty yards or so, and, grey, oily waste flows slowly and smellily past. By Indian standards the street is almost empty: a few three-wheel motorcycle rickshaws, bicycles with bells, a pram (also with a bell), the occasional private car and a steady stream of packed, ramshackle buses weaving through cows, calves, the odd dog and a duck.

A young couple haggle over the price of thin and shiny metal kitchenware watched from a cramped brick lean-to by two anorexic cows, their scavenging over for the day. Is the cud they are chewing mostly paper? It seems so.

Monks in plum robes with yellow socks and shirts, the Tibetan women in smart dresses with a tuck in the back and fashioned from much heavier material than the lighter, brighter saris of the native women, move purposively. A lama follows us spinning his prayer wheel, chanting in a low voice. We arrive at the brilliant, whitewashed stupa and join the worshippers circling the wall into which are fixed, in groups of four, large prayer wheels. An old man in front of us sets the *om mane padme hum* mantra spinning as he processes. For one circumambulation I try to cease looking with tourist eyes. I want to feel with these people the pain of their exile. Jhampa says his mother intends to circle the stupa 100,000 times before she dies: her daily dose is thirty revolutions.

We fall asleep to the deep-throated blast of the lama's horns, the barking of dogs and the chirp of a single, lonely cricket, my mind briefly registering that Tibetan Buddhist culture is poles apart from that of its neighbour and present host, Nepal, which is Hindu and bears the ineradicable marks of Western influence. Nepal is another place, another culture and certainly 'alien soil' for Tibetans. We from the West are more aware of their similarities than their differences and need reminding that these are strangers in a foreign land and subject to the stresses of refugee life.

The school we have come to visit is attempting to straddle this cultural divide, giving its pupils the language and skills to make their way in their new home, and at the same time keeping alive their cultural roots. Jhampa, a Tibetan in Nepal, contradicts normal Nepalese practice by being 'soft' on punishment. His teachers are not allowed to touch their charges, a restriction some of his indigenous teachers find irksome but one which appears to be in keeping with the Tibetans' own attitude towards children.

Jhampa, a refugee from the age of seven, has written of the situation facing his community:

> According to recent studies conducted by the Himalaya Cultural Society of Nepal many of our rich traditional crafts are slowly

dying out due to 'modern development'. Hundreds of young and
skilled craftsmen are switching from their professions into more
easy and fast-earning jobs such as working in small factories and
restaurants or as tourist coolies. Some remain jobless.

A shared tradition, from which Nepal has departed as a result of
Westernising pressure, could be restored through Tibetan example.
Traditional crafts could prosper.

> Handicraft and vocational training would turn them into happy,
> useful and self-supporting members of our society. The school
> seeks talented children from poor and needy families, especially
> from the remote parts of Nepal. Once they complete their
> schooling they will be able to return to their respective villages to
> teach and help their own people.

The following day, a Sunday, we are Land Rovered to the school.
We stop abruptly at a smart, new, three-storey building. As we
uncurl from the ride the school band, mostly drums and flutes,
strikes up.

We have to bend low so that two quite tiny children can
put white silk scarves, the welcoming gift for an honoured guest,
about our necks. Dolker escorts us to a room on the second floor
which has been beautifully prepared for us. We would rather be
here risking illness than staying in a hotel. The children disperse,
some to swim, some to play. One weekend a month they return
home if parents live near enough. Some of these parents work
close to the border with Tibet, their business not always legal.

The rising gong bursts through the mists of sleep at
4.55am, and soon chatter and song accompany the children's
morning chores. Breakfast for us is steamed buns with jam and
yak's cheese, and a choice of sugared Indian or salted Tibetan tea.
The children change into uniform, white trousers for the boys,
green tartan skirts for the girls, with blue shirts and dark blue ties
that have a light blue diagonal stripe. They line up in the courtyard
and file in for morning assembly. Prayers are sung, concluding with
the Peace Prayer that we say at lunchtime at the Small School. The
date on the blackboard is written in Nepali, Tibetan and English. It
is April 15th 1991, my birthday. I had completely forgotten that I
would be fifty-one today: another world, another time.

It is difficult to assess the quality of teaching. The
atmosphere is warm, the children friendly and polite and as lively
as they ought to be. The teachers are firm but not strict. Jhampa

says that some of his teachers are old-fashioned in their approach. The better ones can easily be lured away by the promise of bigger salaries.

The children here range in age from three to eighteen. Three is too young, but three toddlers have been dumped on the school by parents who are away 'doing business'. They are treated with great affection by both the adults and the other children and take their places at the head of their files in the courtyard where the rule is the shortest at the front!

Baba is the youngest. He has an exciting morning. First, he pours ink over himself and thus is kept, blue-handed, with the staff during their tea break. He then gets involved with a peddler of suspect ice cream. In one morning he can make his bibbed trousers look as though he has been wearing them for a week. They are fresh every day.

He is tame with the staff, shy with strangers, and usually ready for a game. He still wets his bed if not woken in time, and has to be reminded during the day to go to the loo. However, he takes his responsibilities as 'head of the queue' seriously, and stands firmly to attention when the children wait in the courtyard to file into meals. At first he found it difficult to sit in front of his food while the prayer was being sung. Now he sits with his hands together like some innocent monkey.

Jhampa and Dolker show us the trees they have planted: firs, willows, pride of India, lemon, orange, and mango: over a thousand in all. There is rice growing in the Valley. Here barley is ripening fast.

The teaching situation is complicated by the fact that some of the older children have had only a few years of education. Nepal has over 75% illiteracy, and although primary education is available in towns and a large number of villages it is not universal. These are some of the lucky ones. We have passed several small carpet factories where the less fortunate weave away their youth.

As we talk the children, this being the Saturday of our first week, slip away, some to swim in the river, some to play and some to catch up with their washing, also in the river. They have all changed out of uniform and are relaxed and noisy.

I sit with the teacher of music. He is a flute player. He has six descant and four treble recorders in the cupboard but they are unused because he doesn't know the fingering. I draw a finger chart and give him a lesson in Western notation. To another teacher I show a few basic guitar chords so that the two guitars can also be brought into use.

Jhampa tells a story

Jhampa and I talk through his problems. Unsurprisingly, the raising of money is a major concern. He has had to borrow to put up the buildings, which are solidly constructed, substantial and smart, and is being charged 3% per month. Fortunately a group of friends in Cornwall is raising money for him.

The water table is rapidly falling and the newly excavated well is sometimes dry. The pump needs frequent repair. The result is no water in the loo for long stretches at a time. It is usual for us to have to forego our morning wash. Flush toilets of the squatting type have been installed but lack of water renders them most unappetizing.

The electricity supply preoccupies him. The lights are dim until 10 o'clock at night because the service comes first to the neighbouring village. If he can bring in a three-phase supply the village will also benefit, but they are too poor to contribute towards it.

I learn about his past. He escaped from Tibet with his father at the age of seven. Over his right breast his father wore a large amulet stuffed with all sorts of objects believed to have magical properties. This no one was allowed to touch. On rare occasions his son might stroke it, having first washed his hands. His rifle had also been out of bounds. When father and son stopped for the night he would hang the amulet high in a tree with the gun next to it.

At the border he discovered he would have to surrender his weapons so he greased the metal parts, wrapped them in felt and buried them in the mountain, making sure that Jhampa would be able to recognise the spot. He thought that within a year the Dalai Lama's army would drive the Chinese out of Tibet. The arms remain buried.

Jhampa is working hard to produce a textbook but cannot get agreement on the curriculum. He is also trying to persuade the heads of other independent schools to start a training college. The government college opens only when there are enough students, has been closed for the most of the previous year, and is now closed because of the elections. Despite this catalogue of challenges, Jhampa remains positive and cheerful.

I won't bore you with the details of driving a rickety Volkswagen through Kathmandu streets or of trying to negotiate a post office that makes the Indian system seem a model of streamlined perfection. But I will tell you about the living goddess.

Here in Kathmandu we discover temples run as family businesses and visit one, that of the living goddess Kumari. She is chosen from among the silversmiths and installed in her own temple. There the family of the girl, as young as five, selected for her fearlessness, for being able to recognise her predecessor's clothes, and for having thirty-two distinctive signs of Divinity, is supported by the government and enjoys the people's offerings. When her periods start, or even if she bleeds, she is pensioned off with a large dowry. Unfortunately there are not many men who are prepared to marry an ex-goddess. We stand with the worshippers and wait for her to appear at a window to wave to us. We are not disappointed. She is wearing fancy clothes and sports stylized make-up.

INDIA

From Nepal we move on to India. We have been to this land of mystics and mountebanks, of sadhus and saddos, of sacred sites and sickening sights before. This time our visit has been organised by the Gandhi Peace Foundation in order for us to discover how far Gandhian education has progressed. I have already mentioned one school we visit, Lakshmi ashram in Kausani, in a previous chapter.

Kausani is in the foothills of the Himalayas. We drove there in a typical rickety Indian bus that wheezed as it climbed and jerked with each double-declutch. The journey to Jaipur in Rajasthan is quite a contrast. Firstly, our companions are of a different class, speaking English, reading Jeffrey Archer, inviting us to lunch at the Taj hotel. Luggage is put in the boot in exchange for tokens. I miss the excitement of climbing onto the roof to manhandle our rucksacks. The drive is a little smoother than the one to Kausani but a lot hairier. Shortly before Jaipur we pass eight lorries that have been involved in accidents, six are on their backs and two have had a head-on collision that couldn't have left the drivers alive.

In Uttar Pradesh the sugar cane harvest is in full swing. In Rajasthan bullock carts give way to camel carts piled high with straw. Our eyes are held captive by the vivid primary colours of the women's clothes, bright blues, greens, yellows and reds. The flowers along the roadside share the yellow and red which, together with the blue of the sky and the green of the fleshy-leaved trees, afford a perfect match.

We make our way to the Seva Sangh office and find ourselves in a nature cure clinic. Vinoba stayed here, which seems some sort of seal of approval. At the time of his visit the ashram was out in the jungle. Now it is part of the sprawl which surrounds and drowns the old pink city. We are hosted by Rameshwar Vidyarthi who, with Siddharaj Dhadda, has organised a meeting for me to address on the philosophy of the Small School. The audience is made up of 35 men and one woman, some of them quite prominent in education. The Vice-Chancellor of the university chairs it.

Afterwards I interview Shri Dhadda, a veteran of the peace movement. When I learn his full story I realise how lucky I am to be granted this interview. He was born in 1909 and became interested in the Gandhian principles of peace and non-violence while at university. He practised law in Bangalore and then in Jaipur but gave this up to join the Quit India Movement in 1942. He was imprisoned for two-and-a-half years.

The success of the Movement led to his being appointed Industries Minister for the State of Rajasthan. When he realized that the political situation would require him to compromise his principles he resigned from the Congress party and joined the Sarvodaya Movement ('universal uplift' or 'progress of all').

In 1951 he established a Sarvodaya Ashram in Khemal, a small village in the Rajasthan desert. He experimented in various ways to bring about a peacefully co-existing community.

In the late sixties he served as the Secretary General of Bihar Relief Committee, organising aid to the drought-hit state. As president of All India Sarva Seva Sangh of Wardha, he opposed the Emergency, which led to his incarceration in jails across the country for nearly two years. What was the Emergency?

Veteran political leader Jayaprakash Narayan had called for an end to growing misgovernance and corruption under the Congress Party regime. His 'Total Revolution', addressed predominantly to young people, generated tremendous popular support and pushed Indira Gandhi into a corner. At the same time the Allahabad High Court declared Mrs Gandhi's election to Parliament null and void. Her response was to declare a State of Emergency.

After the lifting of the Emergency, and the subsequent formation of a new Government, Dhadda was offered the second highest constitutional position in the country. Needless to say, he declined it.

Shri Dhadda's achievements are considerable. Training schemes in spinning and weaving, painting and printing for poorer sections of society – women, untouchables and tribal communities – have led to remunerative employment, larger incomes and better education. The introduction of new tools has increased efficiency. He has also been involved in house building, irrigation schemes and agricultural improvements. In 2002 he received the Jamnalal Bajaj Award for Constructive Work.

I found the following in the *The Hindu* newspaper:

CHENNAI, SEPT. 23 [2004]. Protests are being staged in various parts of the country against various issues, but here is a senior citizen, Siddharaj Dhadda (96), who is leading a movement against multinational soft drink majors in Jaipur.

During his recent visit to Chennai, the freedom fighter, in an interview to *The Hindu*, said the country was promoting capitalism, rather unabashedly in the name of development.

Mr. Dhadda is concerned over the threat posed to groundwater table allegedly by the Coca Cola plant in Kaladera, about 40-km from the capital of Rajasthan.

Noting that the manufacturing plants of soft drink majors across the country guzzle lakhs of litres of water, Mr. Dhadda, who still retains the spring in his feet, accuses them of contributing to water scarcity.

At least 20 villages neighbouring Kaladera are facing water shortage, says the freedom fighter who turned down the Padma Bhushan award last year and participated in a similar campaign against Coca Cola's plant in Plachimada, Kerala.

He questions Coca Cola's version that only two of the four borewells at the Kaladera plant were being used and estimates the population of the villages at about 10,000.

He never gave up campaigning.

The following morning I talk to one hundred-and-thirty B. Ed final-year students about the role of the teacher. The premises are extremely depressing. The young women listen attentively to what I have to say, but some of the staff are politely critical. We are shown samples of the students' work: visual aids and project books. It could be the GCSE coursework of a conscientious but dull 16-year-old.

It seems that Gandhian activities no longer receive the respect they once had. On June 7, 2014, the Jaipur Development Authority (JDA) sealed the premises of this Sangh, which had been in existence on its own land since 1959.

They threw out all the residents and their belongings, cancelled the allotment and took over their land. The insensitivity of the JDA team, led by its officials Pawan Arora and Subhash Mahariya, was such that in the scorching heat of 47 degrees, one resident who had recently delivered a baby, was asked to leave the room by evening, locking the kitchen and adjoining rooms so that she could not even be fed... The 80-year-old Secretary of the Sangh, Rameshwar Vidyarthi, together with his wife, living in one room of the premises, were thrown out with their belongings and are now on the road...The intention of the JDA was clear, to grab the property of the Sangh, convert it into real estate and grant it to land sharks. (National Alliance of People's Movements)

From Jaipur we take the Chetak Express (average speed 20 mph) to Udaipur where, as the Ubeshwar Vikas Mandal received my CV only the day before, a small meeting is hastily convened. A former foreign minister, a director of education, the head of the Gandhian school, and the principal of the domestic science training college listen politely, but their response is typical of bureaucrats. The organiser, Kishore Saint, is disappointed but he should have invited a different sort of group if he had wanted a different outcome.

The next morning we set out in a jeep for the hills. The driver stops twice to buy flowers. He requires roses to offer to a god. On the previous trip the engine, which was new, had broken down in a field. He wished to avert another such tragedy and so, at a temple in a village near to our destination, the blooms, wrapped in large leaves, are handed with a rupee to the temple attendant, a wise move. The engine gets extremely hot but it doesn't break down. On the other hand, his technique of freewheeling downhill nearly results in our sliding off the road on a bend. We are preserved by the power of the petals.

The hills here have been stripped bare. We come to a patch of newly-planted trees, and a new well. The trees are small but healthy. It is a good beginning, but the reforestation task seems enormous. A meeting of villagers is quickly called and we are sat on a rug under a tree. A village elder welcomes us and tells us how, as a small boy, he remembers going into the jungle, where now there is scrub, and of seeing the animals there. Village life had been a happy one.

Then the contractors arrived and paid the villagers to cut down and carry away the trees. They needed the money and did not see the harm in it. Now they understand it was a wrong thing to do. The absence of trees has resulted in this loss of water. With help from the UVM they have dug the well we have seen.

Kesu, our guide and driver, tells us that engineers had said there was only enough water for domestic purposes, not irrigation, but the priest, who had selected the site, had assured the village there would be plenty for the land. They believed the priest.

We are given tea, rich with unadulterated fresh milk, and invited to spend the night but move on to a second village where a similar meeting takes place. The well in this second village is like a small swimming pool and will certainly irrigate the land. A pump house has been built. Men and women sit separately, but an innovation brought about by UVM means that women contribute to both the discussion and decisions. The women's leaders in both villages are forceful characters.

UVM realises that unless women are brought into the mainstream of the labour movement there is no labour movement worth its name. Amongst the poor all women work. Their priorities are income, fuel, fodder, a lowering of the maternal and infant mortality rates, and safe drinking water.

Up, and South to Ahmedabad in Gujarat. The students are somewhat lifeless and I am not happy with the way the lecture goes.

The upside of our visit is a long interview with Ela Bhatt. She was a lawyer, daughter of a judge, who at the age of thirty-nine established the Self Employed Women's Association (SEWA). Then 98% of Labour in India was in the unorganised sector: self-employed home-based producers, artisans, casual workers, marginal farmers, and unpaid family labourers. When we meet they are still outside the purview of legislative protection and of Social Security. She realised that they had to be brought into the mainstream of the Labour movement.

The Registrar of Trade Unions asked her, 'How can you call it a trade union? There is no specific employer/employee relationship. Against whom are you going to agitate?' She replied that the purpose of the trade union is not only to agitate but to create solidarity of producers and workers who have to fight, not an individual employer, but the many policies antagonistic to them.

> The legal definition of 'workplace' does not include the home. Because the woman does not have a specific employer she is not a worker. Therefore there are no minimum prices fixed for piece work. We have to question the very concept and definition of 'employer', 'work' and workplace', even 'viability'. Whom do you call viable? We take a woman's project to the bank and they say it is not viable.

Downtown street markets were disappearing. Vendors and hawkers who had been there for at least three generations were being thrown out. From the Supreme Court they obtained a licence for the area to be made into a pedestrian zone. The Supreme Court declared street vending to be a fundamental right. A lot of fireworks were let off in celebration.

The most common problem for women: a shortage of
capital, with exorbitant rates of interest, and exploitative rents for a
sewing machine, or a handcart, or a handloom. They thought credit
facilities should be given them through the banks. At that time,
1973-4, the banks did not know who the small borrowers were.

The banks started giving loans to SEWA members but
during the Emergency there was a moratorium on debts. These
small people said 'We need not repay. Indira Gandhi has forgiven
all our debts.' The banks did not learn. So the members asked why
they could not have their own bank. Within six months they had
collected the necessary share capital. In 1974 the SEWA Bank was
formed. At the time of our interview there were about 30,000
savings accounts. The repayment rate was around 94-95%. These
women, illiterate, unorganised, scattered and rural, had established
a viable financial organisation.

> We are working in another desert region on the border of Pakistan
> and there we have so much support from the local people because
> the land is so barren that whether you take it or don't take it
> makes no difference. Last year they planted more than five lakhs
> of trees (500,000) and for the first time more than 50% of them
> survived. The previous two years the saplings did not survive. The
> Forest Department was not able to raise any saplings, though on
> record they did, but they had to buy from us to show that they
> had raised something.

In 2007 she was invited by Nelson Mandela and Desmond Tutu to
become an Elder, 'a group of world leaders [chosen] to contribute
their wisdom, independent leadership and integrity to tackle some
of the world's toughest problems'.

Our next stop is an agricultural college at Sanosara,
Gujarat. We take to sleeping outside. It is much cooler, but a
mixed blessing. Shortly after 5am the crows have singing practice,
at least I assume it to be that. It might be barking practice.
Whichever it is, they don't get any better at it and after three-
quarters-of-an-hour give up, flying off in waves. They are
succeeded by a bird with a single-note chirp: much more
harmonious. By now the stars have totally disappeared and the sky
is colouring behind the two coconut palms in a romantic sort of
way. These are all that are left of a whole avenue of coconuts and
500 mangoes that were taken by the drought of 1987. People cried
at the destruction of the trees. Though they brought water in by

tractor the trees could not be saved. One of the schemes being promoted by the agricultural college is drip irrigation, imported from Israel. There is a saving of 70% over the usual watering system.

Land that was stony and unproductive is now bearing pomegranates, guavas, melons and lemons. One farmer, only 35 years old, has been so successful that he has three farms and a large shop in the city where he sells farming gear. He is the local agent for the drip system.

Another farmer, who has improved his cattle with the college's help, is experimenting with his own cross-breeds. He has also benefited from the drip system for which financial help is available from the government. Unfortunately the small farmers do not take advantage of it: it's the bigger farmers whose wealth increases.

This has helped them develop another sideline: polishing diamonds for a Belgian firm. The crowded workshops we are shown are unhealthy places. There is no protection for the boys to prevent them inhaling the fine diamond dust. The stones are small, as is the pay, two rupees per diamond. But it is sufficient, apparently, for them to save enough to bribe an official to get a government job without a degree or, I suspect, without matriculation. So even in this village where the farmers are successful there is a desperate desire to escape to the city.

The idea that increased food production will benefit the poor, or that an increase in farmers' earnings will trickle down, is proving illusory. Money moves up, not down, and the rich get richer. When, for instance, the government announces grants for those who hold fewer than five acres a landowner will divide his land into five-acre plots and register them in the names of family members, then collect the grants. Sometimes there is no money left in the kitty for those who genuinely have only five acres.

We move on. The train to Bangalore stops at a small station for the taking on board of water, tea, coffee and various snacks. Another train lies alongside us the nearest carriage of which is being evacuated by the police. Someone has been killed and the body lies on the floor. Murder is in the air. As we left Ahmedabad the previous morning news of Rajiv Gandhi's assassination had quietened the crowds and shut shops and banks. The view of our compartment companions is that this will change nothing because he was killed for local, not national reasons. It might even reduce the violence between the major parties.

With mounting trouble in Bihar and UP, and the general disillusionment with politicians, it would seem to an outsider that some drastic change needs to take place. But what? All the Gandhians we speak to believe that power needs to get down to the local level, but they discuss this in theoretical, not practical terms.

We have had difficulty getting seats on the train to Bangalore. Our host has been able to get us one berth under the VIP quota. We fear that one of us will be chucked off the train. In our compartment is a family of four going to a wedding. They have only two reservations. The conductor makes them buy a third for a bribe of Rs.100.

We might have to share a bunk, quite a problem as they are no wider than my hips. It is easy enough for a Gujarati to suggest sharing: they have no hips. Fortunately for us a young man has an argument with another occupant and storms off the train leaving a spare bunk, so we get a second for nothing, thus saving both our cash and our consciences.

The train arrives nearly six hours late in the station serving Bangalore and we have to get a *tuc tuc*, into the city. Three things are remarkable: there are not, as in Delhi, hordes of people camped by the side of the road; secondly, the streets are wide and clean, and the buildings large and prosperous; thirdly, there are restaurants and bars selling liquor, something unheard of in a prohibition state like Gujarat. This is much more like a Western than an Indian city. The driver takes us to a small hotel which is cheap and clean.

We get up early to catch the bus only to discover that there is a strike on. It is the day of Rajiv Gandhi's funeral and buses and trucks are refusing to go into Tamil Nadhu. This strike might continue for seven days. A taxi driver wants Rs.1000 because it is so dangerous. We settle for 800 and set off with three young men in the front seat of his Ambassador car, there to support each other on this hazardous journey. Of course, as I suspected, we encounter nothing but empty roads.

We visit several other schools in several other villages, a fairly depressing experience. Finally we arrive at Reaching the Unreached, the project for which Keith and Caroline Walker worked before they came to the Small School. We are still in Tamil Nadu at a small place called Kallupatti, west of Madurai. It is the beginning of June 1991.

We meet Brother James Kimpton, who takes a while to warm to us, but then is generous with his time and shows us the projects for which he has been responsible, and they are quite a few for he is an architect, artist, economist, medical worker and administrator rolled into one. More than that, he is a visionary development worker. He began his community development work in India in the early 70s. I was impressed by two aspects of his work in particular, his care of widows and orphans and his building programme.

A request from a priest to take four small children, three girls and one boy who was five years old, created a dilemma.

> At Boys' Village we did not take girls or boys younger than seven. I told this to the Priest and got on my motorbike to go back to Boys' Village. Half way there a 'voice' told me to go and get those children. My response was, 'What will I do with them?' Again the voice said, 'you will be shown'. This is how our whole family-care system started.

He founded Reaching the Unreached.

He employed a widow to 'mother' this family and gave her a small house. He began giving houses to widows on condition that they look after about seven orphans each, thus solving two problems with one neat stroke. He rescues abandoned female babies. The number of families soon increased to ninety-five. Now

Brother James

there are four Children's Villages, four teenage girls' hostels, two boys' hostels including one for HIV+ teenage boys. By 2011 there were 955 boys and girls in full-time care.

Bro. James has managed to design and build solid, basic houses that are cheaper and better than those constructed by the government. Unhappy that asbestos was being used in the making of roof tiles he experimented with coconut fibre. When we visit they are making 300 a day, enough to roof two houses. A house can be completed within 15-20 days from the day of measurement, and that includes the application of whitewash and paint. As well as the tiles, RTU makes its own concrete blocks using local ground-up granite. The cost of a house is £250. By 2013 they had built 8,476 houses and drilled 95 bore wells, for Brother James is also a water diviner. No wonder he received an award for his development work.

Education is another of Bro. James' interests. He seeks to create an 'active learning' environment in which students learn not only from a single teacher, but from each other and from visitors. It's a philosophy instilled in the pupils from a young age. The younger the students are, the less emphasis is placed on teacher-centred instruction. At the beginning of each day groups of children are given a problem and they work in threes or fours to solve it. Those who succeed earn stickers; those especially clever earn crowns and tiaras.

This project is the brightest spot, with the school at Kausani coming a close second, in our two-month tour of Indian schools. Unfortunately that amounts to very little. Government control of the curriculum and the exam system between them squeeze out any concern with values, spirituality and creativity that teachers might have. Gandhi's call for an education of head, heart and hands has become an echo from the past.

MALAYSIA

From Chennai we move on to Malaysia. For the moment we have done with schools. We are here to see the two camps set up for Vietnamese refugees. Our first visit is to Pulau Bidong camp on an island off the coast of Terengganu in the South China Sea. It opened in 1978. At its peak the camp held 40,000; now in 1991 there are about 5,000 Vietnamese. Makeshift huts two and three stories high have been constructed from the salvaged timbers of wrecked boats, plastic sheets, tin cans, and corrugated iron sheets. There is a village feel about it. We discover four large coffee shops, each showing videos, and numerous smaller eating places: three bakers, seven tailor's shops, stalls selling biscuits and sweets, vendors flogging cigarettes. Many refugees have plots on which they grow vegetables and flowers, and trees are flourishing. The first impression is of a rather poor town in which people are both working and pursuing leisure activities. We sit on the beach in the afternoon. Young men play ball games and young boys show off their acrobatic abilities or swim. In the evening we drink iced coffee to the sound of Simon and Garfunkel while watching crabs being hunted with torches. I could be forgiven for thinking that this might be a low-cost holiday resort, an Eastern Butlins.

Penny Dane, one of our Refugee Action workers, is seconded to the Malaysian Red Crescent in Sungai Bisi, the other camp, which is only 10 km from Kuala Lumpur and surrounded by a fence with a watchtower. Space is at a premium. Task Force, a government-appointed body made up in the main of police and prison officers, has moved in too many people in order to pressurise UNHCR into putting up more buildings. The school, once used for second-language teaching, has been taken over by housing. There is little opportunity to run shops or businesses, or to grow vegetables or flowers. Even when the building programme is complete, the 12,000 population will be hard pressed for space. This is bound to increase the stress level in the camp.

The slow rate of screening is also a pressure. It is at least two years before arrivals can expect to be screened, with three to six months wait for a decision. The acceptance rate is about 30%. Refusals are allowed to appeal, and a further 10% are being given refugee status. So 60% know they will not be resettled. They may choose voluntary repatriation. Those given refugee status are themselves responsible for finding a third country willing to accept them.

There are two consequences. The first is that those resettled will have been in the camp for at least three to four years making it difficult for them to adjust to their new environment. In the event, about 240,000 were resettled from Malaysia to third countries; 9,000 were returned to Vietnam; none remained in Malaysia after 2005. The programme lasted more than thirty-five years.

During our visit we talk to members of the social work team, staff at the schools, and Vietnamese, including the camp leader. Three problems are uppermost in our discussions: abortions, violence, and screening.

Abortions are being performed, at a price, by one or more women in the camp. The procedures are primitive and dangerous. There is no possibility of legal abortion. A contraceptive campaign is under way.

Members of the Vietnamese security force abuse their positions of trust. Task Force members have powers of punishment, including detention. Punishments often seem arbitrary and there is no opportunity for Vietnamese to get an independent hearing. UNHCR seems not to be interested.

Many tasks, in particular teaching, are undertaken by Vietnamese staff. Their efficiency is impaired by their own screening and settlement worries.

We are impressed by the work of Penny and her team who avoid both duplication and the playing off of one worker against another, a problem in the other camp.

The demands on the team are going to increase and Col. Shehabi, in charge of the program, is obviously worried. We therefore tell him that Refugee Action will be renewing Penny's contract in October, which is a great relief to him. She and he are anxious to receive more workers. Their immediate problem is that some NGOs, such as VSO and World Concern, are pulling out of Malaysia. There are 700 unaccompanied minors in the camp and I want to see if we are able find someone we can send out to work with them.

Col. Shehabi invites us to a meal. A brigadier is among the other guests and discussion at the dinner table is a little stiff. However, afterwards we all sit in front of the TV for a karaoke session of sentimental Western pop tunes. It is a bizarre experience seeing senior officers let their hair down.

There is one other bizarre experience and that is encountering the durian fruit in the forest near the village where Din, Penny's husband, has his family home. Carrying durian onto aircraft, or smuggling them into hotel rooms is strictly forbidden, such is the strength of the scent/stink that they give off. I take up the challenge and find the taste not unpleasant. Julia's palate is less than titivated.

It is now time to move on, and from refugees we return to education.

JAPAN

We were not intending to visit Japan but Simon Piggott, a *Resurgence* reader and contributor, offered to organise a lecture tour. He has lived there for many years and translates film reviews for a newspaper. The fees he negotiates for my lectures more than cover our expenses even though Japan is not cheap. We are, however, being hosted along the way and only once have to put up in a hotel. In this we are extremely lucky as most visitors never get to stay in a Japanese house with a Japanese family.

The suburbs that surround the centre of Tokyo city consist of a mass of small communities, the houses low and higgledy-piggledy, in narrow streets festooned with electricity and telephone cables. The houses are not neatly arranged in rows because the orientation of each house is usually decided by the priest. Also they are numbered in the order in which they were built, not their position in the street.

In Tokyo we stay with Nobuo and Kuniko Hiratsuko, friends of both Simon and of June and Satish. We are surprised to find that they have no TV set, and neither do many others whom we visit or with whom we stay. They have an old-fashioned washing machine. The shops seem not to stock the streamlined automata or the hi-fi equipment made by Japanese firms and so sought after in the West. On the other hand the cotton-covered loo seat has a heating element in it, a novel luxury.

I won't bore you with a list of the towns and cities in which my lectures are given. Simon proves to be an effective interpreter, and the programme of slides goes down well. Alternative schools, we are told, are not legal in Japan, though we do come across a few. So it is a bit frustrating for those who would have liked to have taken a more flexible approach to schooling to be inspired by our example but feel unable to follow it.

We take time out from lecturing and board the Shinkansen bullet train: destination Hiroshima. Our hotel lies close to the Peace Memorial Park and the A-Bomb Dome. It is August 5, the day before the day of the blast. The next day it is the early, quiet gathering that we attend.

Priests of several faiths participate in early morning ceremonies. On the altar bottles of beer and sake (rice spirit) sit among the flowers and vegetables. The Shinto priests are smart and well drilled; the Anglican and Catholic priests are a bit of a shambles.

Thousands of paper cranes, folded by children from around the world, have been sent as tokens of peace. These youngsters have been inspired by the example of Sadako Sasaki who hoped that by folding 1,000 cranes she would be cured. The

Children's Peace Monument is a memorial to her and to the thousands of other children who died.

We retreat before the crowds arrive for the main ceremony, passing the Pond of Peace, the Flame of Peace, and the TV cameras set up to get shots of wreaths being laid through a hazy shimmer created by the flame. As we wend our slow way back over the bridge small boys in cub's uniform hand us chrysanthemums, symbols of lamentation and grief. Despite this solemn reminder of man's inhumanity to man we leave knowing it has not halted the development of weapons a thousand times more powerful than the atom bomb. When will we ever learn?

We move on to Fukuoka, gateway to the southern island, where we are met by our friend Takako, accompanied by two parents and three teenagers, who present us with a box of cakes. This is quite a contrast to the reception Takako received when she came to visit us in Hartland. On a dark November evening she descended at the coach stop in Bideford with no one around, and nowhere to shelter, in the hope that someone whom she had never met before would pick her up.

She drives us to a small Buddhist monastery in the hills overlooking the city, and sets to, preparing an enormous meal, refusing all offers of help. She showers us with presents from her mother and a bottle of sake from her father. We set about catching up.

When she returned from her trip to Europe and the US she did not see any of her friends for a month. Making sense of her experiences was a slow process. Her mother had accepted that she was not going back into a regular teaching job. Takako toiled in a café for four or five months to earn enough to live on. She was also working with teenage school-refuseniks, and this brought her into contact with a child psychiatrist a third of whose clients are school-refuseniks and who wants to see an alternative for them. She chairs our meeting. Parents with whom Takako has been having monthly meetings are present, as well as some members of the education department. I do my best to encourage the creation of an alternative for these unhappy teenagers.

My final talk is in Oshika, a village of similar size to Hartland, in the mountains of Nagano Prefecture. Simon has his fairly primitive house way up above the village, but we take cold mornings, cold washes and the compost loo in our stride. We have a few days for relaxation and exploration.

We visit the nearby city of Iida for a Puppet Festival. Pupils from a junior high school present part of a Kabuki play. Three boys manipulate each of the male characters, and two girls the female. One boy is responsible for the head, which often has moving eyes and mouth, and the right arm. A second controls the left arm, and the third the feet. Coordination between them has to be extremely precise. The narrator sits to one side, with a musician playing the *biwa*, and does all voices in a sort of *singspiel*. The most impressive aspect of these 14-year-olds is their concentration and stillness.

Two marionette performances provide an interesting contrast, illustrating the different ways in which Japanese and Americans regard life, entertainment, the universe. The US show is skilful, slick and shallow.

Despite the fact that the Americans occupied Japan for several years it seems their culture is not appreciated, with the exception of the song 'You are my sunshine' which always receives a positive reception, particularly from older people. English reserve and our self-deprecating humour seem to be much more to Japanese taste. In the visual arts it is the French, I would say, who come nearest to the Japanese aesthetic. In architecture no one comes close. We Westerners design and build houses from the outside in, the Japanese from the inside out.

We have been introduced to several important Oshika villagers and the turnout for my talk is pretty good. Our hosts are particularly touched by the coincidence of our names, for Hartland is 'land of the deer' and Oshika is 'great deer'. Such signs bode well in Japan. I am approached by one of the village council members who tells me I should bring the Small School to Oshika. That would be much too expensive, I reply. He makes a generous commitment: 'if you can get your school to Japan we will meet all your expenses here'. That is a challenge I cannot resist. We agree a date for the following year.

It interests me to try and work out why I make this sort of crazy commitment. I suppose the first thing to note is that I make most decisions quickly. I trust my gut feeling. I am attracted to undertake projects that others hold are impossible or, at least, difficult. Once a decision is made I pursue it with energy and with little thought of failure. On the plane home I start working out the logistics of a three-week visit to Japan.

That wasn't half a sabbatical!

It is October and I am back home teaching. I receive a letter from Matsuo Yukihisa, the Mayor of Oshika, confirming the village council's approval of the scheme and with 'the full support of the whole village'.

> The realisation of this plan, more than anything else, will bring the children of our two villages closely together, and provide rich food for developing their hearts and minds. It will be a large gift from us for the children to whom we will (one day) entrust the future. In this sense, we extend our heartfelt invitation to all at your school. Indeed, we await your visit to our village with intense eagerness. Lastly, please give our regards to everyone. We pray for the health and happiness of you all.

Persuading our teachers and parents is not hard, and the youngsters, of course greet the prospect with huge enthusiasm.

Parents agree that they will pay or raise £100 for each child. The rest of the money I beg from two Japanese charities, though it isn't until Easter that all the yens are in place. We are going for the last week of July and the first two weeks of August.

John Elford, the editor of Green Books, lives in Hartland and has recently married a Japanese wife, Eriko. She teaches us a few basics with the aid of the BBC Japanese language and culture course. Exploring food is exciting for some and somewhat worrying for others. With the exception of one girl, all sign up for this adventure. We lose one boy who, seeing his mother cry, jumps off the coach as it is about to leave. His father wants his money back but coach and plane are already paid for. We are thirty-six youngsters and five teachers.

Transport to the village goes smoothly and we receive an enthusiastic greeting. A large empty building has been turned into a hostel for us. Farmers bring rice, vegetables, cheese, eggs and butter. Melons and succulent peaches, that in the city command high prices, arrive by the tray load.

If some of the party have had a worry it has been about food. In fact one young girl, who will later run an upmarket restaurant, is so faddy she has brought a second suitcase filled with cornflakes. As we are catering for ourselves for most of the time there is really no problem. We have a repertoire of acceptable dishes. Some want to be more adventurous and a group, led by Andrew, is formed to hunt down unusual-looking comestibles in the local shops to be daringly consumed by the Adventurous Eaters' Club at 11 o'clock at night.

Homestays have been arranged for one weekend, and this has been a bit of a worry for some of the organisers. However, everything goes smoothly, the evaluation reports showing this to have been a very happy experience. In fact, for many of our party this is listed as 'the best thing for me'. Hosts go out of their way to provide pizzas, burgers and other western-style foods. It is the language barrier and the heat that cause the most distress.

The village is noted for its theatre, Oshika Kabuki, officially recognized as a 'cultural treasure'.

> Kabuki theatre is primarily seen in Japan's major cities, with the top stars being celebrity figures. But there is another side to the kabuki world: rural kabuki. In the Edo era, travelling kabuki troupes would put on performances in villages in the countryside, introducing kabuki theatre to the peasants. With few other forms of entertainment existing then, in some places kabuki caught on and the local people would start up their own kabuki theatre groups. The most famous of these 'rural kabuki' theatres is in tiny (population 1,400) Oshika Village. (Nagano Tourism)

Katagiri Noboru, Chair of the village Education Committee, told a local newspaper that he wanted 'to teach the children the fun and interest of traditional local drama'. Workshops are organized and we learn to apply stylised make-up, to make stylised movements and to wield a sword. I am just as excited as the youngsters when I am dressed to kill and am handed a massive sword.

Maya learns to wield a sword

The school, in its turn, has brought three of the Chester cycle of mystery plays directed by Julia. We recruit the animals from among the primary school children and set up a workshop in the local school, painting animal masks, fashioning costumes, and building an ark. It is the school holidays but the classroom is packed and buzzing as paper and cloth are cut, glued, sewn and painted. The kids are excited as they practice animal antics.

An afternoon is spent rehearsing on an outdoor stage in a wonderful old wooden building. Unfortunately the rain forces us to transfer to the indoor theatre which does not have quite the same atmosphere.

Simon has arranged for us to visit Iida, the city where Julia and I had the previous year dipped into the Puppet Festival. There we are given an all-purpose platform under an awning. Our all-age audience seems to love our offering of Noah and the Nativity. (In Oshika we also performed Adam & Eve.)

Women of the village teach flower arranging and conduct a tea ceremony for us. We do some work on the land with hand tools, which the boys, used to tractors, undertake with a good grace.

A select group accepts the invitation of the local monk to early morning meditation. We attend several zazen sessions in the Zen temple. We face outwards. Behind us the monk silently paces. He carries a stick with which, if he spots anyone nodding off, he delivers a wake-up call with a smart thwack on the shoulder.

A small group of students rises at 4am on a Thursday morning. They are driven up the mountain, alighting near the top. They have seen deer and now inhale the strong scent of pine. They hear a sound which they do not recognize. It is the chatter of monkeys. The guide points out a plant that is said to make a cat go mad if it eats the leaves. A salamander scuttles off at speed. The sun is beginning to touch the mountain opposite as they return to the vehicle. Driving by the river they spot an eagle gliding along the tree tops. It looks magnificent with its huge wingspan and air of superiority. They arrive back at the hostel at 6.30 just as everyone else is getting up for breakfast.

At the other end of the scale are the workshops in *taiko* drumming. Some of the younger girls are dwarfed by their instruments but beat away with gay abandon. This is strenuous stuff and not everyone can stay the course, though some look as though they could carry on all night.

There is one worrying incident. One of our pupils is not around at tea time. Maya has gone wandering off by herself, trekking up the mountain, either ignoring or forgetting the rule of three. Our hosts are worried and begin to get together a rescue party, something they usually only have to do in the winter. There are bears in the mountains. Before the rescuers can set off Maya appears and rushes into my arms. She had got lost and now needs comfort and reassurance. It is sometimes necessary to

Katherine beats it

hold a child (it is sometimes necessary to hold an adult) and that trumps any political correctitude. She won't need to be told off, nor reminded about the rule of three.

The 14th of August is the day of the Oshika Summer Festival. There is food, music and a magnificent firework display, followed on the 15th by a *sayonara*, a farewell, party. There is a buzz about a return visit, a real challenge for a Japanese village school. They rise to the challenge, and a year later Oshika schoolchildren appear in Hartland, but for a shorter time. The letter Simon sends to the Small School on their return to Japan reads:

> We arrived back in Oshika in the early hours of this morning (June 21). During the bus ride from the airport we handed out questionnaires, and glancing at comments, I can say that, from our viewpoint, the trip was an unqualified success. Everyone wants to visit Hartland again, at least two people would like to live there, and so on. The warm, generous and understanding attitude of the homestay families seems to be the biggest factor, together with the friendships made during the week-long programme, and the flexibility, and variety of the programme itself. How can we thank you for such a wonderful experience? I hope that the group visits of last year and this year can now be further developed by

individual or family visits, and look forward to any suggestions you may have.

Subsequently we had a very enjoyable day in London, getting mixed up in the Gay Rights March, with visits to National Gallery, British Museum and shopping in Covent Garden. Thank you all once again. None of us will ever forget the marvellous time you gave us.

Japan is a really excellent destination for a school party. It is completely foreign and at the same time is safe and clean, important when considering the sensitivities of young British teenagers. Most African and Asian destinations would be much more challenging. So quite by chance we were in the right place at the right time with the right people.

A woman at the Iida Puppet Festival, impressed by the Chester Mystery plays, asked me if we had any more plays up our sleeves. Yes, we had recently put on Shakespeare's *The Tempest*. Could we bring it to Japan? She, Miss Yuko Ioki, would like to help organise a tour. Did I hesitate? I am afraid not.

Angels on the Temple stage

Chapter Seven

Bard & boards

EACH SUMMER A REPERTORY COMPANY sailed into Guernsey to take up residence at the Little Theatre in St Peter Port. The plays were mostly formulaic farces of the Brian Rix variety, or mysteries of the Agatha Christie kind, though once a season amateurs were recruited to make up the numbers for a Shakespeare play. Otherwise it was the standard eight-handers written for repertory companies. I went whenever I could.

Roy Dotrice, a Guernseyman famous for his one-man show *Brief Lives*, led the company, which included his wife and daughter, and whether playing the lead or the butler he stole the show or, at least, the scene.

The only plays mounted at Elizabeth College were Shakespeare's, one a year directed by Major Micky Manchester. As I could sing my first part was as Ariel in *The Tempest*. When my voice broke I joined the nobility as Duke Senior in *As You Like It*. This was, of course, typecasting. Duke Senior doesn't let anything get him down. Even though Arden is cold, windy, and rugged, it seems like the Garden of Eden to him because, in Arden, he finds 'books in the running brooks,/Sermons in the stones, and good in everything'.

At Lampeter I was again involved in two productions. In Ibsen's *An Enemy of the People*, I was merely one of the crowd. The other production was of a William Douglas Hume farce, *Master of Arts*. I played the Revd. Hildebrand Williams DD, a headmaster, and borrowed the Principal's frock coat and gaiters. He and the Censor wore semi-lunar specs. The curtain went up on me in an armchair, my face hidden behind a newspaper which I slowly lowered. The clerical garb coupled with the semi-lunar spectacles brought the house down. Out of such small triumphs we build a theatrical history, or could do if one omits my inability to keep a straight face.

At Ripon Hall I appeared as Launce, servant to Proteus, with Crab, a live dog, in *Two Gentlemen of Verona*. I also directed two Gilbert and Sullivan productions, *Trial by Jury* and *Utopia Ltd*. These were diversions. I had no Thespian ambitions. That said, church services are a form of theatre and officiants need some of the attributes of the actor, but the means must not become the end. Then, in my Hackney training parish, I recognized the potential of the theatrical genre in work with young people.

Some sort of presentation by members of the youth club would bring about group cohesion and provide an opportunity to offer something to the community. An aspiring pop group with a Beatles-style line-up that rehearsed in the church rooms was happy to become involved.

In Bristol a church youth group had premiered a passion play called *A Man Dies*, which incorporated dance and pop music. It was televised. This was just what we needed. With the help of Harry Manning, a parishioner who danced professionally, we put it on in the School Hall. It was loud and a great success.

Wishing to harness the adrenaline it had created I immediately launched the idea of a Nativity play, and set to work on the script. *Man Born* was first performed at Christmas, 1966.

Once, long ago, in the spring of civilised man,
a young girl sang.
She was the pearl of her village, toast of the town,
pin-up of the young men, and some of the old ones too!
But her hair danced and her eyes shone only when she caught the eye of the carpenter.
He was her man.
He smiled at the gay peasant girl as she sang her way down the main street of Nazareth in Galilee,
and he gently stroked the wooden yoke he was making for a team of oxen.

Not a care in this out-of-the-way corner of the Roman world.
Not a care.
Mary's voice rose over the hills, floating across the lake.
She felt the baby inside her move, and her joy increased.
Whatever's he up to?
She laughed, and dreamed, and sang.

151

Tina Stringer reviewed it:

> The church's sanctuary became a large open stage where the sacred story was mimed, but the action burst into and around the audience and involved us in the drama. Voices boomed from loudspeakers, projected slides of the changing scenes flashed onto a huge backdrop, and the whole was held together and kept moving by the folk-style music. Lively and singable, the songs and carols caught exactly the mood of haunting sadness that goes with the razor sharp excitement of the birth in a stable. (*The Tower*)

The Revd. David Partridge, a curate at St Martin-in-the-Fields, invited us to take part in a Royal Command matinee performance at the Theatre Royal, Drury Lane. Harry Secombe was playing there in *The Four Musketeers*. We had to work around a huge mechanical carbuncle, a combination of crane, forklift, and grabber, which filled the centre of the stage. Despite inflexible lighting and poor projection of our images the cast bathed in the warm glow of royal favour.

Man Born lasted about three-quarters-of-an-hour. The next venture would be a full evening's worth. The parish was involved with Christian Aid so 'hunger' seemed an appropriate theme. To explore this I used the story of Jonah and the whale.

Jo Jonah is 'a folk dramalogue in four movements'. In a trial scene our hero condemns himself for his indifference to the starving millions. He tries to escape by going on a cruise where he enjoys a life of triviality and licence. He is thrown overboard and rescued by the whale in whose belly he is quizzed by his host. Jo eventually repents, reforms, and makes a vigorous plea for the hungry two-thirds of the world. The audience is not told how this is to be done. It it something that they have to work out for themselves.

As members of the inexperienced young cast might either not remember their lines or not be able to project well enough we put them in simple masks and recorded their speeches. The shy would be reassured and the show-offs hindered.

Chris Coward, who taught dance at Edith Cavell School, I had known in Guernsey. She choreographed the whale scene for dancers from her school. They carried eight six-foot high white ribs lit by ultraviolet floods to suggest the whale's interior.

Chris's husband Geoff taught drama at Borehamwood. He agreed to direct the movement. I took charge of the music and played the double bass. Three projectors threw images onto a large screen. The production was financed by the young people themselves with the profits going to Christian Aid.

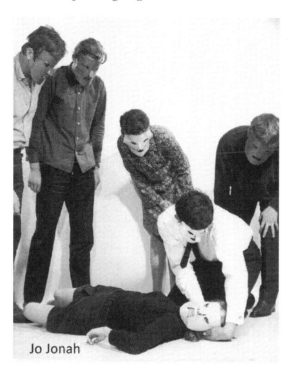

Jo Jonah

Southwark Mothers Union learnt of *Jo Jonah's* success and filled the Queen Elizabeth Hall twice, with two overflow performances in Southwark Cathedral. Urged on by Geoff we decided to take the production to the Edinburgh Festival. We were welcomed by St Mary's Anglican Cathedral, a wonderful space in which to perform, and we all bunked down in a church hall.

Reviewing the Edinburgh production in *The British Weekly* Brian Cooper wrote:

> The biblical Jonah is demythologised into Jo Jonah, a Mr Everyman of 20th-century Britain: a respectable family man, looked up to by the neighbours whose comfortable status-conformity values he unthinkingly follows. Yet he glimpses a hungry world's needs, and his conscience puts him on trial: himself both prisoner of his own values and judge of the world's needs and his own response to the world's cries.

He tries to drive past the hungry masses as they queue for food – but in his 50 mph Mini he has to drive for three-and-a-half years, ten hours a day, before he escapes their cries. This was perhaps the most powerful image in an excellently zestful effort aimed at stirring all our consciences towards a Christian response on world poverty. Forty very enthusiastic youngsters, good folk singing by a tireless group, clear narration, and an imaginative use of slides all made for a memorable occasion which ought to be repeated in churches throughout the country.

With this production we had upped our game, making greater demands on our performers and giving them an experience of success and an appreciation that was new to many. The script was published by REP Ltd, a Pergamon company.

Our next effort was *The Passion of Judas Iscariot*. Judas was not quite the villain he is usually made out to be. Elgar offers a sympathetic portrayal in his oratorio *The Apostles* and I wished to do likewise. It is important that youngsters appreciate alternative readings: there is never just one interpretation of Biblical stories.

The Passion of Judas Iscariot is a tragedy for it shows the way in which an enthusiastic follower misunderstands the motives and intentions of his leader. The problem is this: if Judas were an evil man, why was he ever chosen to be a disciple? And if money were his only motive for betraying Jesus, why does he return it and commit suicide? The answer given here is that Judas was sincere, but he became impatient with Jesus for not declaring himself to be the Messiah who would rid the country of the Romans, that he took matters into his own hands in order to force Jesus to act, and that his plan misfired badly.

The first performance was in the Central Hall, Westminster. The other three performances were in Anglican churches, one of which decided that the script should go to the Bishop of London's censor, a requirement at the time for any text not in the Book of Common Prayer or the Bible. The censor was not happy. He wrote:

> This play is such a good idea and is so well written that it cannot just be rejected out of hand. At the same time it must be clearly stated that the play cannot, in its present form, be recommended for performance in any Church in the Diocese of London.
>
> Basically the idea is sound: England is imagined, in the future (and pretty near future?) to be under domination of communist Russia, and Russia has appointed a Governor called Pilate, in London...

154

...but the author has equated the Chief Priests with the Bishops of the Church of England, and those Bishops come in for very rough treatment in the text, where they are described as 'bloody bishops', 'pukeworthy punks' and 'slimy bastards', are shown jostling for places at table, loving to have their rings kissed, and so on. London, Durham and Bath & Wells are named.

With regard to the inclusion of the Bishops in the play, there are two objections: first, the obvious one that the play is, by inference, saying that all our present (or near future) Bishops are like this. If the author believes this, he should either get out of the Church, or tell the Bishops to their face just what he thinks of them. If he does not believe that Bishops are like this, then he is doing a great disservice to the Church by putting on – in a Church building – a play which depicts the leaders of our Church in this hypocritical light. The mention of some of them by name is unpardonable.

The second, and perhaps more serious objection, is that 'Bishops' are not an adequate substitute for 'Chief Priests'. One can believe in the possibility of a Russian invasion. Can anyone in their senses imagine that Russian overlords would put Anglican Bishops in charge of an occupied state?

In order to receive permission for performance in Church, the play should be rewritten to exclude reference to 'Bishops'.

I went to see the reverend gentleman and pointed out that bishops in a State church are political: some sit in the House of Lords. Confronted, he retreated on most of his objections on condition that I make it clear that no present holder of the office of bishop was intended. The sees were changed to Chipping Sodbury, Borehamwood and Bognor (Dickens would have appreciated this choice!). Before the performance in St Martin-in-the-Fields I addressed the audience: 'I have been asked by the Bishop of London's Censor to point out that in this play no present holder of the office of bishop...' at which point guffaws from the pews prevented my ending the sentence.

I put a note in the programme:

A word must be written about the bishops. They are the Pharisees of the story. It must be remembered that the Pharisees were very respected members of the Jewish community, that they were sincere and led lives that were considered good by their contemporaries. Jesus' attacks on them must have shocked the crowd and his disciples just as much as it shocked the Pharisees themselves.

My next play, *We will suffer and die if we have to*, was written for the Martin Luther King Foundation at the request of Canon Collins. It was first performed in the Queen Elizabeth Hall on July 4th and 6th 1969 by a multiracial youth drama group based on St. Martin-in-the-Fields. We rehearsed in the crypt.

Much of the script was a group effort. Ideas were offered to the group, or raised by the group, and then experimented with or improvised on. I crystallized and polished up the results for, as Peter Brook wrote, 'There is eventually a need for authorship to reach the ultimate compactness and focus that collective work is almost obliged to miss.' (*The Empty Space* p.35)

In no way is this sort of theatre a pre-training for drama school. It is a different kind of theatre. In Prague there is a puppet theatre that presents Mozart's operas. The music is recorded. It is amazing how quickly one forgets that these are puppets and gets caught up in the story. Fat, middle-aged prima Donna Annas and wobbly Commendatores are much more likely to hinder our appreciation than puppets are. In our youth productions the youngsters are not trying to 'be' the character they are playing. Like the puppets, they just go through the motions. The audience quickly adjusts to this convention.

In *We will suffer and die if we have to* we felt confident enough in our cast to dispense with masks and recorded dialogue. The play explores the historical antecedents of the situation in the US. It opens with an impressionistic statement of the problem, followed by rules for keeping slaves down. In church they are exhorted to lie low. The Whites begin to polarize into Northern and Southern camps leading to a stylized Civil War. Lincoln frees the slaves, who realize that they have nothing to cheer about. A mother gives birth to two children, Martin Lucky and Malcolm Crossby. They represent the ideas of Martin Luther King Jr. and Malcolm X.

The second half opens with a mime to a recording of Martin Luther King's 'I have a dream' speech. Malcolm is not impressed by this vision and loses himself in Harlem, ending up in prison. There he hears Yacub's history, a myth concerning the origin of the races, and becomes a Black Muslim, filled with hatred for the 'white devils'. Martin counters the hate which Malcolm preaches with a message of nonviolence. At the same time he tries to stir the Blacks to action.

The stage is the world of the Blacks, the auditorium contains the comfortable seats of the Whites. The Whites must be persuaded to give seats to the Blacks. The 'real' Malcolm X is shot. The nonviolent Blacks move forward in another effort. A slide of Martin Luther King is on the screen. A shot rings out and the picture shatters. (Both violence and nonviolence have led to violence.) A recording of the speech Martin Luther King made about what he wanted to happen at his funeral is played. The cast move into the audience asking for a leader.

The cast was made up of both black and white youngsters. We mixed them up, some blacks playing Whites, some whites playing Blacks. Rehearsals were real explorations of racial issues and of the violent and nonviolent alternatives. Unfortunately I have no reviews of the QEH or the church performances. I was too busy. The script was published by REP and has sold well in the US.

It was my next production that demanded the greatest effort because of the research that was required. I was approached by the General Secretary of the Bible Reading Fellowship to provide a play as part of their Golden Jubilee celebrations in 1972.

To compress the message of the Bible into a play I considered an impossible task. To present extracts in a pageant form would be to diminish it. It seemed more in keeping with the spirit of the Bible Reading Fellowship to examine the effect of the Bible on particular people at a particular time.

The central figure in *The Crown, the Mitre and the Book* is John Wycliffe, who was responsible for inspiring the first two translations of the Bible into English c.1382-95 (there was a previous one in Anglo-Saxon). Protestants have made a hero of Wycliffe. In fact, what little is known about his life indicates a man of mixed motives. Disappointed at not getting preferment, he challenged the worldliness and certain doctrines of the Church with considerable vigour and, sometimes, venom. Against the power of the Church and the power of the nobility Wycliffe released the power of the Bible. His was not a solitary voice, and the urge for social justice, articulated by the Poor Preachers, the Lollards, as well as by the friars, together with the social conditions themselves, came to a climax in the Peasants' Revolt. My play looks at society in the time of Wycliffe, the 1360s to 80s, and presents, after the mediaeval manner, the issues of the day and the response of one who took the Bible seriously and tried to apply its teaching to these issues.

The Crown, the Mitre & the Book

Characterization, as in the mystery plays, is two dimensional. Individuals are not as important as the ideas for which they stand. Costume is symbolic and actors play several parts. Plays have their own conventions, time-scale and logic. The people of the Middle Ages, too, had their own world-view and particular concerns. Nevertheless, I hoped that the audience would find many parallels with some contemporary problems of society, and ideas relevant to our church and our world.

Once again there was trouble. For the Revd. Thomson at the BRF the script was too radical. He passed it on to a medievalist at Balliol College, Oxford, who responded that

> the play is based very closely on original contemporary documents
> – at points it is almost documentary. Much of the message that is
> put across, through the documents turned into speeches is, as I
> said, untrue to the 14th century – but no more so than Eliot's
> Becket in *Murder in the Cathedral* is untrue to the 12th century. I
> think this is fair artistic licence.

It was pleasing to have my research blessed in this way for I really had invested time and money in a pile of dusty tomes. To set the scene I turned the opening of William Langland's *Piers Plowman* (c. 1370-90), which paints a picture of people of the time, into verse:

A warm May morn in Malverns hills the magic is begun.
I see a splendid tower rise up against the blazing sun.
A great gulf holds a dungeon black, with deep dark pits below;
Between them lies a smooth green plain with people high and low.

Some plough, some sow to grow us food, such food as gluttons waste;
While others in their modish dress show vanity with taste.
But many out of love of God live penitent in prayer:
A hope of heaven and fear of hell make holiness their care.

Yet others choose to live by trade, much better off are they
(In worldly eyes such seem to thrive). Some harmless minstrels play
And sing their honest lays, unlike those babbling, vulgar jests:
Fantastic half-wit tales they tell such as St Paul detests.

Foul, filthy-talking, begging tramps, their bellies crammed with bread,
Survive by wit and fight for ale; fill honest men with dread.
While palmers speak of pilgrimage to Rome or Compostela,
Their tales of shrines and miracles aggrandizing the teller.

The story takes in the Good Parliament, in which the Commons flexes its muscles and appoints its first Speaker; the machinations of John of Gaunt; the debauchery of monks; the unsocial behaviour of students; the radical lectures of Wycliffe; the coronation of Richard II; the Peasants Revolt; Wycliffe's exile to Lutterworth.

For this production we built a modern version of the cart on which medieval guild members performed their mystery plays. I recruited players of medieval instruments and the choir of Waltham Abbey to provide the music. As the folk group was redundant Bob and I were able to act in the play. I naturally took the part of the Archbishop.

Diana Collins reviewed the production for *Christian Action News*. The play

> progresses in a series of linked sketches, each highly symbolic, and involving music, mime, song, pageantry and dance as well as the spoken word. This method is very successful in conveying the wide significance and complexity of the action that takes place. A piece of 14th century English history, and an aspect of man's continued search for the kingdom of heaven, reverberate down the centuries, and the echoes continue with you long after you have left the hall.

In essence, the story is sadly familiar. The abuse and rivalries of power, combined with the pursuit of the spurious national glory through overseas war, impose an intolerable burden on the people; discontent and misery abound, and, into this fertile seedbed is scattered the bursting seed of the revolutionary gospel.

In one sense, you could say that the point of this story is the point of Christian Action. This is that a true reading of the Scriptures must lead to a demand for social justice, and the dream of an egalitarian world in which 'all men work together for good'. And however often this aspiration is frustrated and betrayed – as it continually is – it never loses its power, in every generation, to inspire men and women to action.

The play conveyed the idea attractively, truthfully and forcefully… the show went with a real zing, and the stage management was remarkably effective… And the two final scenes, the most important, and often the most difficult in any play, were particularly and imaginatively successful.

The author's powers of invention never flagged. I thought, too, that the music was particularly good in creating atmosphere, and in both illuminating and carrying forward the story, while giving obvious pleasure to both performers and listeners… A most enjoyable and stimulating evening.

With a large cast recruited from several sources, and the large cart that took up a lot of the Queen Elizabeth Hall stage, it was never going to be possible to perform *The Crown, the Mitre and the Book* in a variety of churches, as had been possible with previous productions, without making serious changes to the script. We had come to the end of an era.

Visiting St Paul's Cathedral during a lunch break I was struck by how like a circus ring the space under the dome is. That fathered an idea: a circus nativity. I arranged to have the space for one lunch-hour shortly before Christmas.

In Paternoster Square – now, thank God, no longer with us – a group of assorted circus artists assembled. A couple pushed a baby in a bouncy pram. There were jugglers and clowns and acrobats. From the Square they processed into the Cathedral. In the Whispering Gallery the star, a breather of fire, drew them on. The holy family set themselves up in the middle of the dome circle. The rest of the cast juggled coloured balls, blew bubbles, walked on their hands, and with similar delights offered their skills to the newborn babe. It was great public theatre, the only fly in the wine being the response of two vergers to drops of paraffin falling from the flame breather's mouth. They scurried hither and thither with rags to mop up the drops. I am not sorry to report that this was another event that divided opinion. What, after all, are cathedrals for? For Mrs Thatcher to celebrate a Falklands 'victory'?

I have written no more plays since, nor acted in any, but I have produced and directed them. In this I have usually been helped by Julia whose parents, Barbara and Michael Meiklejohn, played an important role in Canada's amateur theatre in the years before a professional theatre was established there.

My first effort was Edward Bond's *The Sea*, a dark comedy set, appropriately, on the East Coast and presented in Bradwell. I learnt to be wary of amateur drama queens of both genders.

The years working with refugees left no time for involvement in extra-curricular activities. Things changed when we arrived in Hartland in 1983. I had met John Arden when on my way to India and liked his work. I find it sad that his plays have now fallen out of favour.

With Margaretta D'Arcy he wrote *The Business of Good Government* for a church in Somerset. It is the best nativity play I know. Most of our cast were not used to acting but we managed to pull off a couple of performances that were both thought-provoking and entertaining, such is the high quality of the writing.

Another of their collaborations, *The Royal Pardon*, was presented a few years later with parents and pupils of the Small School. The authors had themselves directed the first performance at the Beaford Arts Centre, our North Devon local, with Maureen Lipman, Tamara Hinchco, Roger Davenport and Nigel Gregory in the cast. These were professionals. We were amateurs but the D'Arcy/Arden style of rough theatre meant that we could be just as entertaining.

When I first arrived at the Small School drama was in a poor state. We progressed with playlets written by pupils and scenes from *Alice in Wonderland*. One Special Week we took *The Caucasian Chalk Circle* by Bertolt Brecht as our subject. With the younger group Julia tackled the main part of the play in summary form. With older pupils I worked on the final trial scene. The performance was promising.

The English Shakespeare Company, brainchild of the Michaels Pennington and Bogdanov, was presenting the full cycle of Shakespeare's history plays, *The Wars of the Roses*, at the Theatre Royal, Plymouth. This was an opportunity not to be missed. We took the whole school, stayed in the youth hostel for the week and went to every play. This was quite demanding but, because it was quite demanding, it could be presented as a challenge.

To make things easier I arranged for the company to run a workshop for us on the theatre stage on the Tuesday morning. In this way a relationship was built between our youngsters and the actors. 'Who do you fancy?' leading into heated discussions of merits and demerits in terms of both appearance and ability. From then on closer attention was paid to the details of performances.

Pupils had been encouraged to learn a speech from one of the plays. Maya chose 'Once more unto the breach, dear friends, once more', Henry V's great speech before Harfleur. Maya was young and small, and the organisers sceptical when I begged them to set up the scene. They did, and were astonished when Maya filled the theatre with her call to arms. That was a great moment.

Before each performance I made sure everyone knew the basic plot of the play. As the week progressed they got more and more into the stories, assisted certainly by the downward progress of the vain, fat knight Falstaff, and the arrival on stage of a tank that in Henry V burst through the backcloth bearing a banner inviting us to 'Fuck the French!' It was the general juvenile opinion that Richard III was the best of the cycle. I don't believe it was. What had happened was that ears had become attuned to the language, and this play was the final offering. I learnt an important lesson because, if understanding Shakespeare is a matter of ear training, then the more Shakespeare our students are exposed to, the more likely they are to appreciate him.

Back in school there was a rook-like chorus clamouring to put on a play, one by Shakespeare of course. This was the outcome for which I had hoped. But which one should and could we tackle? One in which there could be a considerable amount of type-casting.

I began with Simon Rodway, a storyteller. His creative writing GCSE project was a Tolkienesque tale that had seventy-one footnotes, most of them giving the etymology of words that he had invented. I could see him as Prospero weaving his spells. Ruth Clarke had the fresh innocence and beauty that marked her out as Miranda. Maya Kumar Mitchell could dance and act but could not sing. As someone else could sing for her she became Ariel. Justin Morrison had the rough accent and body language ideal for Caliban. That was the four principals cast. *The Tempest* it would have to be.

The Tempest is the last play Shakespeare wrote, and one of the most effective. Harold Goddard identifies its three central concerns: liberty, love and wonder. Each is set against its perversion: licence/liberty, lust/love, banality/wonder. At its conclusion Caliban is freed from his enslavement to Stephano the drunk, Prospero discards his magic arts and Ariel is freed from service to Prospero. On the way we are shown a whole gamut of power from the demonic tyranny of the witch Sycorax to the utopian commonwealth of Gonzalez.

Ariel is the one who brings about a transformation, prompting Prospero to abjure his rough magic and forgive his wayward brother. 'Forgiveness' is the key that unlocks the prisons in which each is trapped. And though we may not go as far as Miranda in describing this as a 'brave new world', we may begin to appreciate humankind as 'beauteous' when it allows itself to forgive and to be transformed by forgiveness, though we are never sure that Prospero's brother is transformed.

Simon, Ruth & Maya

Nearly the whole school was involved in the play which we put on at the Bideford College Theatre in December 1989. Caroline Lucas reviewed the production:

I wondered, waiting for the play to start, if the evening would seem a very long one. The first few minutes dispelled these doubts: the storm burst onto the stage, and for the rest of the play I sat entranced.

It was a simple and classic production. Costumes, lighting and music were individually excellent. No gimmicks were needed to hold our attention; the freshness that the actors brought to the story was enough.

Simon Rodway's Prospero carried the production with a committed and powerful performance, but I was particularly moved by Ruth Clarke's Miranda, one of the best I have ever seen. She had a gentle sweetness that made Miranda's innocence quite believable. These two had a stillness that was nicely set off by the quicksilver dancing figure of Ariel as interpreted by Maya K. Mitchell.

That was quite a triumph for a school of 30 pupils and a powerful weapon in the armoury needed to persuade others of the positive aspects of small schools.

I wanted a suitable vehicle for Ruth Clarke's talents and settled on Brecht's _The Good Woman of Setzuan_ (PC title: _The Good Person of Szechwan_). Brecht in his epic and dialectical theatre tries to subvert any emotional content a story may have. There are contradictions in people and in social situations and portraying this is crucial. 'The bourgeois theatre's performances always aim at smoothing over contradictions, at creating false harmony, at idealization. Conditions are reported as if they could not be otherwise.' (Brecht _Gesammelte Werke 16_ tr. Willett.)

Three gods descend on Szechwan to discover whether it is possible to live on earth and be good. If they can find some good people the world can be left as it is. 'Is there any need for social change?' is Brecht's question. The bumbling trio keep lowering their expectations so as to achieve a positive outcome.

Only one person responds to their request for accommodation, and that is the penniless prostitute Shen Teh. She receives a $1,000 reward with which she buys a tobacconist's shop. Being good-hearted she allows herself to be sponged on by down-and-outs and other wasters. To protect herself she invents a cousin, Shui Ta. 'He' throws out the family to which she has given shelter. Brecht's argument is that in a capitalist society human beings can only be good if they are simultaneously bad. Hence the world must be changed.

Shen Te comes upon an out-of-work pilot, Sun, in the Park. He is about to kill himself. She falls in love and attempts to support him, but he proves to be just another sponger. Shui Ta has to be re-called to rescue her. Shen Te becomes pregnant. Shui Ta remains on the scene, setting up and running a tobacco factory, her pregnant bump being interpreted as 'his' prosperity. Shen Teh's disappearance leads to Shui Ta's arrest and trial. Shen Teh reveals to the gods, as judges, that she and Shui Ta are the same person and that everything she did was motivated by three things: a desire to help her neighbours; love for her lover; and to save her son from poverty.

The gods make themselves scarce, deaf to her cries that to be good as well as to survive means that she has had to divide herself in two. For Brecht this illustrates the bourgeois split between the private moral self and the public business self, a consequence of capitalism. As Shen Teh climbs the ladder from poverty the family she throws out descends it to join the *lumpenproletariat*.

Audiences are expected to respond with their minds more than their hearts. But as Brecht realised, for audiences to approach his plays in this way they might require some training.

I found a script that deviated from this outline by introducing opium. When Shui Ta kicks out the family they leave opium behind, the sale of which gives her the wherewithal to buy the factory. Instead of Sun becoming an employee of the factory he becomes an opium addict. It seemed to me that this change of plot added a dimension that would resonate with a contemporary audience so I incorporated it.

Before we went public we gave a performance to the drama department of North Devon College. It was a disaster. On the one hand the action was slow, with pauses between speeches. On the other, the students in the audience did not appreciate or even understand the argument. They were bored, not discomforted. I am fairly confident that my players did, at least, understand the arguments.

For the next few days we worked hard to speed up the performance, and in this we succeeded. Fortunately the audiences at the Bideford College Theatre were more appreciative of what the play was trying to say, even if they disagreed with the message.

Three of our productions were joint ventures between pupils and adults. *Toad of Toad Hall* was great fun. *The Prime of Miss Jean Brodie* required a delicate handling of the affair between the art master Mr Lloyd and the teenager Sandy because youngsters don't always make a distinction between acting and real life. Not that anything untoward actually arose in this instance but one has to be cognisant of the possibility. In *The Crucible* the girls were great, going off their heads in spectacular style. The difficulty came between two of the adults. John Proctor had some professional acting experience but his mastery of the script was not always secure. Judge Danforth, the pretentious, officious and selfish villain of the piece, required precise cues. The confrontation between them in the trial scene was too real, and tricky to direct.

My favourite adult production was of *A Resounding Tinkle* by N.F. Simpson, an absurdist concoction in the spirit of the Goons and Monty Python. There is no plot, just a series of events that set the scene for memorable one-liners and non-sequiturs. The extraordinary and impossible are treated as perfectly rational everyday events.

A Resounding Tinkle

Bro and Middie Paradock have a penchant for debating politics – someone comes to the door to ask Bro to form a government – for hiring comedians to entertain them and for having an elephant delivered annually. Comedy such as this is difficult to rehearse. The first few times everyone falls about with laughter but, as rehearsals proceed, members of the cast begin to wonder whether this isn't a huge mistake. They require constant reassurance. However, come the day, and within seconds of the delivery of the opening lines audiences in the Plough were in fits of laughter, even crossing their legs. The challenge for the actors, if the laughs are to keep coming, is to keep straight faces.

A much more serious challenge arose from Julia's and my half-sabbatical. Could a cast be assembled to take *The Tempest* on tour in Japan? Was our work good enough to show abroad?

A tour of Japan would be strenuous, and too much for younger members of the school. In any case, the principal characters had moved on to higher things. Word went out to them and expressions of interest in a revival flew back. I decided on an age range of 15 to 20 years. To make up the numbers we would recruit friends of those who had been involved in the first production. Thus was born the 'Tempest Project' which soon became the 'Small School Youth Theatre'. To give it a modicum of clout I recruited Adrian Noble, the artistic director and chief executive of the Royal Shakespeare Company, and Sam Wanamaker, founder of the International Globe Centre, as our patrons. The British Council in Japan also gave their support.

Miss Yuko Iioki committed the hosts to meeting all expenses in Japan, including a flight from Narita to Fukuoka. Funds in the UK were much harder to come by. Some parents made substantial contributions and friends of the Small School also donated. The Daiwa Anglo-Japanese Foundation, the Youth Exchange Centre (funded by Sasakawa GB) and the Foundation for the Arts and Sports gave significant support. Finally a benefit performance at the Plough Arts Centre raised £500. We were able to borrow swords, beards, wigs, footwear and tights from the Royal Shakespeare Company, which was a great help.

Miss Ioki had the money raised and the programme organised when the project came under threat: cancer had incapacitated her. Her courage inspired helpers to join in the project. She said that organising our visit gave a focus to her determination to fight the disease. Shortly after we returned home she went into hospital asking for another play the following year to keep her going.

We met at Easter for three days of rehearsals when much of the action was set and attention given to the understanding and speaking of Shakespeare's verse. The main rehearsal period was from July 1st to the 14th. For the first three days we had the services of Stephen Powell, a professional director. This did wonders for group cohesion and the raising of the energy level. We also had a half-day make-up workshop and an introduction to Japanese language and culture. We worked a six-and-a-half day week for 12 hours a day.

All the costumes were made by Hannah Rodway. She was amazing. She would cut a pattern from newspaper just by looking at her subject: she had no need to measure them. I had sent her on a one-week course to learn how to make authentic Elizabethan costume, and now gave her £300 to spend on materials, mostly brocades and velvets. Olaf Bayer, son of a well-known potter, made half-masks for the court group and other props.

The journey to Japan was uneventful but at Narita airport tragedy struck. As we approached customs an officer spotted our sword bag. I explained that they were not weapons but props for a theatre production, uttered the magic word 'Shakespeare', removed the padlock from the bag and a sword from its sheath to show that it was slightly rusty and blunt. I thought I was winning the argument until an officer – there were three on the case by now – tested it with a magnet. The police were called and the offending weapons confiscated. I said that they had been lent us by the Royal Shakespeare Company. I could not let them out of my sight. 'Royal' seemed marginally more impressive than 'Shakespeare' but I was getting nowhere slowly.

Julia was at the JAL desk successfully negotiating seats on the early flight to Fukuoka and getting worried by my non-appearance. The JAL girl spoke several times to customs officials and each time put back the departure deadline by five minutes. The policeman, who took thirty minutes to arrive, told me I required a permit. I asked him to forward the swords to his colleagues in Fukuoka and I would negotiate a permit there. I could not get a permit because I was not Japanese. Only Japanese sponsors could obtain one. I said the sponsors were in Fukuoka and repeated my request. No, a permit had to be obtained before the weapons arrived in the country. There were now only fifteen minutes to take off. Reluctantly I accepted a receipt and a telephone number and abandoned the bag for a seat on the plane.

Swords play an important part in *The Tempest*. Ferdinand draws one on Prospero and is disarmed in both literal and metaphorical senses. Antonio and Sebastian draw them to kill Alonzo and Gonzalo and are frustrated when Ariel wakes the latter up. Alonzo, Antonio and Sebastian draw them on Ariel, who mocks and makes the swords 'too massy for their strengths'. These lords are powerless in the presence of the forces that Prospero has at his command. They rush off, swords drawn, raising in Gonzalo's mind the possibility that they will kill each other. He sends Adrian and Francisco after them, sword in hand. When members of the court are led into Prospero's magic circle by Ariel I have them holding empty scabbards. When Prospero reveals himself to them, and he and they are reconciled, I have him returning their swords to emphasise the trust he is placing in them.

At our first venue a helper offered to find replacements. He returned with plastic jobs about 18 inches long. I could imagine the audience chuckling if these were to be drawn on stage. A second excursion was more fruitful and produced an armful of rapiers from a fencing school that had experienced a similar confiscation when returning from a trip abroad.

Our first two performances were organised by Kawai, private schools that hired two theatres. After the performance I spoke about the place of theatre in education, followed by a question and answer session. The audience then divided into discussion groups, each with two members of our party. The exchange was lively and lasted for one-and-a-half hours.

Our youngsters were being treated like stars, showered with flowers and badgered for autographs and photos. Simon even had flowers sent to the hotel, which made up somewhat for the loss of his money at Moscow airport: he was in the habit of losing things. We discovered that for many of our audience this was not only their first experience of Shakespeare but their first experience of live theatre.

The enthusiasm of audiences was a great relief because neither the Japanese organisers nor we ourselves were certain that we could hold an audience with a play in a foreign language.

The Tempest
in a disco

In Iizuka city the performance took place in a large classroom and was attended by many of the homestay families. The play made a terrific impact in this confined space. Members of the cast, watching from the side, were surprised at how much the play had come on, in particular the clowning which was raising quite a few laughs.

It became increasingly clear that the attraction for the organisers had been the Small School, and that more money had been put up for my talks/lectures than for the play. So each performance had to be prefaced and followed by a speech. I also gave lectures in Kobe, Shiga, Kobuchizawa and Tokyo.

A Shinto Temple in Kyoto blessed us with a dance and gave us sweets and sake.

The Harvard-educated interpreter supplied for my lecture at Shiga was an associate professor of English and religious studies. He knew none of the plays of Shakespeare, but worse, did not understand, or did not agree with, what I had to say about education and, I was told, mangled my words and my thoughts.

Tenki-mura, an arts group, organised a performance in the garden of a Zen Temple. Through the gateway we climbed a steep flight of stone steps, the place for ritual rising on the left at the top of them. The temple reveals itself as you ascend. First you see a roof of solid thatch, then the faint glint of gold from the shrine

170

room, then a long veranda platform. Small trees and shrubs and neat paths make for a beautiful garden. On the right a bridge crosses a long pond, swarming with carp. Two small thatched shelters with a sitting platform under them add to the restful atmosphere. What a set this garden was to play on!

For this performance we worked with a *biwa* player who introduced each of the characters, gave a synopsis of the plot, and thrashed the strings of his instrument, like a cross between a lute and a banjo, with a wooden plectrum the size of a scallop shell, to represent the storm. This proved to be a most enjoyable and fruitful innovation. The performance started just before dusk and, with discreet lighting, proved most magical. Maya/Ariel in particular responded to the space and the setting with imagination. She did indeed do her spiriting lightly. From an artistic point of view this was the high point of the tour.

I was impressed by the professionalism of the cast who worked without a prompter and who had honed the performance down to 1 hr 45 minutes with no gabbling or cuts.

The zazen meditation session organised for the following morning was a little perfunctory: the monks had joined in the party a little too enthusiastically, though we did not mention this to the Radio 4 interviewer who spoke to Ruth and me for their Kaleidoscope programme. There was a lot of media interest and TV coverage in five of the cities we visited.

Kobuchisawa, Miss Yuko Ioki's home town, was the place and time for relaxation. Here we gave only one performance in five days. The mayor, an architect, keenly supported our visit. He was looking for ways of keeping young people in the community and wanted to organise exchanges with us. He gave a reception lunch for the whole party, a superb feast for the leaders, and attended my lecture, the performance and the *sayonara* (farewell) party.

The performance was at the smart Risonare hotel. It was to have been on a terrace but rain forced us into the Atom disco, together with a rather crushed audience of over four hundred. It was not an easy space but the coloured lights did wonders for Prospero's cloak and Ariel's costume. In the audience were a dozen of our friends who came over from Oshika, the village that had hosted the Small School the year before.

When we began the tour the court scenes, with three of the cast on a university drama course, were the strongest. The drama students were competitive in their approach. By the fourth performance Prospero, Arial and Miranda had responded to the challenge and were dominating the proceedings effortlessly.

At an evaluation session the crew were asked to identify the best and worst features of the tour. They were mostly humorous:

> the bus driver falling asleep and Rob shouting, 'farewell my wife and children'.
> a room full of swivelling chairs which we careered around on like dodgem cars
> Ian locked in the shower without his clothes
> singing 'Mull of Kintyre' as we left the dentist's house
> the bus taking half-an-hour to turn a corner
> when the biwa player got totally pissed and sang 'Wild Things'
> the monks getting up with a hangover
> Rob collapsing backwards into the cold plunge bath after the sauna
> Tim throwing up on his plate at the kindergarten
> someone wearing a baseball cap with a kimono
> Simon clutching bouquets of flowers
> a 20-foot model parsnip on top of a tall building
> a 23-foot high blow-up of Arnold Schwarzenegger
> musical lighters and toilet roll holders.

It will come as no surprise that we agreed to return the following year with another Shakespeare play. Now they knew the quality of our work, and that we could communicate Shakespeare to an audience with little English, they were promising better theatrical resources, though we had no complaint about those they had provided. I hoped this would mean my not having to give lectures.

The commitment, hard work and good humour of the participants was impressive. The group was a joy to be with. They certainly gave flesh to the proposition that the development of individual creativity need not be at the expense of responsibility to the group.

Should we tackle *Twelfth Night?* It had gone down well at school. Would the humour be appreciated by the Japanese? Doubtful, so we settled on *The Winter's Tale* which, like *The Tempest*, is a late play. Shakespeare has been criticised for defying the classic unities of time, space and compactness of action: there is a sixteen-year gap between the two halves of the play. It begins in Sicily, then jumps to Bohemia and back again. This did not worry me because I know how, in music, the bringing together of diverse and contrasting material can result in a satisfying total experience.

Impressed by the contribution the *biwa* player made to the performance of *The Tempest* in the Zen Temple Garden I determined to use him in this new production. At various crisis points in the plot the action was halted for Kyokusei Katayama, the *biwa* player, to tell the audience what was happening. So, for instance, when Leontes has ordered his young son Mamillius to be removed from Hermione's presence the actors freeze and Katayama-san describes what is going on with each of the characters.

This approach accords with Japanese sensibilities, for whereas in a Western drama things get louder and faster at a point of crisis, in Japanese theatre it is usual for the pace to slow down so that the situation can be properly mulled over. It worked.

The costumes were designed and made by Abi Johns, only sixteen at the time. Again I gave her the money and let her get on with it. Now a French teacher, she has a sideline in making bride and bridesmaid dresses.

I shall not bore you with the details of this second tour because it was much like the first except that I managed to limit lectures on education to two. There was, naturally, a request from our hosts for a further tour the following year but the cast asked if we could do something different back home.

It seemed desirable to take a break from Shakespeare. Next in line was Brecht. We had previously worked on *The Caucasian Chalk Circle*, and that had gone well. This time there would be no messing with the script, except to rewrite the words of the songs for which I was composing the music.

Like *The Winter's Tale*, Brecht's play is in two distinct parts. The first shows how a servant girl, Grusha, becomes engaged to a soldier, Simon, and then rescues the son of the executed Governor during a palace revolution. She flees with the infant to the northern mountains. After many trials she marries a man who pretends to be an invalid in order to provide for the child.

Part Two tells the story of Azdak who wishes to confess to a crime. When he gets to town he finds himself accidentally placed in the chair of the Judge. In the judgements he makes he comes down on the side of the poor. When the Governor's widow takes Grusha to court for the return of her son he employs the

Chalk Circle test, associated with the judgement of Solomon, to determine the true mother. Because Grusha cannot bring herself to pull the child out of the circle Azdak finds that she is the real mother (even though she isn't). He divorces her from the invalid so she can marry Simon.

Organising a tour of the West Country was far more difficult than taking the theatre group to Japan. Most venues were not good at publicity and we played to some small audiences. Was it Brecht's plays that were unpopular? Was it distrust of an unknown amateur group? Or was it a dislike of theatre?

Our final gig was due to take place at the Tavistock Wharf. When we arrived there we were told that the theatre was in financial difficulties and had had to close. Nobody had informed us of this, and because this was our last performance, we insisted that the theatre be reopened. The cast toured the town to drum up an audience. We played to about two dozen people, but that we didn't mind because what was important was for us to do this thing together one last time. It had become a group ritual.

Kathryn Leat &
Justin Morrison
Caucasian Chalk Circle

The most rewarding performance was at an alternative holiday camp on the edge of Exeter. A large tented theatre and several workshop tents were made available. For the performance the theatre was full with the exception of the front row. Just as we were about to begin it filled with a group of potentially noisy teenagers. They had the power to put off our actors. 'Sing them into silence' I urged, and we stood at the front of the stage and belted the opening number at them. From that moment they were captivated.

The day had been extremely hot and one cast member was ambulanced to hospital with heatstroke. The rest of the crew covered for him, taking his lines and doing his scene shifting. This expression of corporate responsibility was important as a sign that we had succeeded in building a team out of a disparate bunch of teenagers.

That was 1995. There would be no further productions because students now had to pay for their university education. They couldn't afford to give up five weeks of their summer holiday when they might be earning money to see them through the next academic year.

The Small School Youth Theatre ended with one of Brecht's most vivid creations. I thoroughly enjoyed this work even though the demands on time and energy were enormous. These I willingly gave, not for personal gratification or glory, but because I see the theatre, not just as a powerful tool for educating performers and audience, but as a place where all the possibilities that are open to us as human beings can be explored.

The curtain has come down and it is time to move on.

Chapter Eight

Christian Action

WHEN I WAS YET A LOWLY HACKNEY CURATE I was invited to become a trustee of Christian Action, a huge and unexpected honour for one so young. Its chairman, Canon L. John Collins, was best known for his leadership of CND. Closer to his heart was Christian Action which had emerged in 1946 out of the concern of a group of Christians at Oxford, where he was Dean of Oriel College, that Christian principles should guide the reconstruction of society after the horrors of war. To enable him to develop his vision Clement Attlee, the PM, had him appointed to a canonry of St Paul's Cathedral. Among those who helped him launch Christian Action were Victor Gollancz, the publisher, George MacLeod, the founder of the Iona community, and Lord Longford. Their first act was to demand the repatriation of illegally-held prisoners of war who, according to the Geneva Convention, should have been sent home on the cessation of hostilities.

Fast forward to 1968, a year of violence: violence in Vietnam; violence in the American South; the assassination of Martin Luther King Jr. and Robert Kennedy; the invasion of Czechoslovakia by Soviet troops, and trouble on the streets of Paris.

March 8th: University of Warsaw students march for student rights and are beaten with clubs. By March 11th the general public have joined the students and there are violent confrontations with the police.

March 17th: an anti-war demonstration in Grosvenor Square, London, ends with 86 people injured and 200 demonstrators arrested. Three government ministers are physically attacked by students protesting against the Vietnam War.

May 6th: 'Bloody Monday', one of the most violent days of the Parisian student revolt. Fighting is intense. Barricades are set up and the police retaliate with gas grenades.

There is student unrest in Germany that would to lead to the Baader-Meinhof Gang, which morphs into the Red Army Faction.

Canon Collins and I knew that we had to respond to this eruption of violence. Students in particular needed to understand and adopt the principles and practice of nonviolence or the clamour for change would end in bloodshed and a shift to the political right. The answer we came up with was a school of nonviolence. A comprehensive concept of nonviolence as a moral philosophy, a way of life and a practical social and political force, and not merely as a technique of protest, would be taught. We were excited by the idea. Who might we get to help us with this?

John had met Satish Kumar the previous year when on his peace pilgrimage. He was now in Germany on his way back to India. John invited him to return to England. Satish and I agreed to work together to establish the London School of Nonviolence. As a curate at St Martin-in-the-Fields I could ensure that we had a place to meet that was central, accessible and free.

A little later I was offered the post of Director of Christian Action. Anti-apartheid work was becoming increasingly demanding and John no longer had time to run it himself. He remained the Chairman, so I got to know him quite well. He was an imposing figure, tall with a narrow aristocratic head, a large nose, a shock of wavy grey hair, expressive eyebrows, and usually with a pipe clenched between his teeth. Special Branch kept an eye on him and the *Daily Telegraph* anathematized him, impeccable credentials.

The aims of Christian Action, which were to translate the teachings of Christ into practical action in local, national and international affairs in social, political and economic spheres, found a good deal of support, but since its inception, whenever it particularised and focused on some concrete issue a number of good Christian people defected. However, support was never sought at the expense of action. It was a guiding principle that we should not campaign on an issue without doing something to tackle the problem to which we were drawing attention.

Christian Action's post-war reconciliation projects included the bringing over of the Berlin Philharmonic Orchestra, arranging international work camps and the setting up of a home for refugees suffering from TB, all initiatives that had their critics. But perhaps Canon Collins' best-known work has been the establishment of the International Defence and Aid Fund for political prisoners and their families in Southern Africa: South Africa, Namibia and Rhodesia. Over a period of twenty-five years more than £100 million was smuggled into South Africa for the defence of thousands of political activists and to provide aid for their families whilst they were in prison.

John was very security-conscious where the anti-apartheid work was concerned. The Defence and Aid Fund was apparently the only anti-apartheid organisation not penetrated by the South African Bureau of State Security (BOSS).

On the domestic issues for which I was responsible John offered a sympathetic ear. Unfortunately conservative trustees who had problems with some of the things I was doing were also able to bend it. It was normally possible, at my sherry-time sessions, to steer him from the soft option to the thornily radical and relevant course we needed to pursue. It became a bit of a bore, though. His trust of others was not always well-founded.

Michael X came seeking financial support for his new centre on the Holloway Rd. He claimed he had converted from Rachmanism to nonviolence. He had fooled John Lennon and Yoko Ono and now set his sights on the good Canon. 'Oh no, John!' was my response. When Michael was hanged for murder in Port of Spain in 1975 I was relieved that my nose had not been fooled by a rat that could be smelt from the Mile End Road.

This was my first experience of running an office. I soon realised that two members of staff had to go. Canon Collins had given one, a South African, a job as a way of helping him. This sort of 'help' is a grave mistake. Give help, certainly, but in a more appropriate way. We bought him building equipment and he blossomed. Hard on his heels to the exit was an ineffective press officer. Project staff could tell their own story.

It became clear that my secretary was perfectly capable of answering many of the routine enquiries herself. Dictating letters is an inefficient use of time. We divided the mail. I typed my own replies and she answered hers in her own name. She was no longer a secretary but a personal assistant, a novelty in the early 70s.

A campaigning organisation puts out a considerable amount of printed material. We invested in an offset litho printer and an IBM selectric golf ball machine: we were in on the earliest days of desktop publishing. I hired a series of designers straight from college, an interesting experience as their portfolios were stuffed with the same exercises. We were able to produce posters, booklets and a new monthly eight-page newsletter within the existing printing budget. The duplicator was dumped.

HOMELESS IN BRITAIN

Homelessness was an established Christian Action concern. The Notting Hill Housing Trust had been given the money to buy their first house. They later used this money to found Shelter. Meanwhile CA concentrated on the plight of single homeless women, with a project in Lambeth and another in Bethnal Green. I wanted to expand our Homeless in Britain work and employed the Revd. Nick Beacock, who had been instrumental in the setting up of Crisis at Christmas, to run it. With David Brandon as our consultant things began to move.

Following the success of the TV drama *Cathy Come Home* in boosting the launch of Shelter we approached its author, Jeremy Sandford, to write something similar that would highlight the plight of single homeless women. He visited our Lambeth house and talked to the residents, to the staff and to David. He also talked to the Cyrenians. The result was *Edna the Inebriate Woman*.

Edna is on a treadmill (David Brandon's term). From sleeping rough she moves on to a spell in a psychiatric ward where she is given electric shock treatment. She takes to the road again. A purposeful minor infringement of the law results in time in prison where she is out of the rain and cold. Finally she experiences a period in a hostel, similar to ours in Lambeth, where she is treated with respect and given help. The hostel is closed down following complaints from the neighbours. Edna is back on the road.

It went out in October 1971 as a BBC 1 Play for the Day and won a British Television Academy award for Best Drama Production, and a Best Actress award for Patricia Hayes in the role of Edna. Critics were divided in their views of the film and of Jeremy's book, *Down and Out in Britain* (NEL 1972) published at the same time. Neither work persuaded the public to give us financial support. Help came from another source.

I was approached by the Vicar of St Paul's, Covent Garden, the actors' church, with an interesting proposition. He Chaired the Theatre Girls Club, a hostel in Greek Street, Soho. It had provided accommodation for young women working in the theatre, usually as chorus girls, who previously had not been paid during rehearsal time. Now their economic situation was much improved and the hostel had no takers. At the next committee meeting Nick and I were elected as members. I took over as Chair, and everyone except Nick resigned. We now had a hostel for 45 single homeless women in the heart of the West End.

The Chairman of the ILEA Schools Committee, Canon Harvey Hinds, took us to court on behalf of the landlords, claiming that the premises were being used as a drug addiction centre. The judge found that this was not the case, and though we had acted illegally, he would allow us to continue with the work we were doing as it seemed to be in the spirit of the charity's original sponsors. Harry Secombe and Dame Flora Robson helped launch an appeal fund to meet our legal costs.

This was not an easy project to run. David Brandon reported that a suicide in January 1972 symbolised the main problems. Maureen had broken down the office door with a hammer in the early hours of the morning and taken all her own Tuinal tablets, leaving a goodbye poem on the kitchen table. Then she dragged herself upstairs and died outside David's bedroom door. Jeremy Sandford included her poem in *Down and Out in Britain*.

> I feel myself slipping away,
> nothing more can make me stay,
> I must destroy the physical me,
> so that my spirit can be free.
> I must go, so that I'll find
> my sanity, and peace of mind.
>
> The memory of the me that lingers on,
> must not be a sad or unhappy one,
> I am not worthy of your sorrow.
> I could not live to face tomorrow,
> my heart is full of love for you,
> and sadness for my failure too.

Residents regularly landed up in drug dependency units, remand homes, mental hospitals and casualty units. It was other residents, rather than the staff, who kept in touch with them. By the end of the first three months they were helping each other, accompanying one another to hospital or the labour exchange. As was to be expected, there was screaming and violence. Other residents treated such anti-social behaviour with considerable tolerance. Fortunately the neighbours were unlikely to complain.

Sir Keith Joseph, Secretary of State for Social Services, visited 59 Greek Street. He had been a founder of the National Council for the Single Woman and Her Dependants in 1965 and seemed to be impressed by the work we were undertaking. He asked what we would do if the government gave us the same sort of money as they gave to the Salvation Army. I replied that we would refuse it. We needed to be completely free to criticize government policy, for we believed that our job was to show how problems might be tackled, not to take from government the responsibility for meeting them. As Nick Beacock wrote, Homeless in Britain

> seeks to initiate campaigns or projects in those areas of the field in which there is a manifest injustice or an urgent need which is being ignored. At the same time, we seek to set up projects that will be essentially experimental in their development, and not fall into the trap of duplicating other projects in the field of single homelessness. Further, one of our objectives is to see that responsibility in the long term is carried by the community, (whether local authority or central government), so our task is to spread our experience and, where right, to hand over initiated work to the appropriate organisation.

The following week the DHSS issued a circular to local authorities entitled *Homeless Single Persons in Need of Care and Support* which called on local authorities to experiment with a variety of residential houses and day centres. 'The prime need is for more extensive experience of ways in which this difficult group can be helped'. It described houses like our Lambeth Shelter and 59 Greek Street, saying they should be as non-institutional as possible.

> Some of the most successful experiments suggest that somewhat unconventional provision may be helpful; it is likely to be difficult to encourage people to stay if staff provides an obviously rigid or disciplined environment. A flexible system, accepting residents

with a minimum of rules, and providing a genuinely homely environment should be the aim.

You could have been reading a description of Christian Action's homeless work!

I made one important discovery. Working in residential projects is extremely demanding. By putting in proper support and supervision we increased our social workers' workspan from an average of six months to two years. Such support does not come cheap but it is much more effective than a regime of tick boxes and paper reporting.

In the summer of 1973 Nick Beacock left Christian Action to become director of the Campaign for the Homeless and Rootless, (CHAR). It was not long afterwards that Christian Action did, in fact, hive off the homelessness work.

TENT CITY

In 1968 an estimated 10,000 people were sleeping out in Green Park, left open as an experiment. Because of complaints from local residents this was not repeated in the following year and patrols on it, as on St James's Park, were doubled and the railings reinforced. Baroness Llewelyn-Davies told the House of Lords that it was well-known that there was a phenomenal shortage of proper accommodation for visitors.

The problem for Christian Action was that young visitors were taking up places in hostels for the homeless. The London Tourist Board claimed that they had the matter in hand. They were able to help people, 'provided they are willing to pay £1 or more, and don't want to be right in the centre', two conditions unacceptable to most young tourists. The Central Bureau for Educational Visits and Exchanges summarised the situation on behalf of interested organisations.

> While government has been involved in much trouble and expense enclosing central London parks this summer, it appears no thought has been given to attacking either the basic problem or the worsening situation that could well develop this summer as a result of the park closures.

This statement brought no official action, and so it looked as though London, in the summer of 1970, would be faced with thousands of foreign youngsters wandering through streets and parks looking for a place to kip. I persuaded Christian Action to adopt a threefold programme that would: give practical help to our young visitors; draw attention to the problem; and provide us with the information to propose a suitable solution. This was a personal project.

A radio appeal for accommodation in private houses brought a good response. We asked for church halls and obtained three. The ILEA was happy for schools to be used, but heads seemed at the mercy of their caretaking staff. The few who offered help laid down conditions that made Auschwitz seem like a holiday camp. No schools were used. The three church halls were our main resource. The Revd Roderick Wells, of St Mary's at Lambeth, wrote:

> The project went off very well this summer and was a useful education point in our parish life. Certainly it was well accepted by a majority of people, and I'm sure a repeat performance next year would be thoroughly acceptable.

A hut/office provided by John Laing and sited in the courtyard of St Martin-in-the-Fields, Trafalgar Square, was at the heart of the project. It was staffed from 10am to 11pm by two paid workers and a number of volunteers, all recruited from among those we were trying to help. The hut was easily spotted by those searching for somewhere to sleep. It became a centre for baggage dumping and general information. Vouchers were issued so that individual church halls did not have to handle money.

Several times we sent people to the London Tourist Board bureau and each time they returned unable to get anything for less than 10 shillings. We also sent people to sleep in the parks. They reported that the police were proficient at moving them on.

It is difficult to convey the spirit that pervaded the project. One of our workers, John Hunt, wrote:

> Money would be collected, food bought, cooked and then shared between as many as possible, particularly those with little money. Music, too, fostered a great feeling of unity. Most nights singing would continue until the early hours.

From the last week in July until the end of August we found accommodation for over 3,500 people. To 1,000 of these we gave questionnaires in English, French and German. Most were completed. Thirty-five nationalities were represented, the majority coming from the USA, closely followed by West Germany. There were twice as many males as females. No accommodation was provided for British citizens. The age range was sixteen to thirty. The average age was twenty-one. Half could only afford between five and eight shillings, and a quarter of them nine to twelve shillings. Seventeen Americans had no money at all as it had run out before their charter return flights were scheduled. Where possible we employed them on the project.

I had enough material to write a report, *Unwanted Visitors*. But where could we go from here? The Department of Education and Science commissioned a feasibility study into using a Crystal Palace site for a hostel.

The problem as I saw it was that accommodation was needed only for the summer months. Users of a new hostel would have to pay for the cost of it being empty for the rest of the year. There were always the church halls, those with the necessary lavatory and washing facilities, but most of them could hold only a small number of mattresses. Filling them with young people from overseas meant they would be unavailable for parish uses. At this point it struck me that a hostel in tents was the answer: it would be seasonal and it would be cheap. I now had to persuade others to support its creation.

The Metropolitan Police were predicting that in 1971 2.75m young people would visit over the summer period. As this was a London problem I went to the GLC with *Unwanted Visitors*. After a considerable amount of discussion, and a certain amount of publicity, particularly over local radio, the Parks Department agreed to help us set up a tented hostel next to the football pitches at Wormwood Scrubs. We were offered the use of a building that had changing rooms, showers and lockers in it. Ealing Council granted us planning permission. I bought fourteen second-hand army tents, large marquees, though I had to compete with aid agencies who were responding to the needs of refugees fleeing the genocide in Bangladesh, and four hundred metal bunk beds and mattresses discarded by the prison service.

Members of the press were invited to be present at the erection of the first tent, and a number of photographers and reporters turned up. The team who were to help me with poles, pegs and guy ropes, however, lost their way. Photographers snapped each other pulling on ropes. Coverage was mostly positive, except from the *Daily Telegraph*. Their reporter roamed through the nearby estate asking parents whether or not they feared for their daughters' safety. Did they know that the second largest group would be Germans?

Tent City could accommodate over 500 people a night, some of them using their own tents. Local youngsters, who might cause trouble, were barred. At the end of the summer season the project was deemed a success.

I had given strict instructions to the Tent City manager, an enthusiastic young man, to keep an eye open for drug taking. Alert to the problem he caught a whiff of sweet-smelling smoke. Squatting cross-legged in one of the corridors a hippy type was puffing away at a roll-up. He snatched the fag from the offender's lips and stamped on it with a great grunt of disapproval. He had ferociously destroyed a herbal cigarette.

In 1972 I appointed Barnaby Martin to take over responsibility for Tent City. Because of the effectiveness of the previous year's work, the GLC Parks department offered us the use of football changing rooms on Hackney Marshes as well. There we set up Hackney Camping for those who had their own tents. At the Acton site the London School of Nonviolence established an Alternatives Tent with a programme of speakers almost every night. Barnaby also started our own meal service because the prices charged by an outside caterer the previous year had been exploitative. We provided a complete meal for 25p. To receive money a bowl was left out. There was no significant failure to pay.

One of those using Tent City that summer was Clive, an 18-year-old American. He had been picking fruit for Tiptree Preserves on a farm near Colchester. Wet weather meant that they were making little money. In three weeks they had only two days' work, yet had to pay for food and for accommodation in Nissen huts divided into four double-bunk cubicles with 50 beds in each. Over 300 evening meals took more an hour to serve. Lunch consisted of 'three lousy sandwiches'. A strike in the fourth week led to a rise from 7p to 9p a basket. Strawberries lasted for one further week. Clive was skint and took a room nearby to await money from his father. While he was there some articles were stolen from the camp and he was arrested. Police realised that he was innocent, but because he had no money on him, refused to release him. After three days in Chelmsford jail a friend sold his sleeping bag for £4 and gave him £2. The police took £1 off him to pay for a train ticket to London. He arrived at Tent City with £1. We helped him out until money arrived for him from the States. He and I talked long of his fear of returning to the US to face the draft.

Through Tent City I became involved in an organization dealing with American refugees, referred to by others as 'resisters and deserters'. Because of the war in Vietnam many young Americans left home to avoid the draft. Others, already in the forces and stationed in Europe, came to the UK seeking asylum. Draft resisters were allowed to stay.

One deserter from the American Air Force had served in Vietnam where he was shot up. In hospital he had a recurring nightmare in which he was firing at children. He was told that he was going back to the front. He fled. He had no peace of mind in hiding. Who could be trusted? Should he be caught he would be sent either to a stockade or to Vietnam. He needed psychiatric help but did not get it.

Deserters were seized by American military police that had absolute authority in this country and could deport their prisoners to the States without reference to the British police or any other authority. The Visiting Forces Act was in direct conflict with the statutes on political asylum. These deserters surely had a well-founded fear of persecution for reasons of political opinion. Czechoslovakian deserters, on the other hand, were designated 'refugees' and received with open arms. Tent City was more than a holiday camp.

I was amused to read on the internet that 'Originally Tent City people squatted the Scrubs to provide the camp space. The then GLC was brave enough to grant legality to the site.' (Maxine Lambert, who was in charge when the project closed, quoted by John Locke). It was to correct such historical errors that I embarked on writing my memoirs. At the same time I was reassured by it: I had not become part of the thing that I had created.

Why had no one before me suggested a tented hostel as an appropriate solution to the youth accommodation crisis? Once I proposed it, it seemed so obvious. I think this is true of creative output generally: a work of art can be nothing other than what it is. In its own way it is a perfect statement.

Two years after I left Christian Action Tent City made a loss. I seized the moment and persuaded Christian Action's chairman to hive it off. Barnaby Martin and I established Tent City as a limited company with its profits made over to a new charity, Tree of Life. It never made a loss again. I remained chairman of these two organizations for several years. By then I was Head of the Hartland Small School. At the beginning of the summer season we took pupils to help erect the tents and prepare the site, in return for which Tent City paid for visits to theatres and museums. This mutually beneficial relationship continued for several years.

Googling recently I came across this post by Kevin Grentert.

> My girlfriend and I got stuck in London on our way to India in 1986. We stayed one night in a graveyard, trying to save money, then discovered Tent City, which was the cheapest place in the city at the time. It was hilarious and fun.

In 2000 around 27,000 bed nights were recorded. In that year the lease came up for renewal. The building needed considerable repair and upgrading. Hammersmith and Fulham Council could not afford to keep it in a habitable condition and refused to renew the lease. The site closed. However, thirty years is not a bad lifespan for such a venture. It had, in any case, had its day because by the new millennium young people had more spending money and less desire to experience basic living. Tent City's passing is not to be mourned.

RADICAL ALTERNATIVES TO PRISON

Back at the office I was approached for help by a group calling itself Radical Alternatives to Prison. I could not give them money but I offered them office space and office services. They were reluctant to be associated with an organisation that had 'Christian' in its title, but once they understood our involvements, and saw that we were not engaged in missionary work, they became a CA project. Their booklet *Alternatives to Holloway*, which we published in 1972, was a thorough and detailed advocacy for rational and humane alternatives to prison, with a view to the eventual abolition of imprisonment. They were years ahead of their time. After nearly fifty years Holloway is finally to close but their recommended alternatives will not see the light of day.

Prison is the pivot of our penal system. Huge capital and resources are tied up in these institutions, and apparently ineradicable vested interest in maintaining them and in building more. Yet prisons are expensive, they isolate the offender from the community, they are training grounds in crime, they create new problems in the rehabilitation of the offender, and the effect is not educative but negative. Isolated from family, friends and society, degraded and embittered, offenders are unlikely to survive well in the society they confront when they emerge from prison. We could learn from the Scandinavians.

Since 1971 there has been an open prison on Suomenlinna Island, Finland. In 2013 about ninety-five male prisoners, serving time for theft, drug trafficking, assault, or murder, were approaching the end of their sentences. Staff and prisoners ate together. There was a gym and a barbecue pit. Prisoners could earn between €4.10 and €7.30 an hour, and with this money could rent flat-screen TVs, sound systems, and mini-refrigerators. They could also spend time with their families in Helsinki. Like all prisoners in Scandinavia they were allowed to wear their own clothes. Officers carried no batons, handcuffs, Tasers or pepper-spray.

Here in the UK we have a long way to go.

THE LONDON SCHOOL OF NONVIOLENCE

The opening of the LSNV on 30 January 1969 was assisted, publicity-wise, by the publication of Satish's book *Non-violence or Non-existence (Christian Action Publications)*. The school met for three or four nights a week. There were three courses on aspects of nonviolence. The fourth evening was devoted to occasional speakers. These included EF Schumacher (*Small is Beautiful*); Lanza del Vasto, founder of the Gandhian L'Arche Community; John Seymour (*Practical Self-Sufficiency*); Teddy Goldsmith, editor of *The Ecologist*; Dorothy Day, founder of the *Catholic Worker*; Leopold Kohr (*The Breakdown of Nations*) and many others.

John Papworth, a turbulent Anglican cleric, had been imprisoned for anti-nuclear protests, and through the magazine *Resurgence,* which he founded with EF Schumacher, Leopold Kohr and Sir Herbert Read, and its successor the *Fourth World Review*, he urged 'a revolt at ground-floor level by the people'. He believed global war and ecological disaster could only be averted by scaling down military, industrial and commercial institutions. Small societies could not afford nuclear weapons, nor could they consider sacrificing millions of their citizens and still survive.

John addressed the economics of nonviolence. What is economic justice and freedom? What is the role of money? What are the roles of agriculture and industry? These questions all lead to a consideration of the goals of economic life. As John wrote at the end of his summary of the six lectures he gave during the first session of the school,

> ...if man wants an alternative to the forms of economic life that now afflict and oppress him he must surely begin by insisting on a scale of organisation small enough to enable his moral insights to play their full part in its workings.

John returned to Zambia where, for the next nine years, he was rural development adviser to President Kaunda. With his departure abroad *Resurgence* passed into the hands of Satish Kumar via a businessman unable to continue giving it financial support.

Geoffrey Ashe, the second of our regular contributors, was a fellow of the Royal Society of Literature and had written a biography of Gandhi.

In his five lectures he sought to relate nonviolent principles to the western radical tradition, especially British, with attention given to William Blake and the prophetic vision, the poetry and practice of direct action in Shelley and Owen, the non-Fabian radicals who were Gandhi's English friends, the theory of the Servile State (Hilaire Belloc), and the theories of the romantic revolutionary GK Chesterton.

Our third lecturer was Dr Fred H Blum, a refugee from the Holocaust who became a psychotherapist and then an Anglican priest. With Bishop Stephen Verney he founded The Abbey, Sutton Courtney. Fred explored the concept of nonviolent sociology, the science of society.

> ...To speak about labour markets, about supply and demand, about money markets, about people playing roles unrelated to something essentially human, about politics as a game of power, to think (and feel) in these terms as all of us do to a lesser or greater extent is violent. Our basic way of thinking about man and society today is violent because it limits our thoughts to a frame of reference which destroys human growth and development and violates the dignity of man as a human being. (Fred Blum)

At this time Liz and I were living in a small community in Bow, East London, with another couple, a single woman and a single man: Buss House. Though a community might be created simply to live more cheaply, to get round the housing problem, or to afford more luxuries, I saw Buss House as offering the possibility of putting into practice some of the implications of nonviolence that might lead to the creation of a more just and humane society. The community is 'the kingdom now', an island of new standards and a new lifestyle that challenges the old.

In a community there is bound to be conflict between the demands of the group and those of the individual. It provides an opportunity to discover how such conflict might best be resolved. If one is to live according to standards not generally accepted by society then the support of a group is absolutely essential for all but the most single-minded toughs. The community should witness to the entitlement of everyone to a fair share of the world's resources, and to do this by its members holding all things in common, and by sharing with others that which is in excess of what is necessary for its basic needs. This, of course, entails its members discovering what their basic needs are, and the best way of meeting them.

The six of us were interested in Fred Blum's approach and accepted his invitation to meet monthly with him and his wife, Arna, to explore these issues in greater depth. This was, personally, the most important spin-off from the School of Nonviolence.

We also spent a summer running a guest house in Carradale, a picturesque village on the east side of Kintyre, for a woman for whom it had become too demanding and who wanted it to become a peace centre. In the Autumn I ran courses on Nonviolence there.

For various reasons, including cancer, the Buss House community did not get very far in giving flesh to Fred's vision.

Satish announced that he was returning to India to take part in the centenary celebrations of Gandhi's birth and to set up a development project. He was leaving the LSNV in my hands.

Several of us decided to join in with some of the Gandhi celebrations. I bought a Land Rover. It was orange, a holy colour in India. I replaced the engine, had a large rack welded to the roof, and installed a Calor gas cooker. Ten of us took our seats.

Travel was fine until we reached eastern Turkey. There we hit a corrugated dirt road which had to be taken either quite slowly or at high speed. Whichever one we chose there was always dust. As we passed near and through villages small boys threw stones at us.

The journey through Iran was uneventful, but we arrived at the Afghan border just after it closed at about 3pm. In our cynical way we thought this was done to get customers for the hotel. We slept on carpets in one big room heated with wood we had to buy.

As we arrived in Herat the sun was setting, a magical moment for all the senses: the tinkle of bells worn by the horses, the whiff of smoke wafting up from cooking fires, and the gurgle and somewhat sweet odour rising from the hubble-bubbles of the white-robed men squatting on the pavement.

After a fortnight we arrived in India, one group among many taking the hippy trail. Only Pakistan, where young men encircled the Land Rover and eyed up the women, had us worried.

The conference we attended was in Bihar at an extensive campsite. Speeches and music were made in huge tents. Thousands were fed with amazing speed. Rice, dhal and vegetable curry, cooked in oil barrels, were spooned from buckets onto banana leaves, accompanied by chapattis, as we sat in four long rows.

The highlights of our trip were meetings with Mother Teresa and Vinoba Bhave. My first impression of Mother Teresa was of humility and openness. She gave us time and invited us to visit two of her projects. The home for the dying was housed in an abandoned Hindu temple. Here rows of those brought in off the street could die with dignity according to the rituals of their faith: Muslims were read to from the Qur'an, Hindus received water from the Ganges, and Catholics were given the Last Rites. 'A beautiful death', she said, 'is for people who lived like animals to die like angels—loved and wanted'.

We also visited the Nirmala Shishu Bhavan, her Children's Home of the Immaculate Heart, a haven for orphans and homeless youth.

Some years later Mother Teresa came to London to launch the Peace Prayer at St James', Piccadilly. I spent the day ferrying her round London while she picked my brains to find a way of avoiding the restrictions that Tower Hamlets Council were trying to place on her house there. She was a wily old bird. Despite her smile she was beset by doubts. In her diary she wrote:

> Darkness is such that I really do not see — neither with my mind nor with my reason — the place of God in my soul is blank — There is no God in me — when the pain of longing is so great — I just long & long for God... The torture and pain I can't explain.

She thanked Jesus for sending her the darkness 'because I have come to love the darkness for I believe now that it is a very small part of Jesus' darkness and pain on earth'.

Why Vinoba? On April 18th 1951 Vinoba had met with the villagers at Pochampalli. The Harijans (untouchables) of the village told him that they needed eighty acres of land to make a living. He asked the other villagers if they could help solve this problem. One landlord offered to give one hundred acres of land. The Bhoodan (Gift of the Land) movement was born.

The response to the movement grew. He was being given two hundred, then three hundred acres a day. He received as a gift the whole village of Mangrath. This launched the Gramdan (Gift of the Village) movement. Some dacoits from the notorious Chambal Valley surrendered to him in May 1960. For Vinoba it was a victory for nonviolence.

Vinoba's movement rekindled faith in nonviolence and human values as advocated by Gandhi. He saw the land as a gift of God like air, water, sky and sunshine. He connected science with spirituality, and the autonomous village with a world movement. He regarded the power of the people as superior to that of the state.

We met Vinoba at an ashram he shared with the nuns who looked after him. We were having a fruitful discussion when unfortunately Barnaby subverted it in an attempt to convert Vinoba to supporting contraception.

Back home I was invited to join Fred and Arna Blum, Moiz Rasiwala, from the Taizé Community, and Chris Sadler in the designing of an Integral Development Pilot Project centred on human values. We met in London, Taizé and Bombay. A visit to a British-run project in India revealed the essential shortcomings of outsider intervention. While a manager from the UK was in charge things went fairly smoothly. As soon as they returned to the UK chaos ensued, equipment deteriorated and people lost heart.

In the light of this and similar experiences, we were seeking to promote 'a project which grows on Indian soil and which engenders its own basic ongoing funds'.

Chris, Moiz and I visited the Friends Rural Centre in Rasulia near Hoshangabad, M.P., a community of about thirty-five families living in a compound of thirty-five acres. Members of staff were convinced that the work done at the clinic by foreign medics should ultimately be done by Indian nationals.

I returned home to face problems that we could do something about and decided to bring from the US Charles Walker, a trainer in nonviolent direct action who had worked with civil rights campaigners and anti-Vietnam war protesters. We wanted him to train stewards for demonstrations that would be taking place in London. We made a film of his sessions which became available for hire.

I tried to persuade the Metropolitan Police that we could prevent violence at an upcoming demonstration by having our stewards protect the Soviet embassy from potential troublemakers but they were not prepared to risk it.

There were a few media involvements. I was invited by Joan Bakewell to be on her team for a television debate on the subject of Peace and Nonviolence. My partner was Rabbi Albert Friedlander of the Westminster Synagogue in Knightsbridge who, when teaching in the US, had taken his students to march with Martin Luther King. Chairing the debate was *The Times'* journalist Bernard Levin. He got so upset with what Albert and I were proposing that he lost his temper and intervened in the discussion, arguing for the other side.

Rabbi Friedlander invited me to visit his synagogue. He took me to a room stacked with scrolls ready for repair and dispatch to new congregations. It was sobering to realize that the dusty, damaged scrolls piled on these shelves were all that remained of numerous Jewish communities in Bohemia and Moravia. Out of the ashes new communities were growing and, because of this, Orthodox scribes were prepared to labour on these documents at a Liberal synagogue.

For another TV programme on the same theme I rewrote Isaiah's 'Suffering Servant Songs' with a 'Mayor' in place of 'God' and a 'Sheriff' as the 'Suffering Servant'. Set to country & western-

style music they became The Sheriff Without a Gun. This is the
first song:

> This new Sheriff I make my right hand.
> By this happy choice I firmly stand;
> pin my badge of office to his vest;
> trust he'll fight injustice in the West.
>
> *He will fight injustice, he will fight injustice,*
> *he will fight injustice throughout the West.*
>
> He will talk straight but not shout out loud
> nor shriek shrilly at the sidewalk crowd.
> One who's fallen he won't cruelly kick,
> nor snuff out a dimly burning wick.
>
> Town and prairie, watch his justice grow!
> He won't crack or let his temper go
> 'till in every state his law prevail.
> You can bet your boots that he won't fail.   (Isaiah 42.1-4)

I was approached by Richard Armstrong, a BBC producer, whose
radio programme Talking of God concluded a series of reflections
on 50 years of religious broadcasting by speculating about the
future. He asked me for a script that might reflect the situation of
the church in fifty years' time. I imagined a Britain that had been
invaded by Arabs, with Islam as the official religion. The church
had had to go underground. Its spokesperson was the Bishop of
Oxford, a woman. The programme went out on Sunday Dec.17th
1972. On the following Saturday my contribution made it to Pick
of the Week. There are still seven years to go before we know
whether it was prophetic.

I was the fourth lecturer in that first year of the LSNV. My
contribution was an exploration of ethics and morality. My
sessions were more discussion than lecture.

I have not argued against resisting evil actions, but with
moral, not physical force. Gandhi and Martin Luther King are the
leaders who most convincingly applied the teachings of Jesus to
the social and political spheres. They, like Jesus, did not hesitate to
criticise those who wield power. But they did not call for the
violent overthrow of tyrants. Their call was to service and to
dialogue, so that there is always the possibility that the tyrant's
heart will be touched. To bring about the transformation of an evil
situation we have to take the suffering on ourselves. And we have
to use our imaginations. One of the great things about Gandhi was

his inventiveness. Who else would have realised that the making of salt from seawater could be such a threat to the British occupiers? When leaders have moral authority they can ask protesters to march, unarmed, on a salt works defended by armed troops. And when these protesters are beaten to the ground then the British, as an American reporter declared, lose all moral authority, just as any moral authority the occupying forces had in Iraq is undermined by the torture of prisoners and the violence that has continued there.

In c.1515 Erasmus made the argument in his treatise on war. (The following extracts are from the first translation in an edition published by the Merrymount Press, Boston, in 1907 and entitled *Against War*.)

> ...ye cannot hurt and grieve your enemies, but ye must first greatly hurt your own people. And it seemeth a point of a madman, to enterprise where he is sure and certain of so great a hurt and damage, and is uncertain which way the chance of war will turn.

> ...But after Christ commanded the sword to be put up, it is unlawful for Christian men to make any other war but that which is the fairest war of all, with the most fierce and eager enemies of the Church, with affection of money, with wrath, with ambition, with dread of death...With these we must continually fight, until (our enemies being utterly vanquished) we may be in quiet, for except we may overcome them, there is no man that may attain to any true peace, neither for himself, nor yet with no other. For this war alone is cause of true peace. He that overcometh in this battle will make war with no man living. (p.45)

EASTBOURNE HOUSE

Should an organisation such as Christian Action be based in the heart of the City? Didn't this send out the wrong sort of message? I began to argue for a move to a more appropriate neighbourhood and discovered a youth centre in Bethnal Green that had been empty for over seven years. The snooker room at the top of the building caught my breath. White flakes of ceiling limewash danced on spiders' webs, like snow frozen in mid-descent: quite magical!

The building required a considerable amount of work but I was sure we could recruit volunteers to undertake most of it. The site included a house that had been the vicarage.

By now Canon Collins had retired as Chairman and been replaced by Prebendary John Drewett, the Rector of St Margaret's,

Lothbury, London. He and I were on the same wavelength – he was a member of the Modern Churchman's Union – and, unlike Canon Collins, he did not waver when pressure was put on him to divert from an agreed course of action. I discovered only recently that it was he, as chairman of the Bible Reading Fellowship executive committee, who was responsible for commissioning my play *The Crown, the Mitre and the Book*. So, with his support, and despite opposition from the two women working for Defence and Aid, it was agreed that we would purchase Eastbourne House and move the offices to the East End.

Eastbourne House
Bethnal Green

With the help of Jeffrey Smith, a structural engineer, we began to recruit a team of workers to transform a tired old structure into both offices and a community centre. Liz, Catherine and I moved into the vicarage.

Eastbourne House was to be not only an office, but have nine thousand square feet for community work. That was to include a theatre that would seat 300 and a whole floor which could be used as a simple conference centre, including mattress-on-the-floor accommodation. The community work might range from free school, much needed in the area – a few years before I had been approached by Her Majesty's Inspectors (for schools) to see whether I would be prepared to run one in the East End –

right through to national gatherings of radicals sympathetic to nonviolence.

I wrote a background document in which I pointed out that we live in a time of change, brought about by the development of transport and communications systems. We have become so used to the idea of change that novelty has become the measure even of the creative artist.

> The change we expect is the change we experience: towards ever increasing complexity, towards greater speed, towards more sophisticated gadgetry, towards labourless work, towards larger schools, businesses, cities and states. In so far as this change involves high levels of energy consumption it is not open to us in the long term. This is not solely because the fuel will not be available: there is still a possibility that it will, though at great cost. It is because 'high quanta of energy degrade social relations just as inevitably as they destroy the physical milieu'. (I. Illich, *Energy and Equity* p.15ff).

Illich argues that energy grows at the expense of equity. It is therefore incompatible with socialism. He believes that the Welfare State, so called, deprives individuals of both initiative and responsibility and makes them completely passive. That is why, throughout the world today, there is no freedom but only the illusion of freedom. There can be no freedom until every man and woman in every community controls their own life.

> When every community runs its own affairs, settles its own quarrels, decides how its children shall be educated, undertakes its own defence and manages its own markets there will be a general renewal of self confidence and ordinary people everywhere will get some experience of public affairs. But today this know-how is lacking at the grass roots level. (Vinoba Bhave)

It is the development of this know-how that I believed Eastbourne House should be about. It was to be a resource centre, a power house to encourage change, not in the direction which is generally accepted, but towards a more participatory and equitable society in which those technological tools that are life-enhancing are encouraged and those that aren't are put aside (and similarly with patterns of work, education. etc.)

The development of a new society means the development of a new humanity, for development is of human potentialities as well as the world in which we live. But we ourselves do not have 'the integral spiritual, ethical, emotional, intellectual etc. awareness which would allow us to say with a good conscience that we are ready for the new world. I, for one, do not feel that I am and yet I recognise that the time for action is now.' (Fred Blum) This meant that the project must be experimental, a device to find answers, which at the same time allowed us to act now as part of that which is to be developed.

Why should Christian Action have been concerned with such development? To begin with, because the spiritual is an essential dimension of this sort of work. This means a Christ-centeredness, which transcends current cultural expressions of religion, and which recognises the possibility of discovering Christ in other religions. It is not to be taken in any exclusive sense.

Though we walk with those who cannot subscribe to our faith but agree with our works this must not be allowed to cloud the fact that we begin with the person and teaching of Jesus. Our devotion is to the humanity of him whom we believe has, more than any other, revealed to us the nature of the divine.

Nonviolence is the way of the Cross. The way of suffering love is the only way to overcome evil: love of the enemy, turning the other cheek, the refusal of revenge, obedience to the command 'thou shalt not kill'. To the world it is a way of weakness, for the world finds it hard to understand that by the cross death is defeated. To try and fit Christianity to the thought of the world is to render it powerless. To combat evil or injustice with violence, whether physical or institutional, is to fight evil with evil.

We must refuse to use what the world means by power, whether physical force, wealth or political position. Violence is natural and normal to human beings and society. It is a kind of necessity imposed on both rich and poor. The freedom offered by Christ is freedom from this necessity. To gain political power is natural, as is the acquiring and storing of wealth. Insurance and pension are necessary for individual and family security. The freedom offered by Christ is freedom from these necessities. That freedom we have to find for ourselves. It cannot be imposed. 'Grace is the law of the descending movement' (Simone Weil): the descent from security to faith which 'takes no anxious thought'; the descent from security to vulnerability; the descent from riches to poverty; the descent from Transfiguration Mountain.

The refusal to hold power is not the refusal to speak to power. If need be we must break down the doors of the powerful and shout the claims of love and justice and 'plead the cause of absolute misery before absolute power in a spirit of imperturbably calm and loving intransigence, without animosity or violence.' 'Our faith should render us free against threats, corruption, amiability and the proffer of honours.' (Jacques Ellul, *Violence*)

The Christian is called to be in this world but not of it. This means that we have a lifestyle that is radically different from those around us. This may appear to be a barrier to communication, and considerable effort needs to be made to overcome that barrier. To reject the ways of the world without rejecting those who inhabit it is difficult. As many take their identity from the corporations or parties or revolutionary groups to which they belong, rejection of their values threatens the identity of those who belong to them. We must reach out to and accept such individuals. To accept them is not to live their way of life. Love for my parents does not lead me to live as they live. But neither does it allow me to reject them. That is a tension in which we need strength to continue living.

To live in the kingdom is to have simple needs simply satisfied, to ask for no more than daily bread. To work for that bread, as well with one's hands as one's mind. To share that bread with those who come knocking and take, in return, their cares and their sorrows.

'Those who are not in the Christian tradition might not understand what has been stated in religious terms, a language which has become well-nigh incomprehensible to the majority of modern men.' (EF Schumacher). I saw it as one of our tasks to translate for them. The language of nonviolence was the most suitable for our purpose. Even the World Council of Churches had begun to use it! Its central committee had commended a statement on it.

Unfortunately John Drewett's chairmanship lasted only a matter of months because on January 19th 1973 he died. He was replaced by another trustee, Michael Graham-Jones, a management consultant. Michael persuaded me that the Eastbourne House operation was going to be so big that I should become the Director of Eastbourne House and retain my involvement with Tent City, but enable someone else to become Director of Christian Action with responsibility for its campaigning work. If I would resign as Director of CA then that would allow them to appoint a successor and I would be given the Eastbourne House post. This seemed sensible so I submitted my resignation, which was accepted. Michael then told me that it had been decided not to appoint me to the Eastbourne House post. Today I could have taken action for constructive dismissal, not possible in the Seventies. Michael was weak, and sided with those trustees who wanted a more 'intellectual' voice. It was that of Canon Eric James 'who decided to channel [CA's] still substantial financial resources into social and political work being undertaken by other groups' (*Daily Telegraph* obituary). The organization ceased to act.

To a large extent this was a generational issue. The trustees had short hair and wore suits. We had long hair, beards and bought our clothes in Carnaby Street. It tickled John Collins, in his stiff dog collar, his black, plain-front rabat, and his tailored dark suit, to be a patron of the likes of us. After all, his youngest son Mark consorted with us and drove with Satish to India. I and the other senior staff were never invited to socialise with any of the rest of the Council, an omission that confirmed the dividing line, a blot on the copybook of a 'Christian' organization. There was one exception. Nick Beacock and I were treated by Canon Collins to a turf & surf dinner at his club, the Wig & Pen, the lawyers' and journalists' drinking den in Fleet Street.

I was not involved in the development of Eastbourne House because I had been moved on, though the building work continued. Christian Action has since ceased to exist. Now Eastbourne House is in the hands of a Buddhist Arts Group. They hire out two floors. On the top floor there is a large, bright, attractive studio suitable for movement-based activities as well as for quieter group work such as meditation. On the first floor is a large hall with wooden floor suitable for circus, drawing, movement/dance, theatre, opera, martial arts rehearsals and workshops as well as for talks/meetings and group work. We had not laboured in vain.

I moved on with a determination to operate at a local, not a national level, on projects, however small, that could make a real difference to people's lives, thus honouring the proposition 'small is beautiful', without taking my eye of the global situation.

Chapter Nine

From Bach to Blake and back

BACH'S COMPLETE CHURCH CANTATAS on a set of CDs: a Christmas present to live for! Fifty discs, one of which will usually begin my day, a most sublime way to break the silence. The incredible breadth of Bach's creativity continues to be a source of wonder and inspiration.

What would life be without music? I listen, play and compose. When passing a house in which someone is practising I pause. I was removing props from the QEH when the pianist Ashkenazy came in to run through his evening programme. Even though he was taking everything slowly it was impossible to tear myself away.

I can envisage no excess to surfeit the appetite, hard rock excepted. Bells, cymbals and a couple of gongs dangle from the beams in our living room that I can beat as I pass. The music room is graced with a grand piano, a harpsichord, two guitars, a guitar banjo, a double bass, and a variety of small percussion, including nakers and a renaissance drum. Because of arthritis in my thumbs I have sold my three clarinets. On the Broadwood grand are a set of crumhorns, a rackett and a shawm. To one side is a full-size dumb keyboard linked to Sibelius, the computer music writing programme.

A silver B flat bass, the largest instrument in a brass band, has taken up residence in the spare bedroom. I am in the middle of mastering it having joined the Hartland Town Band. There is a stand on which to rest it and a small towel to catch the drips.

Music thrived in the family. Grandpa Langley owned a music shop, 'Donaldson's', in Bath Street, Jersey, a shop from which, under its original owner, Debussy may well have obtained his Blüthner grand when living on the island. Grandpa dealt in pianos. He arrived late for his wedding because business took precedence.

He was short, bandy-legged, with a scratchy, slightly unkempt moustache. In his waistcoat pocket he kept a sharp penknife with which to peel a slice of apple for a grandchild or snitch a cutting from a rose bed in a public garden. He played the organ in chapel and, as he had eight children, could take them with him, the core of a choir.

His shop was a rare and magical cornucopia. It was on a corner around which the window curved. Through it I could salivate at several gleaming grand pianos and marvel at the long, mahogany counter behind which were rows of narrow drawers stacked from floor to ceiling and packed with sheet music. The department selling 78s was across a corridor. HMV records were graded by label from plum, through red to black. Big works came in large, heavy albums. Red and black would dominate my imagined collection, not being blessed with the perspicacity to envision LPs, tapes and CDs.

If I was in luck a pianist would be practising Chopin or jazz on the grand piano placed at the top of the stairs. But the ultimate treat was a ride in the piano lift to visit the uprights on the first and second floors.

Grandpa's Guy Fawkes celebration was a bonfire of elderly honky-tonks, a favour to young learners as there is nothing worse for the aspiring pianist than to have an instrument that doesn't respond correctly. The removal of cheap joannas from the market was also a favour to himself.

When I was at Lampeter he sent me a beautiful instrument, a Bechstein reproducer upright with a stack of piano rolls. When I left Lampeter for Oxford the Principal agreed it could remain behind until I was settled in a parish. Two years later I returned to collect it. It had disappeared. Principal and Bursar shrugged off the loss. It was many years before the balance sheet was set right.

In the College attic I had discovered many unusual, dusty artefacts: spoils lifted from exotic climes by returning missionaries. A sandstone statue 2' 6" high, 1' 6" wide and 9" deep of a figure sitting on a beautiful cushion in a meditation posture caught my attention. It took up residence in my fireplace. The Principal let me have it. It came with us to Hartland in 1983 and occupied a niche in the wall of Satish Kumar's garden, appropriate as he had been a Jain monk and recognized it as a Jain figure.

I sent a photo to the V&A museum. Within two days an excited expert was on the doorstep. It was 9th century, from Uttar Pradesh, and in very good condition. The museum wanted it. I settled for the bottom of a Sotheby's estimate. The Principal of Lampeter, consulted over my story, invited me to make a contribution to the College's coffers. I had lost a piano through the College's negligence. A harpsichord seemed fair restitution.

Mother – 'Melba', after the Australian soprano – was a competent pianist. I would listen to her playing Brahms or Schumann as I walked up the garden from school. She was the Guernsey Choral Society's accompanist. My father played the harmonium for the Masons, and second violin in the orchestra of Domenico Santangelo (Santy). Father's piano playing was impressionistic, fine when he and I pawed our way through duet versions of overtures and symphonies crammed into the double piano stool, but not when he was accompanying me in one of the Brahms clarinet sonatas. I hoped my mother would do the honours but he was usually the first to volunteer.

THE SINGER, NOT THE SONG

'Singing fortifies health, widens culture, refines the intelligence, enriches the imagination, makes for happiness and endows life with an added zest.' (Patty Mills) I buy into that. I joined a junior choir but not for health reasons. Miss Le Page's choir had girls in it: Janet Le Tocq and Barbara Allen were the lusted-after stars. We bagged first prize at the Eisteddfod with boring regularity. We also gave concerts in chapels.

At Christmas the church choir sang at dances and dinner parties, a lucrative venture that kept us in ersatz angel dress: red cassocks, starched ruffs and whiter-than-white surplices. We would usually be invited to perform at Government House. Far better than carolling in the rain!

Bored with our standard repertoire, which Eric Waddams aped from Kings where he had been a choral scholar, I arranged contemporary pieces such as 'The Virgin Mary' and 'Drummer Boy' in four parts and assembled a choir of teenage boys and girls.

We pinched a number of the bookings and were even invited to Government House, a satisfying coup. Eric was not best pleased. It did not help that his daughter, Suzanne, was a member of our choir. We raised money for lepers in Africa.

Many years later, attending a course at Schumacher College on 'Performance', led by Anthony Rooley, Emma Kirkby and Evelyn Tubb with Jessica Cash, their voice coach, I discovered some of the secrets of voice production.

Over the fortnight I watched these three women bring about amazing transformations in some of the singers on the course. This gave me the confidence to take on two or three singing pupils whom I wished to save from being trained to sing like opera stars by the age of fifteen. I never charged for singing or piano lessons. I was given plenty of pottery, and CDs of most of Haydn's string quartets.

INSTRUMENTS

Piano lessons began when I was eight. When I was eight piano lessons ceased as I didn't practice. Mother had so hated practising that she determined not to put that pressure on her own children. Sometimes I wish she had wielded the whip.

St James-the-Less had a three-manual tracker instrument. ('Tracker' means that it had a mechanical action.) I had no teacher. Nevertheless, I somehow acquired enough keyboard skill to gain an Organ Exhibition at Lampeter, not for solo high jinks but for solid accompaniment skill.

At school I was keen to learn an orchestral instrument, anything but the violin. Elizabeth College's cupboard was bare. From somewhere they found me a clarinet. That was a bit of luck for I loved the liquid, golden waterfall sound, much to be preferred to the spiky reediness of the oboe or the flittering flightiness of the flute. They also found me a teacher. He was as basic as my instrument, which possessed the old-fashioned 'simple system' arrangement of keys and lived in a homemade, heavy wooden box. The teacher was a former band sergeant from Kneller Hall, the Royal Military School of Music. Refinement of tone was not his forte, but he knew all the tricks for overcoming mechanical faults with elastic bands and sealing wax, and sopping up excess spittle with cigarette papers. He was a smoker. His demonstration of an awkward fingering imparted a nasty taste to my reed and mouthpiece. I aspired to a mellow tone like that of Jack Brymer, then the doyen of clarinettists.

The highlight of my clarinet career was winning the woodwind prize at the Guernsey Eisteddfod with 'Carol' from Finzi's *Bagatelles*. It is a simple piece, with no technical challenges, but what did it for me, said the adjudicator, was musicianship. That remark has stuck. Musicianship usually triumphs over technique. As a consequence of this success Mrs Mitchell, who lived in a grand house up the road from us, was persuaded to buy me a Boosey & Hawkes 'Imperial', a professional-quality instrument. There were two drawbacks: I had to learn a different fingering and I needed a matching 'A' clarinet. Playing with the Guernsey Orchestra required the transposition of passages written for the A clarinet into keys with dozens of sharps or flats. Unrewarding!

A university lecturer partnered me in one of the gems in the repertoire. Frankie Newte was extremely shy, emerging like a nervous tortoise from his flat above the college gate. Occasionally he could be heard playing the piano – he was an excellent pianist – but he could rarely be persuaded to perform in public, agreeing to appear at a college concert and then crying off at the last moment. It was decided that I would invite him to play Brahms' first clarinet sonata with me. He would hardly be likely to let me down. And he didn't. We made a fairly decent job of it. Sadly there has been no opportunity to play the piece again.

A downward progress ended with the College skiffle group, to join which I constructed a tea-chest bass. It was of a superior nature, not because of the quality of the tea or the broomstick but because I used a 'cello string and could produce real notes and not just thumps out of it. A memorable performance in the Victoria Hall to an audience of enthusiastic girls got us an article in the *Carmarthen Journal*. Our renditions of 'Singing the Blues' and 'Peggy Sue' were legendary crowd-pleasers.

At Ripon Hall theological college there was more music, apart from the daily services that is, because among ordinands there were a disproportionate number of musicians. The programmes of four concerts remind me that I made considerable contributions on both clarinet and piano. One of the programmes was written by Robin Johnson in cod Chaucerian verse. After the interval:

Opens our Sport and Jesting onse again
With Colyn Pigkins who 'tis sure would fayn
Giv to us talks on sondrie dalliaunce
Of rhythm, Ungaria and al that daunce
So that he nigh on has us to believe
That hys mistakes are part of author's screeve.
The author in this case is hight Bartock
(I tell you so it will be lesser shock).

At Edith Cavell secondary modern school I met up with Alan Cartwright, possessor of a 12-string Gibson guitar. Pam, one of the girls in the Hackney youth group, could sing well. I resurrected the tea-chest bass and, with Richard, another guitarist, The 'John Four' entered the arena. The tea-chest did not last, however.

My uncle Fred had played the double bass in the Guilford Symphony Orchestra. When he died my Aunt Mona let me have it at a bargain price. As the tuning matches the four lower strings of the guitar it did not take me long to get the hang of it. The bow I never mastered completely, but who needs a bow for folk music? East Europeans, in the main.

Next I went oriental. In India I bought a sitar. The Bharatiya Vidya Bhavan School of Indian Music had recently been established in London. Their sitar teacher was an Englishman, Clem Alford, who had studied for several years in India where he had been acclaimed as 'the foremost European master of the Sitar'. For six months I enjoyed lessons with him.

My sitarfest was a good training for the ear for the frets are movable and have to be positioned accurately. The fourteen sympathetic strings, that is, strings that vibrate when a note is played on one of the main strings, I also had to learn to tune, a useful preparation for when I obtained a harpsichord. I hardly reached the foothills of the complex rhythm mountain, because Clem decamped to Japan, there being a pupil famine.

For my next string venture I scraped the barrel, almost literally, for I bought myself a hurdy-gurdy kit, the string equivalent of the bagpipes. The hurdy-gurdy rasp was so well-suited to out-of-doors performance that Julia would not allow it be played under her roof. In the end I sent it back to the Early Music Shop in exchange for two good recorders.

FOLK & LIGHT

When Pam moved to West London the John Four folded. Bob and Anne Burlington, friends of Alan, could sing. Bob also played the guitar. I knew that Suzanne Waddams, my music master's daughter, possessor of a lovely voice, was about to finish her teacher training. She agreed to join us on condition that I find her a teaching post. It seems crazy now, but I contacted a headmaster in Bethnal Green and he offered her a job. She developed whole-class composition. She would give the pupils a text. They would sing a line together, each devising his or her own melody, and would then repeat it until they achieved a unison. In this way they worked through the lines of the song, which would now have a tune that they had composed together. Brilliant!

With Suzanne the folk group, The Common Round, was born. We provided music for performances of my multi-media 'folk' plays. We undertook residencies at venues such as the Black Bull, Whetstone, and the crypt of St Mary's, Woolwich, and appeared at the folk club in the crypt of St Martin-in-the-Fields. We also did religious gigs.

Thames TV were presenting a series of programmes on contemporary religious music with Sydney Carter and Donald Swann. From the audience I suggested that, instead of adopting the mediocre material being churned out by the 20th Century Church Light Music Group, traditional hymn tunes could be pepped up by simplifying the harmonies. The following week I was on the programme with my double bass showing how it could be done. I remained friends with Donald and Sydney and from time to time The Common Round shared programmes with the latter.

The Vietnamese Refugee settlement programme left little time for playing music but Julia and I did get half-season tickets to promenade at the proms.

In Hartland I joined up with Tim and Debbie Body and Tina Bennett to form a group that played at Taizé services and also at weddings. Tim's orchestral instrument is the French horn but with us he played the accordion and keyboard. Debbie was on clarinet and keyboard, Tina the fiddle and I played double bass and bass clarinet. Our wedding repertoire included a substantial amount of klezmer as well as folk and show songs. Tim and I arranged the music for the group.

APPRECIATION

The BBC's lunchtime concerts, usually comprising an overture, a concerto and a symphony, introduced me to standard repertoire. At Elizabeth College's weekly Music Club I encountered a wider range and was struck by the works of Britten and Shostakovich. That was something in the early 50s. Antony Hopkins' 'Talking About Music' programmes for the BBC became a model for my presentations to the Club.

With the help of Tim Blofell, a large and somewhat awkward fellow-student at Lampeter, I explored late romantic repertoire. Tim decided he wanted to be 'a Bohemian' and asked for sartorial assistance, which was speedily forthcoming from cynical bystanders. He appeared at breakfast in light grey tapered trousers, slightly too short so showing to advantage his luminous green socks. Somehow the trousers had become spattered with iodine, suggesting an embarrassing accident. A loud check jacket was partnered with a bow tie. A monocle being too costly, a lens from a pair of spectacles was substituted. This proved difficult to manage. When it fell into his cornflakes the watchers spluttered into their coffee cups. I appeared to be his sole friend. We sat for hours listening to LPs of Mahler, Wagner, Bruckner and Richard Strauss from a record library in Liverpool.

At the other end of the spectrum were Professor Harris's Sunday afternoon sessions. He had a wind-up gramophone with a horn so long – about six feet – that it had to be supported on a metal pole. The needles were of wood so as not to damage his 78s. Though this was an experience not to be missed we were never at ease sitting forward on the sofa or easy chair balancing cake and tea on our knees. Marks would be deducted, we felt, for crumbs on the carpet.

The outstanding musical event at Lampeter was not playing in the Aberystwyth University orchestra for a Gilbert and Sullivan production but attending a concert in Moscow. I had been selected to join a National Union of Students visit to the Soviet Union in 1958 as a member of only the second group to undertake such a mission. We were entertained by a variety of institutions, visited Stalingrad where we spoke with war veterans, and attended a Burns Night celebration at the University. When a professor started intoning sonorously, 'My luff is loik a hrred, hrrred hrrose', our reaction was similar to that described by Shylock on hearing the bagpipes. We were more respectfully responsive to Khatchaturian's ballet *Spartacus*, then enjoying a successful run. At the Hermitage in Leningrad we worked our way through a stack of decadent impressionist paintings that were piled against a wall on the top floor. I regret not having tucked one under my jacket.

Wandering through the Moscow streets I spotted a poster. I could make out the name 'Shostakovich'. A concert of his music was an attractive proposition. A group of us turned up at the box office door. All seats sold! However, we were semi-official guests so the front row was cleared for us to enjoy Shostakovich's Fifth Symphony and Oistrakh playing the Second Violin Concerto. Afterwards we were taken backstage to meet the composer and the soloist. Shostakovich was reticent. Was he shy? Was he reluctant to be seen chatting to Westerners? Oistrakh was much more forthcoming.

The following day I made for GUM, the State Department Store, and bought all the Shostakovich LPs available: Symphonies 5, 10 and 11, the Piano Quintet and the Piano Trio. Since then I have acquired most of his works. It is hard to overestimate the effect that meeting these two had on my musical taste and its development. It led me to Sofia Gubaidulina, whose 'Seven Last Words' I heard, interspersed with Haydn's take on them, in Tallinn, and whose St John Passion moves me. It won an award at Cannes, where Gubaidulina was honoured as 'Best Contemporary Composer'. Recordings of the work have been largely panned by British critics, who might also find attendance at the Orthodox liturgy 'ultimately wearing'.

COMPOSITION

I had a brief encounter with music theory. I was the only 'O' level music candidate and had to study privately with Eric Waddams, the music master. For 'A' level music I would have needed school time. The Principal wasn't having any of his boys sitting it. It was 'a cissy subject'.

It was at Lampeter that I first began to compose. For the 1960 Rag Revue, *Share my Sixties*, Roger Clissold persuaded me to set some amusing words. I accompanied the musical items on the piano wearing tails, an extravagant bow tie and shoes two feet long. I was playing the fool, but felt I was playing the Fool in a deeper sense. The priestly fool Ken Feit aimed to make fools out of priests and priests out of fools, 'and artists out of both; for the artful, playful and sacred share a common domain'.

I set the Nunc Dimittis for the College choir. We recorded it on one of three heavy, metal-cored discs. Frankie Newte responded positively to this and gave me helpful compositional advice, the only such help I have ever received, though not for lack of trying. I applied for a place on a Dartington Summer School composition course with Judith Weir, but only students were accepted. I wrote and complained on behalf of the mature and she generously gave me an afternoon. We talked through my Blake settings. At the Bath Guitar Summer School the composition class with Howard Skempton, for which I was accepted, was cancelled through lack of interest. In his book *Musical Composition* Reginald Smith Brindle expresses doubts as to whether composers can be made. It is more likely that they are born, which is OK by me as I have had no choice but to teach myself. Or to be born for that matter! Nevertheless, I felt the need for a bit of theory and read Schoenberg, Hindemith and Ernő Lendvai, as well as Brindle, on composition and Gordon Jacobs and Walter Piston on orchestration.

Most of my compositions have been word settings, usually either religious or occurring in one of the plays I was producing. At Crown Woods comprehensive school I formed a sixth-form jazz group to play in school assemblies. Frustrated by the limitations of school hymn books I decided to edit one of my own. For *Sing True* (REP, single-line 1969, keyboard 1970) I wrote the music for a dozen of the one hundred folk-style songs and hymns in the collection. About half the items are modernised versions of traditional words with modernised versions of traditional tunes. Many schools adopted it.

I wanted the book to be suitable for use by Jews, Muslims and those of little faith or belief so I omitted references to the Trinity and appended a note on the use of the word 'God'.

> The word 'God' has been used in many different ways. In earlier parts of the Old Testament God was limited to the land he was thought to have power over. The idea of a universal God developed, and instead of being angry he became just and merciful and finally loving.

> Some picture an old white bearded man sitting on a golden throne. Others describe God as the 'depth of history' or 'depth of

existence'. These, and those who hold a variety of beliefs in between, should have no difficulty in accepting most of the hymns in this book.

How can the rest use the word without doing violence to their integrity? Perhaps you can accept God as a hypothesis, not to explain things but so that we can talk about them, a useful linguistic device. If a group of people wants to express their thankfulness, because life is good, the task is made easier if the thanks can be addressed to someone or something.

The word God can be used as shorthand for all that is good, for 'love', 'mercy', 'pity', 'peace' and 'justice'.

If we are to rise above our selfishness then it is necessary to have a point of reference outside ourselves. Otherwise man outgrows his boots. The idea of God can serve as this reference point. At the same time it can be used to describe the very best in us.

I had an email thirty-five years after the book was published thanking me for this note.

Sing True was launched in the Purcell Room on the South Bank, The Common Round providing the music. We recorded an LP for Pye's Marble Arch label. The pity is that this was a mono recording made just as stereo was taking over. *Sing True* sold 72,000 copies. Royalties were made over to Christian Action and effectively paid my salary as their Director for two-and-a-half years.

At Christian Action I imagined, such were the demands of the job, that music would take a back seat but Cyril Taylor, one of our office workers, was also a Vicar Choral at St Paul's cathedral with a third job as general factotum for Musica Reservata, whose gigs in the Queen Elizabeth Hall I was persuaded to attend. I loved those concerts, featuring instruments that were new to me, playing medieval and early Renaissance music that was also novel. Michael Morrow and John Beckett, who ran the show in a rather shambolic way, were a delight. But even more striking was the soprano Jantina Noorman who could sing like a Dutch fishwife.

This experience of early music came in useful when writing my play about John Wycliffe. I enjoyed setting words in a medieval style. With Cyril's help the necessary instrumentalists were recruited. They were joined by the choir of Waltham Abbey. (More about the play in 'bard & boards', chapter 7.)

At the Othona Community centre in Essex I found that there was no common way for the community to sing the psalms.

C of E members were stuck with Anglican chants. A few might be au fait with plainsong. The sprung rhythm of Gelineau settings had made little impact and Taizé chant had not yet come on line. I decided to fill the gap.

By 1976 I had set fifty psalms and fifteen canticles, some from faiths other than Christian. The choice of psalms was based on a list made by a Ripon Hall worship group. We were used to working our way through the Psalter each month. Despite CS Lewis's spirited defence of this practice we resented having to sing 'Blessed shall he be that taketh thy children: and throweth them against the stones' on the evening of the 28th of the month. Those words form the final verse of Psalm 137. It begins 'By the rivers of Babylon', a psalm that, in a Rastafarian setting, became a pop hit. This is my version:

By Babylon's rivers we sat down and wept,
remembering Zion.
On willows that grew there we hung up our harps,
remembering Zion.
For there those that carried us captive away
called for a song;
our captors required of us joy: 'Sing a song,
a song of your city'.

But how could we offer a song of the Lord
on alien soil?
My right hand shall wither, O city of peace,
if I should forget you.
My tongue will adhere to the roof of my mouth
should I forget you,
not setting the city of God before all,
before every pleasure.

These words have been a regular companion of mine. They were in my heart as I worked at settling Vietnamese refugees. I sang them at a service in Cairo cathedral when refugees were pouring out of Sudan, Somalia and Eritrea, many of them meeting regularly in the cathedral crypt, and again they were with me when Julia and I were working in Ethiopia with refugees from South Sudan.

I sent copies of the *Othona Psalms* to Donald Swann and Rabbi Albert A Friedlander, and more recently, to Archbishop Rowan Williams. The responses were heartening. Donald wrote:

There is a happy modal simplicity about the tunes and their varied tempi; and the quite unassuming language, which you use in verse, fits so admirably. Are all these texts recent? It really beats me how you find ways of putting all this Hebrew into clear language.

This was the Rabbi's response:

I have read them through carefully and think that you have done an excellent job. Needless to say, I prefer the Hebrew version to any translation, but I also feel that the Psalms should speak to many communities and should meet the needs of our generation.

Archbishop Rowan, whom I approached as both poet and theologian, was equally positive, describing the collection as 'an extraordinary achievement'. He also raised some interesting points about 'register' to which I have attended in a recent revision.

The canticles that are part of the collection were controversial as they included settings of words from Buddhist, Hindu and Moslem sources. Many of these were later published separately by Stainer & Bell.

The launch of the *Othona Psalms* at St Martin-in-the Fields was a bit of a disaster, for the printers failed to get copies there on time. In those duplicator days we were able to run off a handful of individual items for the congregation/supporters' club, but without printed music. We had something to sing but nothing to sell. The tape we recorded later was similarly cursed.

As part of the Schumacher College course mentioned above we each had to give a performance. I included a couple of my psalm settings in my programme. Evelyn Tubb liked what she heard and offered to record a tape of them. On my return home I set about arranging accompaniments for a stylistically mixed bunch of nine instrumentalists: Evelyn's partner Michael Fields on guitars; Tina Bennett, a professional viola player and leader of the Hartland Chamber Orchestra, violin and viola; Idan Piercy, a graduate of the Royal Military School of Music, clarinet and violin; Anne Rendell, a teacher, flute; Nick Crump, a founder member of the Hambledon Hopstep Band, recorders and trumpet; Tim Dollimore, a student at the Small School, 'cello; John Keys, a Dorset folk musician, accordion; and Brian Davison, formerly drummer with The Nice, percussion. I contributed double bass, keyboard and clarinet. Evelyn also played the trumpet.

Evelyn Tubb

In the winter of 1993 we spent a hectic weekend in the chapel of the Othona Community centre at Burton Bradstock in Dorset learning and recording seventeen of the psalms. The weather was freezing and road noise, which led us to the verge of recording rage, required the abandoning of some takes. The recording engineer Antony Askew, who had worked for the BBC, insisted on whole takes: no patching. One item, a setting of Psalm 62, 'In stillness my heart waits on God', when we eventually achieved an acceptable post-pub take, had us in tears. I have it on my website.

Roderic Dunnett, reviewing the tape, wrote:

> These are dancing, folk-related song arrangements, such as would grace Taizé, with very attractive instrumental antiphons interspersed, and a modernised text sung by solo soprano (the Consort of Musicke's splendid Evelyn Tubb). Closer to the Song of Songs, like a simple profession of faith, they offer the same ingenuous delight as the Singing Nun, way back in the 60s. In no sense trite: a fresh idea, well worth hearing. (*Church Times*)

We had previously made a mono recording when stereo was the latest thing. Now we were putting out a tape in the age of CDs. That was by no means the worst of it. Beta Productions, friends of Antony's who were producing and distributing the tape, went bust leaving me with a box of fifty tapes. Antony died shortly afterwards. His wife could not find the master tape so I was stuck. I would like to make a new recording but cannot find the funding.

I have continued to work on the collection, a major revision of the text resulting from developments in my theological thinking. I have broadened the range of models, such as 'father', that we use to talk about God. The theologian Sally McFague suggests 'God as mother, lover, and friend of the world, and ... the world as God's body.' They replace those 'of God as lord, king, and patriarch, with the world as his realm'.

A piece of music I wrote for John Lane led to greater things. He was an inspirational artist and writer who in 1966 was appointed by the Dartington Hall Trust to be the first Director of the arts centre it opened at Beaford in North Devon, setting a pattern and programme for rural arts. (He later became Chairman of the Trust itself.) To celebrate John's retirement I wrote a suite for a baroque quintet that, shades of Peter Maxwell Davies, included 'John Lane's Maggot'. Liking it, the Beaford Centre commissioned me to write a piece to celebrate their 30th birthday. I chose nine of Ted Hughes' *Season Songs*, words written in and about Devon, for forces that represented North Devon's musical life.

The soprano soloist was Evelyn Tubb, Michael Fields was the guitarist, the Winkleigh Singers, trained by Roland Smith, provided the chorus. The Hartland Chamber Orchestra was the ground and the backbone. As brass bands are an important part of our musical scene I recruited half-a-dozen players. That was a mistake for they were not the best sight readers and they have their own concept of tuning. Evelyn made up for their shortcomings, however, and the two performances we gave at the Plough, Torrington, went down tolerably well. The Director of the Beaford Centre was a bit more positive, writing that '*Season Songs* was extremely successful with both audience and performers', but he had to say that, didn't he?

THE SHE-FOX OF SHINODA

We come now to the most substantial of my compositions. In other chapters you will have read about the four trips Julia and I made to Japan. Afterwards some friends in Tokyo complained that every time we visited them it was to work. We deserved a holiday. Their daughter had spent nearly a year living with us. Our reward was a pair of air tickets. They suggested to another friend, Simon Piggott, who had been involved in organising our previous visits and had lived in Japan for many years, that he take us to Sado Island.

Located in the stretch of sea between Japan and the Korean peninsula, Sado has a special place in Japanese history and culture. For many centuries it was the island to which people out of favour with the government were exiled. These exiles took with them Noh theatre and other cultural expressions, including

215

puppetry. With Simon we visited Ken Nishihashi, a bunya puppeteer. One evening we were discussing the trip that he and his Saruhachi company had made to London and Edinburgh the previous year. Ken felt that the language barrier had made it difficult for the British audience to appreciate his art. I thought that the narration, delivered in a type of raucous Japanese plainsong accompanied by the *biwa,* a Japanese lute that sounds more like a banjo, might also have been a cultural barrier. Possibly under the influence of *sake* I suggested it might be performed as an opera. Ken, who had said that he sometimes used Western classical music in his workshops, was open to the idea. There was no withdrawing. Sometime before midnight we toasted the project's success. Thus the puppet opera was conceived.

I wanted to find out if there were any Western precedents. Haydn created six operas for the Royal Marionette Theatre at Esterhaza Palace of which two survive. That was all I could discover. There was no tradition into which to plug.

The first task was to create an organisation, Hartland Chamber Opera, so that we could apply for funding for eight performances in the West Country in the autumn of 2000 with a return visit to Japan in the autumn of 2001. Fortunately the new millennium was being celebrated as the 'Year of the Artist'. I was given a grant of £10,000. I managed to raise the rest.

Composing something acceptable to a Japanese audience that might also appeal to a Western one was challenging. Japanese traditional art forms are extremely conservative:

> Theatres in Nagoya were aghast when Yoko Matsuo came calling. Even though she was born in the city and is conductor and director of the Aiache Prefecture Symphony Orchestra, her plan to stage Mozart's opera *Don Giovanni* in the style of Japan's most revered and challenging dramatic form, Noh, created outrage. (*The Japan Times*, May 28, 2000).

Simon Piggott, busy translating the libretto into English, summarised the challenge in an email to me:

> I don't think the play will be a success with Western audiences simply as a rendering of Japanese deep feelings. A personal interpretation is called for. At the same time we must beware of creating a gap between our interpretation and the puppets. I think we are lucky to be working with someone like Ken with his openness to Western culture and keenness to experiment.

This opera for adults tells the story of a vixen, Kuzunoha, who became a beautiful woman to repay an exiled court astrologer for saving her life. They marry and have a son Doji who, when the opera begins, is five years old. One day, working at her loom, Kuzunoha sees through the window wild chrysanthemums which remind her of her previous life. In this reverie she returns to her fox form. Her son wakes, sees her and is frightened. She, returning to human form, calms him and puts him to sleep. She realises she must now go back to Shinoda forest, her natural home. She writes a farewell letter to her husband and fastens it to her son's belt. Then she paints a poem on a paper screen and leaves.

When her son awakes he thinks his mother is hiding to punish him. Father returns, sees the poem, reads the letter and determines to go after Kuzunoha. There is a humorous interlude in which the fox tricks some hunters. Father and son search fruitlessly. Death is the only answer. He is about to kill the child when the mother appears and changes back into human form. Why have they come searching for her?

The She-Fox

Kuzunoha will not return but has two gifts for Doji, a talisman from the palace of the dragon king, to possess which is to possess knowledge of heaven and earth, of time and all things in the world of humans. The second gift is a crystal which, when put to the ear, allows an understanding of the language of animals and birds. His father promises to bring up the child to be a man of great stature and to release Kuzunoha from her suffering. Doji wants to stay with his mother but she blesses him and vanishes. Once again she is a vixen, 'leaping, searching the horizon and quizzing earth and sky in her grief'.

So what about my interpretation? Firstly, I have no problem with folk or fairy tales for adults. Many operas from Eastern Europe are based on such tales. Secondly, I was fascinated by the Buddhist/Shinto elements, particularly with regard to suffering and to the natural world. But, thirdly, I saw also a Western approach which explores the animal/human polarities of our nature and the search for authenticity.

There are few precedents for a Western/Japanese crossover. The obvious one seemed at first sight to be Benjamin Britten's *Curlew River*. But though his instrumentation reflects Japanese usage there is, as he wrote, 'nothing specifically Japanese left in the Parable...that I have written.' He took his musical inspiration from plainsong.

How to create a Japanese 'feel' whilst avoiding pastiche? I listened to old and contemporary music. Is it possible to absorb Japanese influences in the way that composers such as Takemitsu, Noda, Hirota and Satoh absorbed Western music? Or should they themselves – a half way house – be the reference point? I checked out the characteristics of Japanese music. The tone colour of individual instruments is important. They are not expected to blend. Instead of chords/harmony there are 'pillar tones', central pitches on which notes above and below resolve. Set rhythmic patterns appear in the percussion, usually in progressions. Pieces are through composed, unlike Western practise where thematic material is usually developed. There is a set form: 'introduction', 'scattering', 'rushing towards the finale'. The goal is to create the maximum effect with a minimum of material: 'less action more meaning'. The challenge is to the flexibility of the listener, not of the composer or performer.

For my sound palette I chose a flute, doubling on alto flute (with Noh flute and Shakuhachi in mind) guitar (Shamisen, Biwa and Koto), both instruments favoured by contemporary Japanese composers, and percussion. There is a wide range of bell and drum in Japan. We would have lots of it! Wood: five Chinese temple blocks (skulls), claves, guiro, slap, maracas and woodblock; skin: four tuned bongos, a renaissance drum and a small tambourine; metal: a set of handbells, glockenspiel, a child's toy piano, two meditation bells, cowbells and a gong. I also wanted a viola, of which there is no equivalent. You may have noticed that there is no bass instrument. Western harmony is usually built from the bass up. By dispensing with a bass line I hoped to get more of an oriental feel.

Deciding on the singers was relatively easy: a soprano for the mother/fox, a treble for the child and a baritone for the father. The narration they could share between them. That would have pleased Yeats who believed that the Noh technique, in which dramatic and narrative presentation are fused, appeals. As with composing for film, the score had to be written to fit pre-existing action. I was sent a video of a performance with which to work.

Music makes its point more slowly than words, and occasionally I use set forms such as a lullaby and a dance. The puppeteers therefore had to accept that in places the action required some modification to allow the music to have its say.

Ken | Angela

The soprano Angela Henckel had been to Japan with the Purcell Quartet as a soloist in *Dido and Aeneas* and had sung the Queen of the Night and Despina with Opera Restor'd. Her voice and personality appealed. The baritone Andrew Moore was recruited unseen. In 1999 he won the National Federation of Music Societies Award for Young Concert Artists. He sang in the Glyndebourne Festival chorus in 2000 and was being coached by Roger Vignoles. Katherine Leat, treble, was a former pupil to whom I had given singing lessons. She had just completed a degree in architecture.

Nineteen months after the initial meeting we gave our first performance in Hartland. A year later we were in Japan, starting on Sado Island and finishing up in Tokyo. The venues included Harmony Hall, Matsumoto, where the performance was recorded. I sent a copy of the CD to the composer Judith Weir for whose *A Night at the Chinese Opera* I have a particular fondness. There were many positive responses to the work but hers was the most precious to me.

> It makes very pleasant refreshing listening, cleanly written and performed – I like the voices. Most unlike the vast majority of

overwritten new music (what are they trying to cover up?) which comes my way from contemporary composers. I can't imagine a more satisfying thing than to be involved in your own performances like this, going to Japan, etc. Terrific. (Judith Weir)

What of this work's future? It could be performed as a ballet and would be suitable for small venues.

A composing challenge to match the *Othona Psalms* was to set all forty-four of William Blake's *Songs of Innocence and Experience*. Many composers, Vaughan Williams, Britten and Tavener among them, have set individual poems but, as far as I am aware, only William Bolcom has set them all. My approach has differed from all of these.

I had read in a biography of Blake that he was not fond of 'art' music and that he used to sing his poems at house gatherings using hymn tunes, folk tunes or popular melodies such as might be heard in Vauxhall Gardens and the streets. A similar simplicity in the vocal line, with an accompaniment for flute/alto flute, clarinet, trumpet, violin, viola, guitar/banjo, double bass and two singers was my response. Since then I have arranged them for one voice with piano accompaniment.

Apart from Ted Hughes' *Season Songs,* most of my song settings have been of religious words. This includes a Julian of Norwich text and Isaiah's 'Suffering Servant' Songs. These latter I treated in a country and western style, the words having been re-written as *The Sheriff Without a Gun,* a figure almost unimaginable in the modern-day US. I wrote them for a TV programme on Peace. They were sung on air by a folk group.

I have been working on the words of the 'Song of Songs' and they now await their music, though I probably won't get much further unless a performance is in the offing. I need that promise to spur me on.

I am also toying with a nativity story set in a circus, taking visual inspiration from Chagall, in which Mary is a bareback horse rider and Joseph the circus carpenter. The angel is a fortune teller. The music would be in folk style. It would be written for TV.

TEACHING

At the Small School we were keen to promote music, especially as the demands of the national curriculum was putting a squeeze on it. Instrument teachers were in despair. The Bideford Youth Orchestra folded. We would buck the trend.

I splashed out on xylophones, marimbas, glockenspiels and metallophones, as well as untuned percussion, instruments with which we have had great improvisational fun.

Medieval instruments followed: a quartet of crumhorns, a rackett, and a shawm, all in kit form. Fortunately Toby Chadwick, our woodwork teacher, was a trained instrument maker so he was able to supervise the construction, tuning and finishing of them. Those who made them learnt to play them, especially pleasing as later generations complained that they were too hard to blow.

Pam Rodway, a parent and part-time teacher, was so excited by this consort that she persuaded an expert in Italian renaissance dances to come up from Exeter and teach them. A sewing team made appropriate dresses and costumes while I tutored the players in a suite of suitable repertoire. On a hot summer's day it all came together on the lawn of the Bishop's Palace in Exeter.

I encouraged an appreciation of opera. Stories and songs, movement and colour make this form an easy way into classical music. The hurdle is the cost. However, the Royal Opera House, Covent Garden, offered matinees to schools at knock-down prices. With family railcards three adults could each take four children at £1 per head. For several years we attended two operas a year. The most popular was Janácek's *The Cunning Little Vixen*, in part because it was Simon Rattle's daughter's birthday and a barrage of balloons was let loose on us from the ceiling, but mainly because it was such a magical production. The dragonfly, descending like an early aeroplane, set the imagination dancing.

More rarely a group went to the Theatre Royal, Plymouth, for a Glyndebourne production. (It was much more expensive than an excursion to the ROH.) The young performers of the touring company have a freshness that clicks with a young audience. One performance took place within half-term. We signed up for a workshop and were the only school keen enough to break into our holiday so had them to ourselves.

As a teenager I found opera too fanciful. It was *Peter Grimes* and *Wozzeck* that first turned me on. I liked the grittiness of story and music. When the ROH staged Schoenberg's opera *Moses and Aron* I was keen to see it. Rumour had it that Solti, who was conducting, did not know the score. He gave an introductory talk and it was clear that this was rubbish. Why the antagonism? Why is it felt necessary to put down what we do not understand? After a Boulez piece at a recent Prom several men in my row exclaimed loudly, 'A load of rubbish!' Difficult, yes, but not detritus.

For the first performance of *Moses and Aron* the house was about a third full. I went two days later and nearly all the seats were taken. The power of the opera is in the struggle between Aron and Moses, and in Moses' failure to give expression to the inexpressible (he speaks his lines), but that wasn't the draw factor. The production, directed by Peter Hall, contained nudity in the Golden Calf orgy that hit the headlines. It was *Hair* for the well-heeled! What those who went for the spectacle discovered is that it was not that difficult after all because, as with film music, the visuals make the modern, and even way-out, acceptable.

Opera is an expensive medium, and that is a problem. Julia and I can rarely afford to go in London. We made an exception for *The Greek Passion* by Bohuslav Martinu and were not disappointed. Perhaps it is the subject matter – persecuted refugees – that so moved us. Otherwise we usually enjoy the genre on the continent or on the TV. Cine-concerts from the opera house seem to have taken off, but it is still cheaper to buy the DVD.

On a recent trip to the Baltic States we saw *Eugene Onegin*, *Il Trovatore*, *Love For Three Oranges*, and *The Queen of Spades* in opera houses where the best seats are about the same price as the cheapest at Covent Garden or the Coliseum.

Adults in Hartland were interested in broadening their appreciation of serious music so I became a WEA lecturer and for several years ran evening classes, doing my A. Hopkins bit. That was when I began with Bach, or rather with arrangements of Bach. Hearing how Elgar, for instance, orchestrates a Bach fugue gives an insight into his musical thinking, but where it is even more instructive is in the arrangements made by Schoenberg and Webern, and particularly Webern who fragments a line, allocating short phrases to different instruments. He does this to the Ricecar à 6 from Bach's *Musical Offering*. It begins with five notes on the trombone followed by two on the horn and two on the trumpet, a process called *Klangfarbenmelodie* that gives a novel feel to the musical material. (Gubaidulina treats similarly this passage in the opening of her violin concerto *Offertorium*.)

I moved on to Webern's *Five Movements* for string quartet. The second movement, which is only fourteen bars long, I played six times in succession in the belief that familiarity would lead to an appreciation. It did not. In Webern I had met my match. I had better luck with his teacher, Schoenberg and even more luck with Berg.

A lecture by the composer Xenakis at the Bath Festival made me realise that there are limits to the music that I can appreciate. I believe the listener needs to hear patterns, which is what we find in music before the 20th century. (Plainsong is an exception. It does not go anywhere – there is no tension, then relaxation of tension – so it is ideal for setting religious words.) The music of Xenakis sounds random, the deranged outpourings of a dyspeptic computer. On the other hand, repetition has returned with a vengeance. You can have too much of it, as the minimalists have demonstrated.

CONDUCTING

On the Schumacher College course mentioned earlier Anthony Rooley told me that I had to take my music more seriously. It so happened that a group of musicians in Hartland was in the process of becoming a chamber orchestra. I joined as the keyboard player. I was soon jumping up and waving my arms in an attempt to do the job the instrument alone was failing to do. The keyboard was abandoned.

My approach was to play straight through a movement many times to allow the shape to get under the skin and an interpretation to evolve. As we rehearsed every Monday, and gave only three or four concerts a year, the works we played we knew well. We also accompanied choral societies, but those were one-day affairs and never entirely satisfactory.

Though in this approach to rehearsal there is an element of democracy, in the end one has to be in control. Otherwise 'Things fall apart; the centre cannot hold; Mere anarchy is loosed upon the world.' Conducting amateur players must be trickier than conducting professionals. Fail to signal an entry and the player might go on holiday. The trickiest bit is bringing the orchestra in after a soloist's cadenza. Otherwise, the art of accompanying a soloist, I discovered, is fairly straightforward: breathe with them. We programmed a lot of concertos as audiences love soloists.

Another skill I had to acquire was the ability to set the right speed. I practised by checking myself against the microwave clock so that I could accurately time a second. I still do it when I am cooking, and I do it at those street crossings that give one a countdown.

'Baroque' meant tons of Telemann because he does not make too great a demand on the players, and a fair amount of Handel for the same reason, but a lesser amount of Bach. There is tons of Telemann. He published 40 volumes of his works, earning money to pay off his wife's gambling debts. Two Telemann concertos stand out, the one for viola, and one in D minor for two clarinets (chalumeaux). Both are available on YouTube. The recording by Musica Antiqua Köln of the chalumeaux concerto is my top recommendation. However, we began to suffer from Telemann fatigue, though we did not tire of Bach and Handel.

When we started out it would be a miracle if we got through a concert without breaking down once or twice. Over time there has been a tremendous improvement. Our players have been a mixed bunch of professionals and amateurs led by Tina Bennett, a professional viola player who worked in Holland for many years. I have written two viola concertos for her. I wrote a flute concerto for Maggie Strange and a clarinet concerto for Sarah Conibear. Other players displayed a range of abilities, and though individual limitations can often be frustrating it is important to keep in mind Albert Schweitzer's remark that an individual's involvement in music-making might be the brightest part of their life, therefore their continuing participation is more important than the pursuit of perfection.

As in our early days baroque music was our staple diet it seemed important to organize some training in baroque technique. We had a day's workshop with Marshall Marcus, then leader of the second violins in the Orchestra of the Age of Enlightenment, who brought with him several baroque bows. We were surprised at the difference they made. Articulation became much crisper. We tried to hang on to that with our modern bows.

In the evening he played a Bach concerto at a concert we gave at the Beaford Arts Centre. Also on the programme was Aaron Copland's 'Appalachian Spring', the chamber version. There are passages in it where the time signature changes almost every bar. From within the second violins came the complaint that I was not beating it correctly. Marshall contradicted him: I was. That backing was a great boost to my confidence.

We moved on to Haydn and Mozart symphonies, playing whole works, not selected movements. We have not always had all the instruments that a piece required and so I made arrangements for our limited forces. I learnt ways to trick the ear. If you sandwich a flute between two trumpets it will easily be mistaken for a trumpet; a bassoon between two horns becomes a horn. I used a clarinet for the high trumpet in a Brandenburg Concerto (as did Karajan). A member of the audience was puzzled. He couldn't see the trumpet.

Over time we programmed contemporaries such as Peter Maxwell Davies, Gavin Bryars, Alan Hovhaness, Alfred Schnittke, Arvo Pärt and Hodgetts. We also attempted some of the simpler Shostakovich, Prokofiev, Bartok, Britten and Copland works to challenge as well as please audiences and players, though it often happened that what was predicted to be challenging turned out to be not so difficult after all.

I was fortunate to work with the soprano Angela Henckel on a number of occasions, *The She-Fox of Shinoda* being the first. Erwin Stein had arranged Mahler's 4th Symphony for Schoenberg's 'Society for Private Musical Performances'. Angela's voice was eminently suited to the child-like song that is the symphony's fourth movement. The eleven instruments Stern used included piano and harmonium. We had no harmonium, nor a suitable piano, so I set about arranging the symphony for the forces at our disposal. It was not difficult as Mahler's scoring is quite chamber-like in this work. Spurred on by this venture's success I tried a similar approach with Vaughan Williams' 5th Symphony. It almost worked. Although some decent brass players were recruited, two rehearsals gave insufficient time for them to achieve a decent blend. Perhaps I was being a bit too ambitious.

It was astonishing how many of our players knew neither the Mahler nor the Vaughan Williams.

RELIGION and SPIRITUALITY

Hildegard of Bingen: 'Music is the echo of the glory and beauty of heaven.'

Religious words do not necessarily make for a spiritual experience. That is true of many settings of the mass. The requiems of Brahms and Britten, however, are spiritual favourites. This may be because the words they were setting were personal to them and not standard fare. Even Antonio Pappano cannot sell the Verdi Requiem to me.

I have grown to appreciate the *St John Passions* of Gubaidulina and Pärt, the *St Luke Passion* of Penderecki, and Haydn's *Creation* and *The Seasons*. They have for me a spiritual dimension, as do some works without words such as Beethoven's late quartets.

The issue of 'spirituality' in music is a controversial one, as it is in all art forms, and we could spend paragraphs considering Messiaen and Gubaidulina, but I know what does it for me and in the end that is what matters.

And in the end we come back to Bach. Any composer since his time, and certainly anyone writing from a religious or spiritual perspective, must take him as their benchmark. It is spiritually invigorating to begin the day with the master, for

> the mysticism, the richness of emotion, and the amazing beauty of design and melody in Bach's music at its best, are an unending marvel... (Henry Raynor)

> Do people really believe that music leads us astray [St Augustine?]
> and that it does not harmonise with love?
> O no! For who would not consider the worth
> of something which noble patrons value highly?
> Certainly, generous nature draws us with it to a higher path.
> Like love it is a great gift of Heaven, only it is not as blind.
> It steals into all hearts, high and low alike.
> It calls heaven to mind and can tell of the glory of the Highest
> to loving souls.
> Yes, who would deny that love is far stronger than death?
> Music strengthens us in death's agony.
> O marvellous art, you we greatly honour.

> (From Bach's wedding cantata BWV 210, author unknown.)

Chapter Ten

In the steps of Cedd

IN WHAT NOW SEEMS LIKE A PREVIOUS LIFE I spent a month in Pembrokeshire trying to help John Seymour, author of *Practical Self-Sufficiency*, great guru of back-to-the-landers, and exemplar of inefficiency, sort out his desk. His life was a complicated juggling act: book-writing, running a small-holding and public speaking. When at home he was rarely inside the house, more often in yard or field where, in a twinkle of clarity, I suspected he played at farming. His home brew never saw the bottle because he ladled out mugs of it before it was fully fermented. It lubricated his much-used vocal chords and fed his imagination. He was frequently away spreading a simple-life message.

Steeped in his writings, and the TV sitcom 'The Good Life', his disciples attempted to distance themselves from traffic queues and the clock, from paying tax, servicing a mortgage or entertaining double-glazing salesmen by taking refuge in far-flung fields where they could sit under their vine and fig tree with a slice of home-baked wholemeal, a hunk of cheese crafted from the milk of the house Jersey, and a tankard of home brew to wash it down, their children out of sight and mind, busy building tree-houses or searching streams for little creatures whose names were a mystery. In the hands of simple-lifers coin of the realm was likely to have given way to the Acorn.

'In the old days, before you were born, Daffodil, people used to exchange little bits of metal or paper for food and clothes. It was called "money" and some people hoarded it, some people invested it, but most people borrowed it, large quantities of it.' Let me not seem to be superior. I bought into this vision of an alternative.

Some weeks prior to this desk-sorting I had received a letter from the Canon Norman Motley, Rector of St Michael's, Cornhill, asking if I would be interested in the post of chaplain/warden of the Othona Community at Bradwell-on-Sea in Essex. I knew nothing of either Norman or Othona, and wondered how he had come by my name. Perhaps he and L John Collins belonged to the same Canons' Coven.

On an inhospitable winter's day Kate and I drove with Norman from the Eastern fringes of the Metropolis to the edge of the marshes lining the Blackwater River. At first we could distinguish nothing that spoke of 'community'. Unfazed, Norman drew our attention to a collection of Nissen and wooden military huts. One of the latter contained tables, chairs and a kitchen of sorts. In another, heavy khaki tents were piled rather haphazardly. In a third we were introduced to a stack of somewhat damp-smelling mattresses. 'Going to the mattresses' in this context seemed to mean a fight with mould, and with nature raw in roof and floor. The One Redeeming Feature was the chapel of St Cedd, in a field above the community site, built in AD 654 and dedicated to St Peter, a magnet for tourists and pilgrims. Despite the attraction of this solid monument, the invitation to live here all-the-year round with a small group of like-minded crazies we placed firmly on the back burner.

We returned to Wales. Sitting one day in John's office (a phrase that Sir Arthur Sullivan might have set) I opened the desk drawer to the right and my eye was caught by the last thing I expected to see: a postcard of St Peter's chapel, a place that was as far Eastward from West Wales as you could get without boarding a boat. It was 'a sign' of the sort I don't usually credit. This time I couldn't help but take note of a voice calling.

Once again I was responding to a situation that offered itself to me. In this particular case there was slight hesitation, not because it did not fit in with some pre-existing career plan, but because of uncertainty about our ability to cope with such basic living conditions throughout the year. I always try to go with the flow, so career development skills have been unnecessary. The only exception to my acceptance of whatever came along was my turning down of the offer of the chaplaincy of the Forest School.

In China, Taoists imagined a type of sage who responded to the flow of events without weighing alternatives. Disciples of monotheistic faiths have believed something similar: freedom, they say, is obeying God's will. What those who follow these traditions want most is not any kind of freedom of choice. Instead what they long for is freedom from choice. (John Gray, *The Soul of the Marionette*.)

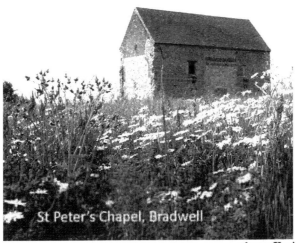

St Peter's Chapel, Bradwell

photo: **Kevin Bruce**

The chapel of St Peter-on-the-Wall is a small building of rough stones resurrected from the Roman fort of Othona: a single, heavy door; concrete slabs on the floor; plain glass windows high up; an indent in the side wall marking the doorway that allowed hay carts entry during the centuries when the building was a barn; a heavy altar of oak, rough with adze marks; solid benches; a circle of candles on a stand: all making for a place of worship greater than its parts, with an atmosphere that can bring atheists to their knees. Norman described his first sight of it in 1946.

> Some tiles [were] missing from the roof of the chapel and the windows were blocked by wooden boards and the earth floor was slightly damp, but the impact was incredible. The sense of thirteen centuries of prayer was almost overpowering. Numinous is a word which most adequately defines what we felt, and what innumerable visitors have felt since.

The moment I entered the building I knew that we were home. There are times when one knows with certitude deeper than purely rational processes and knowledge. We walked back to the car and as the sun set, the chapel appeared, as it very occasionally does, in a faintly pink aura – a reflection of the colours of the sky upon that peculiar stonework of the edifice.

The Diocese of Chelmsford was cooperative. Roof and windows were repaired and a floor of concrete slabs laid.

In the intervening years the diocese has replaced the oak table, which had the advantage of being movable, with a stone altar. They had obviously forgotten that the Book of Common Prayer refers to a Table for the Communion Service, not an altar. A table suggests 'supper'. An altar is a site for a sacrifice.

When Cedd built this chapel on the edge of the Essex marshes it was without the benefit of architect, worship group or diocesan advisory committee. Despite the destruction of the apse, north and south porticos, the west porch and the tower – now only the nave remains – the Visitors' Book carries testimony to the chapel's ability to speak to the soul of contemporary woman and man.

Othona began as an experiment in Christian community in 1946. Canon Norman Motley, like Canon L John Collins, was a chaplain in the RAF during World War II. His style was unusual for he made no distinction between officers and other ranks and welcomed open discussion of 'life, the universe and everything'. His 'Answer Back Meetings' were popular but were met with some unease by his bosses who disliked the name because it seemed to contradict the concept of Authority.

He and his friends had found a comradeship in wartime that lowered many social and religious barriers. They wanted to preserve something of that in peacetime so they began to gather as a community each summer. They found this place with Celtic roots, a Chapel constructed by a Celtic missionary bishop from the stones of a Roman fort: swords into ploughshares.

What might be the attraction?

Community life is as messy as it is rewarding. We call it 'chaordic'; where chaos meets order. It can be intimate but also difficult; it involves laughter and tears. It's a place of warmth and acceptance, but also where people who have nothing in common must learn to rub along together. Every day is a lesson in grace. Members work hard to seek the fulfilment, peace, happiness of every other member within the community... (The Scargill Community)

Do we not all wish to learn this lesson? If so, we need to get together in some way or other to explore how we might do it. The Othona Community, with its commitment to work, worship, study and play seemed as if it might be a place where that could be done.

I wrote to Norman accepting the job of chaplain/warden with only the haziest notion of what it might entail, but simple living and Celtic Christianity were attractive. So on a fine summer's day Kate and I cycled down from London with well-stuffed panniers and, aiming to take possession of our new domain, confidently entered the dining hut. 'Who are you?' 'I am Colin, the new chaplain/warden.' A bewildered and bewildering silence. 'This is Sally. Sally Martin. I am John Hardy. We are the wardens for the summer.'

Talk about awkward! Fortunately John and Sally were relaxed about our unexpected arrival. It was not unusual for Norman to make unilateral decisions and then fail to communicate them to interested parties.

We were shown around the two fields. In the top one was the long hut in which we had introduced ourselves: the dining hut. At the far end of this was the kitchen, divided from the eating area, which could seat over 80, by a serving counter. There were two other long huts, dormitories, one for men and one for women, though families might occupy a room in them.

With people scattered around it the site had a positive feel. It was a fine day: winter weeds had given way to a bright summer dress, quite different from our first experience. The khaki army tents had been erected with two to four beds in each. The mattresses had been aired and distributed. Also in this field were two asbestos-clad Arcons, much smaller pre-fabs that had been produced by Taylor Woodrow to meet the housing shortage at the end of WWII. One of these was the meeting room where the five o'clock lecture took place. Norman's room was in the rear half of the second one; the office was in the front half of it. Behind these was the concrete toilet block with washbasins and showers. There was no hot water, but by the end of a sunny afternoon it was possible to get a warm shower as the tank was on the roof.

Next to this was a wooden shed containing tools; next to that, one in which hurricane paraffin lamps were filled, the glass cleaned, the wicks trimmed, then lit and issued in the evening. That this hut did not go up in flames was a miracle of sorts. If numbers justified it Jonny would start the generator, a temperamental beast, the noise of which, amplified by the hut in which it was housed, offended those who enjoyed the natural sounds associated with the marshes and the sea.

In a heap by the bridge that crossed a small stream – usually dry – and connected the two fields were stacked sections of walls from a temporary building donated by a bank that had used it while their main building was being renovated. It was to be resurrected on a corner of the field marked out by John Hardy, a quantity surveyor, who taught at the local tech.

On the other side of the bridge is the lower field, bounded by the sea wall. In it a small wooden hut and a couple of Nissen huts were slowly sinking into decrepitude. In one was a tractor, in the other, rubbish. One would later accommodate the house cow. This was the field in which the community first met. When the adjacent farm was bought in 1961 the upper field was added to it.

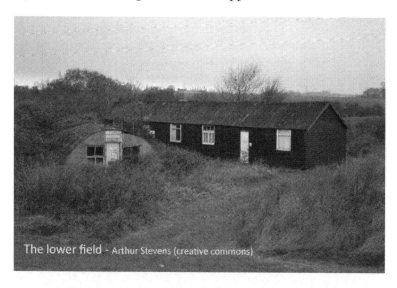

The lower field - Arthur Stevens (creative commons)

Kate and I took up residence in the far end of the rather dilapidated hut in the lower field, a peaceful spot later bagged by Martin Riemer, a committed community member from Germany. The hut was quiet, but cold for, like all the other buildings, it was not insulated. Single planks of wood were all that came between us and the soil below. Our bed was piled high with eiderdowns. Our bodies were untrendily garmented for warmth whenever the sun was low in the sky or clouds covered it.

Rising sea levels pose a threat to the lower field but there are no plans to raise the sea wall. Its stability was recently threatened by badgers, who had carved out their sets in it. They were removed and the wall strengthened. Now they live under the main building, which replaced the huts in the upper field in 1994. [Because I was recently elected Chair of Trustees I cannot avoid bringing past and present together in my account of the Community.]

On our first morning I was up early. It was sunny, with a slight mist over marsh and estuary. From the sea wall I watched, fascinated, as a flotilla of Thames sailing barges, unmistakable because of their red ochre-dyed flax sails, spritsail rigged on two masts with a topsail above the huge mainsail and a large foresail, bore down towards me. They were taking part in the annual Blackwater Barge Match and heading out into the estuary from Maldon. It was a magical experience that immediately confirmed in me the decision we had made to accept Norman's invitation.

Compared with city life, what we met with in these two modest fields was, we thought, about as basic as one can get without descending into deprivation. Yet to those who had been coming to the community for some time life at the camp in the mid-seventies was almost luxurious. Dave Forgan wrote of earlier days:

> Othona occupied what is now known as the lower field where physical conditions were Spartan to say the least. You had to position your bed with care in the original men's hut to avoid water dripping in your face when it rained. Water had to be collected from a standpipe near the chapel – the main water container filled up while we were in chapel in the morning, but other containers were used as well. It took two to carry the larger galvanised bowls along the sea wall, which provided an opportunity to get to know your fellow water carrier. The original dining hut was always more popular than the common room partly, no doubt, because tea was brewed there, but also because the low tunnel-like ceiling provided a more cosy ambience.

> But basic conditions seemed to help people explore fundamental issues together, such as how we could avoid yet more terrible

wars. And what Christians and other 'people who care' (as Norman put it) could contribute to a better world.

Everything is relative. By the mid-seventies the buildings were more substantial, the roofs didn't leak and water came to taps through a pipe. By the early 90s the buildings were so dilapidated that most of them had to be replaced. The new one, of brick and timber, is well insulated and is powered by solar panels and a small wind generator.

In the early days, the notice posted at the entrance to the coastal site read:

> The community meets here for ten weeks annually. People of all nations and various Christian traditions attend – including whole families. The programme, consisting of worship, work, study and play, is arranged in ten weekly sessions. It aims to strengthen international relations; to foster Christian unity; to deepen the experience of a real Christian community; and to study the relationship of faith and life with a view to more positive action in world affairs. It aims to provide recreation of a kind by which the whole personality is nourished in community. It welcomes those who do not accept the Christian tradition, but who care for its values, to come with us.

The current statement reads:

> Othona is an open and inclusive Community rooted in the Christian tradition and drawing on a wealth of other inspirations. We welcome people of all ages, abilities, backgrounds and beliefs to our two centres on the quiet coasts of Essex and Dorset. Through sharing in a daily rhythm of work, learning, worship and play, we seek personal renewal and glimpses of the sacred. In community we explore the relationship between faith and life and encourage one another in caring for the world and its people.

The differences are instructive. The presence in earlier, post-war days, of Germans, Russians, and later Poles, witnessed to a concern for reconciliation. Germans still participate but we have lost the others. Most people coming to the centres now are less concerned with 'positive action in world affairs' and more interested in 'personal renewal', though there is an understanding that the way we live has an effect beyond our little walls.

As time went by the focus on reconciliation with a former enemy faded. By 1973 the UK was one of the twelve members of the European Community that transformed themselves into the

European Union, a development that would make another European war impossible, and one of the earlier aims of Othona redundant.

Norman was emphatic that Othona was not an alternative church. Renewed and inspired, community members were to return to their congregations and act as yeast in the lump. Nowadays many of those who come belong to no church. Othona is likely to be their spiritual home.

Toyohiko Kagawa, the Japanese 'Gandhi', a Christian pacifist, reformer, and labour activist who wrote, spoke, and worked on ways to employ Christian principles in the ordering of society and in cooperatives, stayed with Norman and his family. His vocation to help the poor led him to live among them. He established schools, hospitals, and churches, and is remembered as one the most influential Christian leaders in Japan. He is one of my heroes. He wrote a message for Othona published in an early newsletter. Norman reproduced it in his history of the Community, *Much Ado about Something*.

> I warmly commend the work of the Othona Community – dealing, as it does, with the gospel of Christ in relation to the whole life of man. The Christian faith – Christ – is the solution to all problems: International peace; man in modern society, industrialised as well as agricultural. Jesus is the satisfaction of man's spiritual need, of his material requirements and of his mental necessities.

> The building of true Christian communities which grapple with the whole Christian answer to the modern world is of paramount importance. Such communities strengthen Christians to be more faithful to their witness and do more than most other things to convince non-Christians of the truth of the gospel. In addition, such communities can receive and train newcomers to the faith. This aspect of evangelism must not be overlooked.

> I hope the work will continue and extend – in town and country and abroad – and may be used increasingly by God for the extension of the Kingdom of love and truth.

The training of newcomers to the faith was not overlooked: it was rejected. We have never evangelised in the way that that activity is usually understood. We are of the school that believes that faith is caught, not taught. At the same time we have not shied from addressing issues relating to faith and belief, but in open-ended dialogue. 'Here we stand' is not on the notice board. Discovering commonalities is.

The fostering of Christian unity seemed to be the next reconciliation target. This was given a boost by the participation of the Revd Harold Johnson, a United Reformed Church minister who joined in 1947 and was responsible for introducing many who became key figures in the community. He was a great fan of Bonhoeffer and a keen student of John's Gospel. After Norman's death in 1980 he took on the Chairmanship of Trustees for thirteen years.

The openness of chapel services allowed Quakers, Catholics, Hot Gospellers and Agnostics to worship together, though some, especially the latter, would probably balk at calling it 'worship'.

By the mid-seventies the focus had shifted again. In a letter of June 1975 to the Community Norman expressed his concern about the legitimate needs of the Third and Fourth Worlds that were not being met by European nations. 'We should heed the conservationists, the ecologists, the intermediate technologists, and also the warnings of those who tell truly of the population explosion.' This was at the same time that Kate and I came on the scene and in his letter of October of that year he wrote that 'we can begin to incarnate our concern for intelligent conservation by using more land – in both centres – to produce food: fruit and vegetables, and flowers.'

That is precisely what we began to do. So, to cut a short story even shorter, we found ourselves planting trees – the poplars are now over 30 feet tall, the orchard 'mature' – milking a Jersey cow, collecting hen and duck eggs and turning pigs into bacon. We also fished. The life was caught in words of St Columba, which I turned into a song to sing in the chapel:

Lord, bless us that we bless you,
creator and conserver
of heaven and all its orders,
of land and strand and waters;

that we may search the writings
that give the soul renewal;
that we may read around us
such beauty as will feed us:

that we may find within us
the letters of your loving;
that we may have such living
as any soul will freshen.

At times we kneel to heaven,
at times the psalms are singing,
at times are contemplating
our King, our holy leader.

At times we are delighting
in work that lacks compulsion;
at times we gather seaweed,
at times we go out fishing;

at times we seed and harvest,
at times we feed your creatures,
and feed the poor, our brothers;
at times we sit in silence.

We started acquiring animals. The chickens were rescued birds, refugees from a battery, pink and almost featherless: we named one 'Ovenready'. They had to learn how to scratch the earth, which they did tentatively, like an old lady testing the temperature of the bathwater. We also bought ducks.

One of our small resident group, Adrian, a red-haired, wiry Welshman, was committed to two things: his clarinet and the chickens. I think he regarded the ducks we had – mostly Muscovys – as mess-makers. They were. It could be dangerous to walk about shoeless if you were squeamish because there was a 90% chance that you would get duck poo between the toes.

I like Muscovys. I like their shiny green and black feathers. They waddle with dignity and certainty. Like geese, they eat grass and they do not require a pond.

We were getting a reasonable supply of eggs. Now we wanted our own milk. Norman was not happy with my request for money to buy a cow so I put a jar on the windowsill labelled 'cow fund', and the necessary cash appeared within a short time. The money was there, so no more was said.

I found a smallholder who, having little land of her own, used to take her cows along the road to graze the verges. She had a Jersey, Bambi, with which she was willing to part. We had to have a Jersey as they hailed from my native island. On Bambi I learnt to milk. I loved the early milking in the warmth of the cow shed, my head resting on her flank, the only sounds her breathing and eating and the succession of 'pings' as the milk hit the side of the pail. When her milk started to dry up she was artificially inseminated. Her calf we named Moosli.

As not all of us were vegetarians we needed meat, so we bought a pig. She was baptised Mauline, a combination of the names of our mothers and a hint at what we hoped from her. It was our intention that she would churn up the solid soil in the lower field so that we could plant it. Pigs are good at digging, I learnt. Plant Jerusalem artichokes, a favourite feed, and pigs will snout them out. That, at least, is what John Seymour's helpful handbook advised. Mauline obviously hadn't read it. She ignored the tubers. I had to root for them myself. It turned out that Mauline was the wrong sort of pig, pink and sleek, bred for a cosy indoor life. Outside, she could get sunburnt. She was too highly bred to work for her supper.

We waited for her to swell out with a belly full of piglets. And we waited. Eventually it became clear that she was not pregnant. Her increasing size was merely a consequence of the rich diet of leftovers that she consumed with a great deal of snorting and lip smacking. There is a low success rate with AI for pigs, about 30%. What about presenting our sow to a boar? No farmer will take back an animal from the big wide world to be served for fear of importing disease. Only one path lay before her: she would be on her way to Sugarcandy Mountain. This was a great disappointment to Al who enjoyed scrubbing her down with soapy water – she thought she was already in pig heaven.

We booked her in to the slaughterhouse. The evening before the day of her demise we loaded her on to the back of Jonny's Jeep. Such manhandling she greatly resented and leapt over the side, streaking up the field. I don't think any of us realised how fast pigs could run. Graham grabbed his bike and managed to cut her off on the track. That night she went to bed supperless.

We had a yellow ex-Post Office van. I quickly constructed a partition between the cab and the rear with a sheet of hardboard. Early the next morning I placed a straw bale to act as a step by the rear door, luring her up and in with a bucket of feed. I retreated through the side door with the bucket and most of what she assumed was her breakfast, though now denied her.

Adrian & Mauline

Staying with us was a burly young merchant seaman, an engineer, who offered to accompany Mauline and me to the knacker's yard. We set off at a leisurely pace, but at the S bend on the way into the village Mauline rolled against the side door, bursting it open and exiting onto the road. She quickly picked herself up and began to trot off. A young woman in a nearby garden shouted to her small daughter, 'There's a pig! There's a pig! Get into the house!' I grabbed the bucket of feed and, playing on pig greed, lured her back into the van. We fastened the side door with a rope. The S bend is still referred to by villagers as 'Pig Corner'.

I pulled up at the T junction by the church. There was a crash as Mauline broke through the partition, placing her two front trotters on the engine cover and her snout on the windscreen. It is a design fault in pigs that they have no reverse gear, so we had to lift her back into her place, a tough job. But how to keep her quiet?

I gently broke it to our burly seaman that the one thing that induced docility in Mauline was being scratched behind the ears. He made not a murmur but got on with the job, successfully calming her. Such was his commitment that he began to sing her nursery rhymes and in this fashion we arrived at our destination. There she jumped out and joined, happily it seemed, a handful of more juvenile pigs all awaiting the chop. This sad story had an even sadder conclusion. The abattoir's owner wouldn't give us the meat. Like our mothers, she was too tough.

I concluded that we would be better off buying weaners at the beginning of the season and turning them into bacon at the end of it, so I set about building a home for them. 'Pig sty' is an epithet sometimes applied to a teenager's bedroom. This was to be no slum. I built it with stones specially selected from around the site. The end result was the sturdiest building in the camp. The Karl Marx Pigsty was opened with solemn ceremony. When pigs were no more the roof was raised and it became a dwelling for a human, such was – no! – is its quality, and the cry went up, 'Four legs good, two legs better!' I also added a dairy to the dining hut for Moosli's milk which, being rich, could be skimmed of its cream or churned into excellent butter. Constructed of concrete blocks the dairy was the coolest place in the camp.

> I think I could turn and live with the animals, they are so placid and self contained;
> I stand and look at them long and long.
> They do not sweat and whine about their condition;
> They do not lie awake in the dark and weep for their sins;
> They do not make me sick discussing their duty to God;
> Not one is dissatisfied – not one is demented with the mania of owning things;
> Not one kneels to another, nor his kind that lived thousands of years ago;
> not one is responsible or industrious over the whole earth.
>
> Walt Whitman

Paul and I did a little fishing. At low tide we laid out on the mud a long line with baited hooks. At the next low tide we picked up whatever flatfish had fallen for the bait. Fish was eaten immediately and only by the core group. Not being attached to the power grid – the noisy generator was used sparingly – we could have no fridge or freezer on site. We had a freezer at the farm, but that was a bit of a trek. The farm freezer held joints of pork other than the two legs turned into hams, one through a wet cure, the other salted and then smoked.

How to smoke it? We had installed a wood-burning stove in the dining hut. I put a metal cupboard on the roof over the chimney. In that we hung the joint. We had to take care that we burnt no resinous wood, but otherwise the exercise was successful. That winter we ate Ham with everything, especially with our own eggs.

We decided to grow potatoes in the upper half of the top field. Lawrence D. Hills, founder of the Henry Doubleday Research Association (it became Garden Organic) was our gardening guru. His *Grow Your Own Fruit and Vegetables* (Faber 1971) was then becoming a bible for gardeners, self-sufficiency enthusiasts and commercial organic growers. He advised using comfrey, 'a natural mineral mine', as a fertiliser. Each potato was to be wrapped in a leaf when it was planted. That was all that was necessary. So before we planted our potatoes, we planted comfrey, lots of it. Unfortunately, when the time came to plant the potatoes, the comfrey was not sufficiently developed to be used. We did not see that as the disaster it might have been because there was shortly afterwards a cancer scare associated with comfrey. That was a false alarm: the virtues of comfrey are currently being touted again for external use and as compost. Forty years after we planted them clumps of comfrey still make an appearance in the field.

When we first joined the Community food came in bulk from Kealey & Tonge in London: catering cans of everything from baked beans and watery tomatoes to large packs of dried soup, dried milk and custard powder. On the store shelves were stacked tins of spam – spam fritters for breakfast – that were showing signs of rust. These I buried. Some still regret their passing.

Norman made the ordering and provision of food a personal concern, auditing the order and monitoring receipts. He would keep an eye on the size of servings, getting quite cross if he thought the servers were being too generous. He himself would take small portions, but then he would have several small portions. This did not go unnoticed.

The farm next door, owned by the community, grew wheat. I thought we should make our own flour from it but nothing happened until Kate and I, visiting Wells, spotted a manually operated wheat grinding machine in a shop window. We bought it, and it was fixed to the bench on which food was served. As people queued for their meal they could give the handle a couple of turns. When more flour was required we challenged punters to see who could grind the most flour in a minute. There was never a shortage of takers willing to test their prowess.

We baked bread every day, usually wholemeal rolls. Since that time I have used such rolls for communion, replacing those little white discs that tend to adhere to the roof of the mouth.

Those wafers represent the unleavened bread used to celebrate Passover. I use leavened bread to represent the risen life. Didn't Jesus tell us that we should be like yeast in society? The wholemeal roll is a reminder of this and of everyday life: of those who grow our food and those who prepare it for us. It links us to others in the community and to the soil. The leftover crumbs I scatter for the birds.

Kneading bread and forming rolls is for me an opportunity to meditate. When kneading, hands and lungs work together in a natural rhythm. As I form the rolls I bring to mind the people for whom I am making them. I found myself teaching others how to make bread. It is not that difficult, and quite satisfying. That is why I later introduced the practice at the Small School, not to put Hovis and Mother's Pride out of business.

Though it can be difficult when catering for large numbers – sometimes we were preparing meals for over a hundred people – food should look attractive. I do not mean anything elaborate but I do mean attention to presentation: a scattering of herbs or edible flowers. We also introduced vegetarian dishes and options, a surprising innovation for those brought up on spam fritters.

We fed the body and spirit; we also fed the mind. From the spring through to the autumn there was a programme of speakers and events. In the winter months community members often came down for weekends. Usually we didn't know who was coming. It was a bit like a drop-in youth club for people of all ages.

A leaflet I wrote at the time reads:

> More and more people are concerned to explore the meaning of Community, to discover a living spirituality, to find an appropriate lifestyle, to learn more about healing and caring. These, too, are our concerns. We welcome all, whatever their background or abilities, to share our experience and struggle, and to work, pray, play and study with us.

> We live a simple life in wooden huts (plus tents in summer), a resident nucleus of the Community looking after the animals, growing vegetables, baking bread and responding to the needs of the temporary residents, not waiting on them, but building them into a community for the duration of their stay. We believe that in meaningful work, relevant worship, genuine recreation, and study that has practical application we can find a real sense of purpose and source of healing.

Here, as a sample, is the 1978 programme. It began on Maundy Thursday with a look, over the Passion and Easter weekend, at 'the Giving and Finding of Life'. It was led by community members. That was followed by seven weekend workshops. Tricia Zipfel of the Holloway Tenant Co-operative addressed the question, 'How can we build community? Something that concerns all who are involved in the life of a local church as much as those who are active in areas of social stress'.

Sheila Wilson, a professional counsellor with a Jungian background, explored myths, fairy tales and nursery rhymes to discover how these excursions into inner space relate to one's own life.

By popular request we had a third visit from George Ineson and Catherine Robinson offering a mix of yoga and Tai Chi. George was the founder of the Taena Community in Gloucestershire and Catherine the daughter of the Bishop of Woolwich.

The author Beryl Bye, whose pony books have a strong religious/spiritual element that her publisher, Lutterworth, thought might put some people off, searched for a practical style of living, neither Spartan nor extravagant.

Harold Kersey, an early member of the community and a retired senior probation officer, entitled his weekend 'A Fair Crack of the Whip – Punishment and Forgiveness'.

Two members of the L'Arche Community, the Rev Tim Hollis and his wife Marion, both fully involved in it, talked about the life and spirit of their houses and its application to all communities.

The final weekend workshop of the season was 'God, Men and Things'. John Davies, an engineer by training, had been Chief Executive of the Shell companies. At the time he was working with EF Schumacher as a consultant to the Intermediate Technology Group, a specialist on air and sea pollution.

In the first of the summer weeks we looked at how the World Council of Churches served ecumenism with Rex Davies, who until his appointment as a Canon of Lincoln Minster, was on the staff of the WCC in Geneva. Having explored relations between the denominations we widened our concern to other faiths. Kudsi Erguner, a Whirling Dervish musician, led a 'Sufi Week' with a couple who ran drawing and calligraphy workshops.

This discussion of our relationship with other world religions was taken further by Sir John Lawrence, a community trustee whom *The Guardian* described as 'the nearest to a professional layman that the Church of England has ever had – and a good deal more influential than many bishops'.

An Anglican priest from India, Sebastian Charles, looked at cities, towns and villages with an eye to the 1980s. For three weeks of August we organized music, drama and movement workshops with a number of contributors of whom I was one. Following this Norman addressed the issue of 'Aggression', and then, in a Women's Week, we investigated the role of women in society and the church. For the final week of the season the Bishop of Bradwell, Derek Bond, gave his attention to what would happen to the church when the money ran out.

Two other speakers, who visited us in other years, remain in the memory. John Stewart Collis, a pioneer of the ecology movement, spent the war years in the Land Army. His most famous book, *The Worm Forgives the Plough*, is a down-to-earth account of farming with basic tools. His prose reminded Richard Church, in an introduction to *Vision of Glory*, a compilation of extracts from his major works, of Ruskin. As he was a friend of Kate's father, the poet Martyn Skinner, we were able to persuade him to come to Bradwell. Like Iris Murdoch, who, when researching for *The Bell*, found herself unable to go past the gate of a community she was wanting to inspect, JSC sat in his car wondering whether to turn around and go home. We managed to persuade him that we had one head each and the normal number of limbs. He entered slowly, gradually relaxed and then had everyone in his palm with his storytelling, which was to do with the planting of trees. There is a passage on this theme in *Vision of Glory* that I want to share with you.

> Trees are necessary to our existence because they are the chief guardians of the soil, keeping it stable and watered. In the very ancient past, trees were thought to be spirits or the habitation of spirits, both good and evil, and finally were conceived as simply deities who were the guardians of fertility... This way of thinking gradually broke up and we entered the Era of Economics when trees and everything else were valued in cash. At the height of this economic era the application of science showed how swiftly and completely men could make use of trees in particular and nature in general. We have just reached the end of that period, having found

that such an attitude has brought us to the edge of disaster. We are about to enter what might be called the last act of the drama, when science now discovers precisely in what way trees really are the guardians of fertility after all. This will be the Era of Ecology, the science of achieving an equilibrium with the environment. Thus having come full circle, we are back at the beginning again. But is it too late to make a fresh start? The world is not what it was at the beginning of the story. Half the wealth has gone. Even so, we could save the situation. But are we sufficiently alarmed to mend our ways? (p.157. The original was published in 1950.)

With apple, plum and damson trees we populated our orchard. In the hedges hazelnuts were planted and, in front of the copse that ran behind the sea wall, three walnut trees that would not be cropping for nearly ten years and have now been swallowed up by the creeping grove. We also planted a row of poplars alongside the drive. We were attempting to mend our ways.

Ken Feit was a Jesuit turned itinerant fool who led a three-day workshop on storytelling and celebration 'for teachers, clergy, counsellors, therapists, poets, dream analysts, human beings and all aspiring fools'.

> The term 'priestly fool' is used to describe that person, male or female, who is a discerner of wonder, mystery, and paradox; who celebrates life and death; who is a storyteller and listener; who is a focuser of community (though frequently living on the periphery of the community); who is a proclaimer of the truth (verbally and non-verbally); who is a servant and healer of the poor (powerless); and who re-symbolizes, re-ritualizes, and re-mythologizes for the tribe.

We had met Ken at Wick Court (SCM) where he ran a workshop on white face and clowning. Kate remembers me 'being nonviolent in the field dressed as a clown and being mocked by local lads'. We learnt just how disturbing – even frightening – white face can be. He worked us hard. The highlight of the Othona weekend was an evening session in the Chapel lit by candlelight. He told stories and, as a climax, took a grain of maize in a teaspoon and held it over a candle flame. In his hands the transformation when it popped was magical: almost a miracle. He had realised his intention of making us 'alive to a sense of wonder, mystery and paradox'.

The following Easter, 1979, was the warmest for thirty years, with a maximum temperature of 23°C. Tables were put out on the grass next to the dining hut for Easter Day lunch. Those who were not vegetarians ate some of our ducks, or rather, drakes. The breeding of animals results in a superabundance of males. Each cock and drake wants to assert their rights over every hen and duck, which makes for a miserable life of attempting avoidance on the part of the females. So males have to be culled and I had to learn to do the culling, accepting the disturbing sight of broken-necked cockerels and severed-head drakes trying to fly. However, the deliciousness of the meal soon forced the memory of things past to fade.

In the 70s an interest in alternative technology encouraged an exploration of wind power. In Denmark, and to a lesser extent in Germany, there was considerable pressure for the exploitation of wind energy. One project popular with intermediate technologists was the building of vertical axis wind generators from an oil barrel and car parts. I studied the literature but was not convinced by this. It did not seem nearly as productive as the more usual generator with blades. At the same time there was growing unease about nuclear power plants, partly because of the devastation an accident could cause and partly because the problem of waste disposal had not been solved.

This was a live issue for the community because the Bradwell nuclear power station was on our doorstep. It opened in 1962. Our opposition to it was such that Tony Benn, who was Secretary of State for Energy, and a near neighbour, dropped in to debate the issue while he supped mugs of tea. The construction of a wind generator became necessary as a witness, albeit a small one, to the alternative that we were trying to promote. We erected a wooden tower that rose above the trees. I left before the machine was built that was to go on top of it. Now the tower has gone but a commercial wind turbine has replaced it.

Bradwell power station ceased to generate electricity in 2002 but it will take 102 years before decommissioning is complete in 2104. The plant is a bulky blot on the landscape. Locals have accepted it because it provides jobs. What will replace it? There has been considerable opposition to the building of wind farms in the area, which can't be on aesthetic grounds because few constructions could be more hideous than the concrete carbuncles that housed the two Magnox reactors. However, local opposition to wind farms has been ignored and there is a field of them on the far side of the Chapel and another array on the opposite side of the river. Wind farms are becoming an increasingly important source of renewable energy and are used as part of a strategy to reduce reliance on fossil fuels. But fission isn't finished. According to the *Sunday Times'* industry sources, China General Nuclear Power Corporation and China National Nuclear Corporation are preparing designs for Bradwell for submission to the Office for Nuclear Regulation (in 2014). Other reports have warned that the site is being considered for the storage of nuclear waste. The battle for renewables isn't over yet.

The presence of a permanent core group of six living at the centre changed the dynamic of the Community, which some people resented. Old hands, instead of being the ones who made it all happen, as it was when they came together for a few weeks in the summer, said they felt more like visitors dropping in on an ongoing programme. Not all felt like that. Some, like the Higgins family, made regular and frequent visits and contributed to the work of developing the site. There were also some who did not appreciate the new emphasis on achieving a degree of self-sufficiency and on reducing food miles by keeping animals and producing our own fruit and vegetables, as well as purchasing organic products where that was possible.

Most members welcomed the erection of the Bank. There was a difficulty, however. We had no plans. By measuring the sections that were piled up John got some idea of the size of the concrete base that needed to be laid. Because the walls were designed to overlap the edge of the concrete, precision was essential. It was missed by a few inches. Norman, always on the lookout for money-saving opportunities, hired a couple of Essex Cowboys to erect the building. The roof has never been completely watertight. The walls are reasonably vertical.

This was an era of Youth Training Programmes and we signed up for a team of eight youngsters, supervised by a bricklayer and a carpenter. The chippy was pretty effective; the bricky was useless. Despite that, we put up concrete internal walls to give stability and to provide some sound insulation for the bedrooms. A meeting room was the most impressive part of the project. We built an open fireplace and fitted and polished a pre-loved pine floor. Windows were curtained and, as a final finishing touch, I

247

used my calligraphy skills to paint a text on one of the beams. We had made an ideal space for folk dancing, the weekly concert, and the talks.

Every morning and evening we walked up to the Chapel, whatever the weather. I would have with me my guitar and Adrian his clarinet. If there was another guitarist, perhaps Blind Dave, I would lug up my double bass.

I loved those walks, especially the smell of camomile, crushed by our feet because it grew along the edge of the path. The Essex landscape, flat and open to a vast sky, can be disturbing to those who live comfortably among hills or mountains. Hedges are few, removed to make it easier to sow and harvest wheat or sugar beet in the giant fields that stretch inland from the estuary. For me it brings alive two of my Othona compositions, Psalms 8 and 19:

Creator, praise shall rise from all you've birthed
and earth, rejoicing, join its voice with heaven's.
The wisdom of the child, the baby's cries
rebuke the mighty, teaching them hard lessons.
Through the earth your name is great.

When I survey the skies and search their depths,
where circling stars and moon each dance their part,
I wonder that you keep me in your mind
and hold this child of Adam in your heart.

You made me one with ev'ry form of life
and gave me grace and wisdom beyond measure.
You made me steward over all your works
and to my care entrusted ev'ry creature:

all sheep and cattle, wild and fearsome beasts,
fine feathered birds, and fish from sprat to skate,
with seals and whales and monsters of the deep.
Creator, through the earth your name is great.
(Psalm 8)

The heavens proclaim a creative force
that fashioned the cosmos and shows itself there.
This message is mirrored by day after day
and night after night whispers word of its care.

May words that my mouth may utter
and thoughts that may fill the heart
respond to creation's blessing
and praise the Creator's art.

No speech tells the tale, for words have no place;
all voices are silent, no tears and no mirth;
and yet through creation the rhythms resound,
in echo return from the ends of the earth.

The sky, like a tent, envelopes the sun
which rises, a groom going out to his bride;
a champion triumphantly climbing the skies,
a face from whose features no creature can hide.
(from Psalm 19)

Life at both Centres is lived close to nature. The grounds at Othona West Dorset have been designated a 'Site of Nature Conservation Interest' for their grasslands and wildflower rarities, that include four species of orchid. This is a great habitat 'for all manner of creatures from glow-worms to slow-worms, from dormice to birds of prey, from butterflies to the occasional passing deer'. When humans sleep, rabbits rule.

The house and chapel were built by Adela Curtis, a Christian mystic, and her 'White Ladies' in the 1920s and 30s. A photo shows them occupying a hillside barren of all but 'gorse, brambles and couch grass', which they transformed. Now there are wooded areas with secluded paths and places to sit and meditate in an atmosphere of shaded peace.

Each member of the community she founded lived in a simple hut surrounded by a small piece of land for cultivation. The women wove their own robes, first from the wool of their sheep, then from undyed silk – they had worms and mulberry – or cotton. They collected rainwater, made candles from the wax of their bees, distilled scent, grew organic fruit and vegetables, enjoyed a vegetarian diet and processed their sewage to put back on the land.

Adela, who died in 1960 at the age of 96, was reckoned by Aldous Huxley to be a great English mystic. With her death the community, too, came to an end. The Charity Commissioners passed on the property to the Othona Community.

The orchard is still very productive. Salad is grown in a polytunnel. In small ways Adela's spirit lives on.

From time to time I have run or led events in what is now, after additions and improvements, the more comfortable of the two centres. One such event stands out.

Having completed the first part of the Royal Opera House, Covent Garden's course on creating opera in schools I needed to try out my newly-acquired skills. We programmed an opera week in Dorset. At the first meeting we divided into three groups, each tasked with devising a plot. Immediately a middle-aged couple withdrew: it would never happen. It would be naff.

The three groups returned with their stories. By adopting 'a travelling man' as the main theme other elements of the three stories could be incorporated.

The three groups were sent off again to develop their part of the story and write lyrics for their songs. They then composed tunes for their lyrics. These tunes I harmonized and arranged for the instruments we had available. That left us three days in which to make costumes and props and rehearse. The couple who had excused themselves from participating were amazed at the end result, for this ad hoc group of teenagers and adults had devised and presented a powerful piece of theatre.

Since then teenagers have seemed to participate less and less. God is out of fashion. 'Jesus' and 'Christ' are more frequently expletives, not prayers. Where Jesus is talked about, he is talked about as God, a God that has died. He is not taken seriously as a man. Those who take Christianity seriously – and I count myself as one of them – seem to be regarded as mostly sane but with an aberrant streak, like those who don historic uniforms and re-enact the battles of Marston Moor or Naseby.

The Exodus from the Middle East, with refugees knocking on Europe's door, is a challenge to our values and our priorities. How will Othona respond? The crisis has the potential of uniting altruism with the political so perhaps our study will be re-focussed.

EXPLORING WORSHIP

When I left the Othona Community in 1979 it was with a commission from Richard Mulkern, a community member and an editor with Mowbrays, the religious publisher, for a book on worship. It is a group study guide of twenty-two sessions aimed at giving the laity the tools with which to design acts of worship.

> Exciting experiences in the theatre, the concert hall and the folk club have raised questions about worship, for by comparison the traditional services can sometimes seem boring, the official revisions uninspiring and 'modern' alternatives, trite. It may be that I am too much of a perfectionist or even constitutionally incapable of worshipping. It is reassuring to find that others suffer

from the same dis-ease. This book, then, is written for all who share the belief that only the best is good enough for God, and who would like to find ways of making worship more inspiring. (From the Introduction)

In the chapel at Othona I had experienced what can happen when people are prepared to take risks, to face making mistakes and even to be laughed at. Within a supportive group, away from the expectations and restrictions of their churches, and encouraged by the magic of the place they were able to produce varieties of worship that were alive, meaningful and creative.

What happens when we cease to approach worship as an activity of the mind and begin to allow the heart and the body to make their special contribution? I believe that we come to understood that worship is a form of drama, and even of theatre. When we listen to the heart and the body we realize the full importance of myth, symbol and ritual. These three elements are basic ingredients of theatre as they are of worship.

The intention of the course was that participants discover such things from their own experience, or even discover that what I said about them is false. Because worship in public is a communal activity I felt that the exploration should be a group one. I did not set out to give answers to the questions we might have about worship but to equip members of worshipping communities with the tools to find answers for themselves.

Richard sent the book to David Winter, former Head of Religious Broadcasting at the BBC. He was enthusiastic.

I think this book is unusual, fascinating and potentially a winner. The plan of action is well set out and convincingly argued, clearly based on personal experience, and well related to the situation of many 'religious' people today. I like the emphasis that this is not just a series of exercises or rituals to be gone through, but a genuine experience to be entered into – 'these prayers are to be prayed'. For me the Discussion' spot sounds the weakest point, partly because it reverts to the verbal, which the author has quite correctly said is the chief inhibitor of real worship. (Report to the publisher.)

Unfortunately Richard moved on before the book was published. His successor at Mowbray's was not nearly so enthusiastic and *Exploring Worship* was 'let go' rather than released.

Nevertheless, it was reviewed in the religious press, though each reviewer had reservations.

To one I was too 'authoritarian'. 'If you can see your congregation being happy to lie on the floor in an orange light, doing deep-breathing exercises and semaphoring the Lord's Prayer...' (D. Wilkins) 'I have an uneasy feeling that though this book seeks to open up the entire field of ways in which we might worship, it will present to some people things they might find a little odd.' '...this book may well present a challenge to those groups wishing to develop their meetings in a new and exciting way.' (Jeffrey Yates, the *Methodist Recorder*.) The reviewer in the *Christian Herald* wished that it was more obviously God-centred with more Biblical content. 'Even so, I feel some sessions, properly undertaken, could benefit many worship groups in quite a number of ways.'

Finally Michael Hocking contributed an extensive evaluation in the *Church Times* that contains much that is complimentary, though his suspicion that it is 'American-inspired' is erroneous. He felt I must have in mind 'a group of boisterous, extrovert and highly intelligent teenagers'. Then we come full circle.

> I don't think that I have ever seen such clear, demanding and mandatory instructions by any clergyman writing a book for group discussion; the authoritarian attitude reminds me far more of an Old Testament figure than the usual slightly apologetic Anglican equivalent.

I am not quite sure whether this is a negative criticism or a compliment. I will take it as the latter as I have no wish to be perceived as a 'slightly apologetic Anglican'. I don't see how one can write instructions for an activity without it sounding authoritarian. Here is a sample:

Session 2 begins with Relaxation.

Before you relax, look at your body. Study your hands, feet, arms and legs. Look at your shoulders, your chest, your stomach. Is your body a familiar friend or are you ashamed of it?

Focus on your lovely features... and now on the ugly ones.

Discussion

How do you feel about your body?

Comment

Whether or not we like our bodies (and the majority of people seem embarrassed by them) most of us pander to them. Reacting against this, some Christians have ignored the body and its needs and some have punished it. However, we should neither indulge nor punish the body but take its needs seriously. Learning to relax will be our first step in taking the needs of the body seriously.

silent Lord's Prayer

Thirty-six years ago some people might have found this odd and difficult. I don't think there would be the same reaction today. I like to think that the book was ahead of its time. But then I also like to think that I am not authoritarian. I merely have strongly-held views.

The most positive response came in the Julian Meetings newsletter. Silence, relaxation and meditation 'are introduced in such a natural way as to be helpful to anyone, whether or not they think of themselves as budding contemplatives.'

Finally someone understood from where I was coming.

Chapter Eleven

Refugee Action

THE SEEDS OF REFUGEE ACTION were sown in Save the Children soil.

My involvement with refugees began with a cryptic telegram from Mike Whitlam, Deputy Director of Child Care (UK) of Save the Children. Would I meet him at 1pm on the following Tuesday in a pub opposite the Home Office? No explanation. That would be Tuesday May 28th 1979.

I had applied to Save the Children (SCF) for a job as a community worker in Oldham, a joint appointment with local authority Social Services. I was shown around a run-down estate and told that this would be my patch. There was obviously plenty of challenging work to do, and I asked the Director of Social Services how he would feel if I appeared at the Town Hall with a deputation of residents from the estate demanding improvements to their living conditions. Despite my being SCF's favoured candidate he would have none of me. He seemed to think it was the community worker's job to keep the community down, not stir it up.

The two SCF staff members were embarrassed and promised that if I applied for another post I would be shortlisted. A vacancy appeared in Northern Ireland. I was asked to withdraw my application as they wanted an Irish person, which seemed reasonable. Then, out of the blue, The Telegram arrived.

BOAT PEOPLE

From 1977 people had been fleeing from Vietnam. In 1978 the media carried reports of women being raped by Thai pirates as they sailed to safety. So when a British ship, the *Sibonga*, picked up two boatloads of refugees there was sympathetic press coverage.

Captain Healey Martin reported that he had responded to distress flares and pulled alongside a leaking vessel. Women on a boat twenty metres long and three metres wide were screaming for help. The previous night they had buried five babies at sea.

The *Sibonga* rescued 1,003 Vietnamese Boat People and another British vessel, the *Roachbank*, a further 393. The newspapers whipped up support for theses tragic victims, but it was ten days before Margaret Thatcher, under pressure from her Foreign Secretary Lord Carrington and Home Secretary Willie Whitelaw, agreed that these, along with 1,500 from camps in South-East Asia to which the previous Labour administration had committed itself, could come to Britain. This was quite a turnaround, for Mrs Thatcher had tried to find ways for Britain to avoid responsibility for any refugees picked up by British ships.

Mike Whitlam strode beaming into the pub and apologised for the telegram whose brevity had been dictated by uncertainty. An important decision was just minutes behind him. At the Home Office three agencies, the British Council for Aid to Refugees (BCAR), the Ockenden Venture (OV) and Save the Children (SCF) had been asked to submit plans for the reception and settlement of these 'boat people'. The Home Office wanted SCF's involvement to add professional input, something that they believed was lacking in the other two agencies.

Although SCF had a project for Vietnamese children, run by Robina Brand, they had no experience of settling refugees in this country. A programme would have to be designed from scratch, a rare opportunity. Would I do it? I accepted a six-month contract on the spot.

I had never worked with refugees. I had set up hostels for single homeless women and established other projects, and was an experienced manager. I was looking forward to this novel challenge.

The Government insisted, with the support of BCAR, that the Vietnamese should be settled outside the major conurbations, especially London, in small groups of four to ten families. I opposed this policy. There would be comparatively few Vietnamese coming here and they should be settled in much larger groupings for mutual support, for community building and for access to Vietnamese/Chinese groceries. The Government talked about not wanting to create 'ghettoes' and my views were ignored.

The brief was to take refugees straight into reception centres from the airport. They would be there for three months during which time they would receive English tuition provided by the LEA and paid for by the government. Cultural orientation would be provided by the centre staff. The three agencies would be responsible for finding housing and settling the families in them. The Home Office could negotiate the use of camps, no longer used by the military, as reception centres.

Being committed to a Small is Beautiful philosophy I refused the camp offer. I was aware that a strong negative aspect of the programme for Asians from Uganda, chased out by Idi Amin in 1972, was criticism of the conditions in the five centres holding more than a thousand people. The Ugandan Resettlement Board had another ten centres the smallest of which held 250 refugees. To me even that was too large.

Fortunately Rachel Jenkins, the Director of Child Care and my boss, shared my view that small is beautiful and was prepared to consider a network of human scale reception centres as an appropriate response to the needs of this vulnerable group. The advantages of the 'domestic' centres I was proposing over ex-military camps is that they would give us flexibility; allow for speedy expansion and, more importantly, contraction; encourage diversity in approaches to settlement; make it easier to recruit local volunteers, easier to negotiate with local authorities, easier to involve the refugees themselves in the running of the centre, easier to settle them in houses that were not too far from the centre and thus easier to give post-settlement support. They would also be manageable by project leaders with no previous management experience.

The other two agencies and the Home Office were sceptical: we would not find the buildings and/or it would be hugely expensive. Barry Denton of Ockenden thought it would lead to dependency.

I was not worried, as the representatives of BCAR and OV were, about the cost of obtaining small centres. When I had set up Tent City I had persuaded Hammersmith Council to let us have the site rent free and I believed I could repeat the trick. We managed to obtain our centres, twenty-two in all, of which there were usually fourteen operating at any one time, rent-free.

We were not far into the programme before it was significantly expanded. At a summit in Geneva, called to establish an international resettlement programme, Britain was pressurised into taking 19,000 Vietnamese, well above Thatcher's grudging offer of 1,500. The majority of these came through Hong Kong. Their story differs from that of those who were picked up at sea.

They were mostly ethnic Chinese who lived in North Vietnam, usually near the Chinese border, and are known as the Hoa. They were not Vietnamese citizens – if they possessed a passport it was Chinese – and when the border war erupted between Vietnam and China they were regarded as potential fifth columnists and either sent to remote labour camps or were pushed out by the Vietnamese authorities. They were small farmers and fishermen, usually with little formal education, who had had no previous contact with a Western way of life. The fishermen among them took to their boats, hugging the coast of China, sometimes landing to take on food and water, until they reached Hong Kong. Unlike those who fled from the South the casualty count was low.

The 'boat people' are not one community but at least four, though it is misleading to talk about 'communities' for that implies more cohesion than actually exists. It was often assumed by helpers that their common refugee experience would lead them to help one another. Many resisted this common bond because they wanted to forget the refugee experience. Community organisations, however, have gradually emerged.

The zone allocated to us by the Home Office's Joint Committee was Northern Ireland, Scotland and the East of England down to Essex. This is where we must settle our refugees and find and set up our reception centres. We were the newcomers, and had to accept a realm more suitable for the raising of sheep. Our centres were strung out from Montrose in North East Scotland to Hothfield in Kent; from Devizes in the West to Mundesley in the East. We were naughty: some of these were in BCAR's zone: Devizes closed early and Hothfield was transferred to BCAR.

From where would we get our buildings? Children's homes and small hospitals seemed to offer the best hope. The recent closure of a number of these was to be of considerable help.

We therefore began a systematic approach to social service departments and area health authorities. Having identified a suitable building I played the emergency card: 'I need a decision today' or 'I want a meeting tomorrow'. The Chief Executive of one major Scottish city did not even bother to call a meeting. He sorted it all out in half-an-hour on the phone while I stood by him in his office.

To get the premises rent-free I indicated how my request could solve a worrying problem. They had an empty building that was once a children's home, or a cottage hospital, or some building that would not require planning permission for a change of use. They probably feared that, unless an alternative use could be found for it, it would be taken off them. The cost of keeping it secure was an added burden. My occupying it would take away the worry and the cost. Because I would be doing them a favour, and might have to spend money making the property fit for purpose, I would not be paying rent.

I tell senior local bureaucrats that the Home Office will pay for the provision of language training in the reception centre, and the Director of Education perks up. There is the problem of providing houses for settlement, but the head of housing thinks he can put refugees into properties that no one else wants, so he has no objection. The Chief Executive fancies he can invoice central government for the housing and other expenses. He is mistaken, but I do not disabuse him. All are aware that a positive decision will be politically popular. I get what I want without exception.

One local authority had closed a small hospital, despite a local outcry. Local wrath would have been too great had they immediately tried to demolish or sell it. We were giving the building a popular use, and the local population a cooling-off period. In this case the authority tried hard to get us to pay rent, even invoking a fictitious directive from the DHSS.

It would be cynical to suggest that the element of self-interest was active in all cases, and I would certainly want to proclaim the seminary at Osterley and the Ladymary School in Edinburgh, both Roman Catholic foundations, exceptions, as was the centre in Derby where the Director of Social Services was enormously helpful.

SCF's property man, Denys Bullock, was on the ball. He understood the need for speed and would make his inspection and recommendations within a couple of days of our finding a property. I fixed a setting-up time of three weeks: three weeks to appoint staff and get the building equipped to receive their first batch of Vietnamese.

We needed man and woman power. Our HQ office was staffed by just five people: Mary Smalley, transferred to us from another department and invaluable for her knowledge of the way the organization operated; Jane Lee, an art historian by profession who never took 'no' for an answer; Julia Meiklejohn, my deputy with oversight of financial matters; a succession of three secretaries, Sue Parker, Jackie Heather and Liz Coy, and me.

The appointment of Julia was a small victory. Personnel matters were the responsibility of Commander Taken Gardner-Brown, the Administrative Director. (Many of the senior staff were ex-military or ex-colonial or both.) He brought me a retired Brigadier from his club for interview. On his CV I noticed his membership of several golf clubs. 'We will be on the road for at least three days a week. There won't be time for golf.' It wasn't quite the job for him.

Taken Gardner-Brown was rather embarrassed. 'I think you had probably better make the appointment yourself.' I thumbed through the CVs. One stood out. Julia was an economist, had been research assistant to the Chief Statistician of Canada, had carried out research in Malaysia and India and was working part-

Julia signs the register

time backstage at Covent Garden whilst studying at LSE.

I have never believed in going through the motions of shortlisting for a post if a suitable candidate appears. But I did need to find out a few things about Julia that were not on her CV. Could I work with her? Could she work with project leaders and other staff? How would she respond to the needs of refugees? How would she cope with making it up as we went along? I could think of only one way to find out – take her to a reception centre for a day. So we hoofed it down to Campion House, Osterley, met the staff and refugees and discussed the programme. It all worked out fine, to the extent that, after a few months, her father was able to refer to me as his sin-in-law!

We needed to appoint project leaders speedily. There was a good response to our adverts. As there was no history of running these sorts of projects in this country we could not require applicants to have had appropriate direct experience so we invited most of those who applied to spend the day with us, fifteen applicants at a time. At the first session we outlined the project. Our primary requirement was for project leaders, but we also needed other staff. If at any point an applicant decided they did not want to be part of the programme they were to leave immediately. We expected that anyone still with us at the end of the day would accept a post if offered it.

In the second session applicants spoke about themselves, their experiences, their skills and their hopes, and what they could contribute. Several had travelled abroad, and some had taught in Asia or Africa. One had worked with refugees in Australia, one had been involved in the Ugandan Asian programme in the UK and a third had done voluntary work in Thailand.

At this point we began to distinguish the listeners from those who merely talked. The interesting ones were those who forgot that they were at an interview and joined freely in a debate about ways and means, for we were offering project leaders the chance to run their own show in their own way. Those who wanted to be part of the programme, but not to lead a project, were now asked to identify themselves. They might stay to the end of the day so that newly-chosen project leaders, who would be responsible for appointing their own staff, could negotiate with them.

After lunch each candidate for project leader had an individual interview with Julia and me in case there were matters they did not wish to share with the whole group. We then had a full group session for further questions, after which the interviewers retired to make their decisions. The three of us – Rachel had sat in – were unanimous in our assessments of the candidates' qualities.

We returned and identified those to whom we were offering project leader posts. We explained to those who had been rejected our reasons for this. This is difficult to do but is usually much appreciated, and certainly better than a phone call from a secretary or an impersonal letter. It gives the rejected person the chance to question the decision and sometimes allows for a certain amount of counselling. Rachel Jenkins, my boss, appreciating the appropriateness of this novel process, left the rest of these selection marathons to us.

There is much more to be said about this method, which I have used successfully since, but I want to make three observations: firstly, most of the project leaders we appointed were women – they had generally been employed below their natural ability and welcomed an opportunity to get management experience; they were more prepared than the men to take on short-term employment with no commitment on the part of SCF to re-deploy them at the end of the programme. Secondly, this approach avoids any feeling that the thing has been fixed in advance and allows candidates to appreciate the qualities of those who have been successful. Thirdly, we made only one mistake in these appointments and that was because I failed to follow my gut instinct and gave in when challenged.

The comments of those who went through this process ranged from 'embarrassing' and 'intimidating' (though theses two were successful) to 'it enabled one to conceal one's weaknesses and make the most of one's strengths' from a project leader who adopted the same method when appointing his own staff. 'Most agreed that selection in this way seemed to work well, and allowed the interviewers to see the candidates in the kind of group situation that a large part of the job involved.' (*First Impressions*, RA)

As I hoped, these recruits had different styles of leadership. Visiting their centres I saw how their personalities were reflected in the atmosphere of each project. They all tried to act democratically and involve the staff group in decision-making and action. They were prepared to change their own decisions in response to staff feeling. However, they came to recognise that, in the end, the overall responsibility and final decision lay with them. They began to understand the loneliness of management. 'They do look to you to solve problems quite a lot. You can't share all your uncertainties with them, and there's quite a lot of worrying and thinking by yourself. They expect you to take ultimate decisions.' Another said, 'I'm surprised when staff haven't made decisions on my weekends off, when I knew they had enough information to do it. Things do store up for my return'. There were three exceptions to this. The first was the project leader about whom I had had doubts. When visiting his centre in Scotland we sensed that something was not right, but neither Julia nor I could put a finger on it. Then he was off sick, and I moved in to run the project. Staff, though uneasy, said nothing. They had been sworn to secrecy by their boss. I persuaded them that the interests of the Vietnamese came first and so the beans were spilt. He was a tyrant and a bully. I had enough information to dismiss him.

Two of our project leaders were of Asian origin. Rani Atma, an Indian from Kenya, ran the centre in Ilkley and, when that closed, the one in Bingley, Yorkshire. Minh Phuoc, who was Vietnamese but not a refugee, ran the centre at Pontefract. Both shared a style of management that I labelled 'Asian' that was not always appreciated either by their staff or by outsiders. They tested their staff for loyalty by giving them basic, wearing tasks. Kevin Armstrong worked for Minh. He had been a second-hand car salesman and, on paper had few relevant qualifications. She really put him through the mill. We concluded that she thought little of him. But when she accepted a job back in Vietnam she insisted he be appointed as her successor. The Vietnamese never had a better champion than Kevin, who wheeler-dealt magnificently on their behalf – I never enquired too closely into his modus operandi!

Having passed the test, Rani's staff became her friends. I was impressed with her social work skills. She worked alongside Vietnamese women in the kitchen because the shared activity of preparing food allowed for gaps in the conversation, which could progress from recipes to personal problems. Silence carried no awkwardness or threat. After she left Refugee Action she founded the Asian Family Counselling Service, which for several years I chaired. Relate never really understood that marriage counselling in an Asian context meant dealing with the extended family, speaking to one Grandma in Mumbai and another in New York. Rani became a lay member of the General Medical Council.

The considerable autonomy that our project leaders enjoyed in a system in which there was no 'chain of command' was frustrating for many in the Home Office and the other two voluntary organisations. They wanted to deal with Head Office and often resented being asked to approach a project directly. Officialdom found it equally hard to appreciate that each project had its own way of operating. This uniformity of purpose, but not of operation, I regarded as a strength, not a weakness. A useful spin-off was that, in having to relate directly with the Home Office, project leaders gained some valuable experience in dealing with government departments. They also gained a greater understanding of some of the issues that frustrated all of us.

Project leaders met regularly with Julia and me for a couple of days at one of the reception centres. We slept on the floor. Here project leaders could share problems and juggle with solutions. We had no blueprint for a reception centre. There were, of course, budgetary constraints, and some project leaders needed help with keeping the books and reading accounts. It has to be said that some would have preferred to have been given a manual, but there was not time to write one.

From a management point of view, the advantage of this system, initially forced on us by circumstances, was that a number of possible ways of structuring and operating centres could be tested. At these meetings project leaders learnt from each other. As the programme progressed, the projects moved naturally towards a more uniform pattern of provision whilst preserving their individual flavour.

I fixed, quite arbitrarily, on a staffing ratio of 1:12. Five staff would be required: a social worker, a nurse or health visitor, an interpreter, a housekeeper and a general assistant, all of whom would be resident. This meant reception centres that could take 60-80 Vietnamese.

The inclusion of a nurse/health visitor – we were the only agency to employ them as part of our team – resulted from a belief that local health authorities would have little experience of tropical diseases and that refugees from camps would not be in the best of health. The condition of those rescued by the *Sibonga* and *Roachbank* we took as a warning. *SCF* employed many nurses overseas so there was a pool of returnees into which we could and did dip.

An unfortunate situation at the Devizes Centre convinced us that we were right about employing our own medical staff. I was at the Devizes centre, an empty part of a hospital, when the first group of Vietnamese emerged exhausted from the coach that had brought them from Heathrow. It was early evening. Most refused food, changed into their nightclothes and collapsed in their rooms. A local doctor, sniffing out an opportunity to publish papers on the health problems of refugees from Vietnam, arrived with his bag and a torch and proceeded to examine the terrified newcomers in their rooms and nightwear.

One local health authority quarantined the centre in their area despite the fact that refugees had been screened in Hong Kong for communicable diseases such as TB. Apart from this pair of aberrations, we controlled the health programme. The other agencies relied on local health services.

In January 1980 we organised a medical conference. We found that some Medical Officers for Environmental Health were accepting responsibility for screening. Others, fearing that financial resources would not be available, washed their hands of it. There was considerable confusion, exacerbated by a lack of information from Hong Kong and ignorance of Port Health Clearance. I recommended that our medical staff rely on their own judgement. They held routine clinics, undertook health education and participated in the life of the centre, in one of which the health visitor was also the project leader.

Life could be difficult for nurses and health visitors. One challenge was to do with the taking of blood.

> We managed to get everyone into the bus to go for blood tests except one family. We knocked at the door for five minutes. There was no answer. Fearing that something might have happened we fetched the master key. We opened the door and there were these three figures in bed, a big lump on one side, a big lump on the other and a small lump in the middle. They were fully clothed.

Those from the North believe that blood, once taken cannot be replaced. It could be difficult for the nurse to persuade them to go to the hospital for an antenatal.

> If I insist they say 'I have been the mother of five children. I know better than you. Keep your mouth shut!' What can I do? When I explain to them that the blood is replaced they say, 'No, in Hong Kong they took only a very little. Every time we go to the hospital they take 10 or 20 cc. They want to kill us'.

> A woman who had been settled was about to have a baby. The health visitor called at the time it was due. It had been born two or

three hours before and the father had acted as midwife. There was something wrong with the baby, which was taken into hospital. Within eighteen hours Dad had gone to the hospital, which the Vietnamese call 'death houses', picked up wife and baby and walked out. The baby is doing quite well. The support group had a nervous breakdown. The English worker had to explain to the support group that having a baby was a natural thing.

Other centres had a more positive first intake experience than that of Devizes. For Jo Vaughan, the project leader at Warwick, the greatest thing was the National Front on the lawn waving furiously at the Vietnamese who stood and waved back at this welcome greeting. A similar thing happened at Ilkley. There the Vietnamese took NF members cups of tea.

A major concern of staff was the almost complete absence of an established ethnic community with which the refugees could identify. They worried at the wide cultural divide between the Vietnamese and the host community, with its implications in terms of language learning, employment – many of the 'skilled' Vietnamese found their skills were not relevant in an industrialised Western economy – and the development of social relationships with the host community. Vietnamese refugees had much less control over their lives here than other ethnic minority groups and were going to have to rely on the efforts of the voluntary agencies for support.

Although dispersion made it easier to obtain housing, the areas in which we were settling refugees offered little employment. We knew that most of them would be much better off in cities. Nearly all our centres, therefore, taught their refugees how to go about moving to a city of their choice. When they did move we, unlike the Home Office officials, considered this to be successful settlement for they had learnt to use the system.

Here are two more examples of cultural misunderstandings.

I nearly died the death at the wedding ceremony. The girl was painfully shy. She either couldn't speak or spoke so low the registrar couldn't hear. And he, at one point, became pretty angry and almost refused to go on with the ceremony on the grounds that she was being forced into the marriage. Then voices all round the room shouted out for her to speak up and it was nearly stopped again. Everyone was almost hysterical.

The fights between single men have never been very serious. It is much worse between families. The Vietnamese interpreters keep very cool, however. One doesn't realise how much is posturing and how much is going to develop into serious damage. We have had a few black eyes and cuts but no one has been seriously hurt. But you have to separate them when they are fighting.

It is easy to interpret these stories as signs of an inferior culture. We need to weigh them against those things that horrify the Vietnamese about our own culture. Vietnamese workers have expressed surprise and concern about the ease with which British workers will recommend abortion or divorce. In some cases they have had to intervene to stop it happening because the client did not know how to tell the British social worker that they did not want it. They are amazed at the lack of responsibility within the family, and particularly the way we treat our old people. They take a greater pride in self-sufficiency and do not really understand our attitude to welfare. It is inappropriate to talk about one culture being better than another. They are different, and those differences have to be respected.

SETTING UP A SCHOOL

One thorny issue was English lessons which the government had made the responsibility of the local authorities. Some authorities had no expertise in teaching English as a second language. Some authorities used the programme to help them out of other difficulties. This was often at the expense of the refugees.

The teachers usually taught on site, and in some cases there were clashes between the teachers and the centre staff. However, in three of the centres our staff became involved in the teaching, and teaching staff helped with settlement. The situation was even easier where one of the teaching staff was resident.

Many of the older refugees were illiterate in their own language, usually Cantonese. Quite a few had only a basic working knowledge of Vietnamese. To expect them to learn enough English to deal with doctors, social workers, schools and employment agencies was quite unrealistic. Youngsters, however, were able to learn quite quickly, and this led to some difficult situations. We found cases where a young child was being asked to translate for a parent who was having medical treatment or suffering from severe mental problems.

The majority of teachers were dedicated, cooperative, and followed up their pupils when they settled. The schools to which the youngsters were going when settled reported them doing well, but often this was 'doing well' in remedial classes. It was obvious something had to be done.

In July 1980 we organised a national conference on education involving both the Home Office and the Department of Education and Science. The latter sent six of Her Majesty's Inspectors, which I found slightly daunting. We had three items on the agenda: schooling for brighter teenagers; provision for the 16+ group, and the problems of middle-aged, jobless, heads of family. Unfortunately the solution sought for the latter two problems was 'more government money', one that stood little chance of success.

I floated the idea of a school for teenagers. This was generally well-received. We heard the usual objections: 'boarding schools are elitist and destructive of family life'; 'Such a school would prevent the pupils from integrating'; 'The expense is too great'.

SCF took the 'bright teenager' problem to itself. I have written about the school that we established in the chapter on education.

INTERPRETATION

It became clear to me that our social work was limited by the abilities of the interpreters. If an interpreter does not understand why a question is being asked then miscommunication is likely. Kathy Despicht, one of our project leaders, presented a paper to a conference in Lausanne on counselling in which she gave two examples of mistranslation. 'Parents are paid Child Benefit by the government' became 'parents pay Child Benefit to the government'. One interpreter's comment on another's performance was, 'He changed what she said and made her sound ever so unpleasant. All the refugees are complaining'.

> The interpreters were usually young refugees themselves with a limited command of English and little understanding of the complicated social systems of Britain. They were intelligent and hard-working but they often had unresolved problems of their own, and lacked the emotional maturity or skills to cope in situations of conflict...

The dynamics of any exchange were difficult to handle; either it was very wooden and controlled or the interpreter would effectively take over the role of counsellor, leaving the British worker outside with no idea as to what was going on. When three languages were involved the interpersonal relationships, and transfer of information, could become even less satisfactory. (Unpublished June 1982.)

What if we gave our Vietnamese/Chinese staff some social-work training? There would be a double advantage in this, as not only would it enable us to work more effectively, it would give the Vietnamese community some potential leaders. (In my view it was necessary to supplant the old men who did not understand the new culture and were operating inappropriately.) I was grateful for the strong support for this programme by project leaders Rani Atma (Bingley) and Minh Thuoc (Pontefract).

The two Home Office officials with whom we dealt were keen on this development but couldn't offer any money. However, they turned a blind eye to our taking twenty Vietnamese staff from both SCF and BCAR back into reception. This was at Osterley, near Hounslow. Sally Martin was the project leader and Sandy Buchan a social worker there. In later years he became the CEO of Refugee Action.

Two experienced social-work trainers were hired, Roz Finlay and Suzanne Bang, the latter a Dane with experience of working cross-culturally. The training was intense and revealing. One thing soon became apparent, and caused a stir in British social work circles: social work is culturally specific. For example, home-grown social workers address issues and individuals directly. They look each other in the eye, which Vietnamese would never do.

If a Vietnamese husband is suspected of beating his wife the social worker is circumspect and goes to the neighbours to ask if they have noticed anything. She then visits the couple. Have they heard about the Vietnamese man in Birmingham who has got into trouble with the authorities because he was found beating his wife? It wouldn't happen here, of course. In this way the message is communicated with no loss of face. For a British social worker talking to the neighbours would be an absolute no-no.

Roz described the six-month programme: a comparison of education systems; access skills; developing a telephone manner; role playing and interviewing; assessing; counselling; DHSS and the law; the Health Service; family expectations and the differences in family life – bringing up children, cultural conflict, death; the refugee experience; mental health; the setting up of support groups.

Julia took the para-social workers to France to stay with Tich Nhat Hanh at Plum Village near Bordeaux. We felt it was important that there should be input from a spiritual source.

Tich Nhat Hanh & trainees

The training was very successful, allowing our Vietnamese workers to take on much more responsibility and to free up other members of staff. When the programme ended many found employment with the local authorities with whom they had been dealing, others with local community groups.

REFUGEE ACTION EMERGES

SCF's PR department was not geared up to meeting all the Vietnamese Settlement operation's needs. We needed publicity for projects in local areas that was not forthcoming. In part this reflected a conflict of interest between the project and the local SCF group. We were also becoming increasingly frustrated with SCF's Finance Dept. They made mistakes with salaries, submitted a double claim to the Home Office and had to be constantly monitored by Julia. Not only that but, even though all our salaries were being paid by the Home Office, they were charging an administration fee of 10%.

The solution seemed to be to ask SCF to hive off the programme as a separate organisation. Rachel and the Child Care Committee were persuaded that, as future work would in the main be organizing support for adults, it didn't really fit with the Child Care Department's other work. The committee agreed that the new organization could inherit everything Vietnamese except the school at Bingley and Robina's project for unaccompanied minors.

The next step was to persuade the project leaders to back the idea. Before they did so they wanted to be certain we would get Home Office support, i.e. funding.

Julia and I had developed a good relationship with Home Office officials. When the programme began we found that the other agencies inflated their budgets by about a third. The Home Office then cut them back by about a third. Julia told them that we were not going to play that silly game. Our submissions would be accurate. In fact she was usually within around 1% of her prediction. We could be trusted with money. Our second tack was to discover what problems and pressures the civil servants themselves faced, then to find ways of helping where we could. Thirdly, if it was necessary to make a public criticism, we warned them and gave them the text before we released it so they were never taken by surprise.

Because of these things they trusted us. When we pointed out that they would save the administration fee they were paying SCF, they readily agreed to support us. That brought on board most of the staff.

We had to find a suitable chairman. Rani Atma had worked for Lord Chitnis, the Director of Rowntree Social Services, and she and I went to see him. He agreed to accept the position as long as meetings did not last longer than an hour. He understood the relationship that needs to exist between trustees of a charity and its professional staff. I had worked for charities that tried to micro-manage operations, and where decisions hung in the air between meetings that might be two months apart. That was incredibly frustrating and demotivating.

This choice of Chair had two positive consequences: meetings took place in the House of Lords, which made the recruitment of other trustees easy, and Rowntree Social Services had offices in Poland Street that we could use as a London base. Our Head Office we set up in Leeds to be near our reception centres. It later moved to Derby.

Pratap Chitnis was as good as his word. He and I went through the agenda before meetings which lasted little over an hour. All the business I presented was approved without fuss. One successful project that he and I undertook was the rescue of women and children caught up in the civil war in El Salvador. It was so sensitive that I had to ask clergy friends for money without being able to tell them what it was for. I was touched by their generous response.

The choice of a name for the new organisation was not easy. The 'British Council for Aid to Refugees' is clumsy. 'Ockenden Venture' says nothing about its mission. In the end I settled on 'Refugee Action'. Having been the Director of Christian Action I knew the title to be dynamic and memorable, so Refugee Action seemed the natural choice. I even designed the first logo! The transition went remarkably smoothly.

One of the important differences between the new organisation and the old was salaries. When we looked at what people were earning, because pay was related to qualifications and responsibility, the British had the highest salaries, the British Chinese were next and the Vietnamese staff, nearly all of whom were refugees, earnt the least, and yet the latter probably needed the money the most. To put this right everyone was paid the same. I would have liked to have paid people according to need but that proved a little too complicated to work out.

Once the reception centres closed about half the staff were the trained para-social workers. Meetings took place in both Vietnamese and English.

Running down a programme is often the most difficult part. How do you avoid good workers jumping ship before the programme ends, for instance? I think I can safely say that we managed the run-down effectively. One part of our approach was to cut posts vertically and so I, as Director and wishing to set an example, was one of the first to go, to be replaced by Julia. As I was off to the British Refugee Council there was commiseration, not envy.

THE BRITISH REFUGEE COUNCIL

At the same time as we were going it alone, the BCAR and the Standing Conference on Refugees (SCOR), both founded in 1951, merged to form the British Refugee Council, later renamed the Refugee Council when the Scottish and Welsh refugee councils were established. The Director was Martin Barber. He and I agreed that, when the reception centres closed, Refugee Action would be absorbed by the BRC. (A turnaround, as I had previously been asked by the Home Office, in a conversation in St James' Park that the official concerned said would be denied, if we would be prepared to take over BCAR.) Martin offered me the post of Director of Settlement at BRC. He wanted me to introduce RA practices into his organization.

Although the majority of the BRC social workers based at Bondway House in Vauxhall were well-meaning, they had inherited the culture of BCAR. You don't change a corporate culture by shedding a few staff and adopting a new name. BRC was top-heavy, bureaucratic, wasteful, and in its financial accounting, devious. I felt sorry for Martin Barber because this is what he inherited, not what he created.

I faced a number of critical decisions. I had to sack the transport team. They had been lining their own pockets by selling off donated furniture. I had to sideline elderly Vietnamese staff with little understanding of the problems their community faced. I also had to shut down the camp at Sopley.

Robert Hood, who had run the Vietnamese programme, had warned through the press that there would be riots when Sopley closed, and the police would need to be involved. I was determined that this should not happen. Management had been chaotic. For instance, housing for settlement was handled by the London office and communication with the camp was poor, each blaming the other for failures. Before taking any action I had to see the centre for myself.

SOPLEY

A military camp in a village situated in the New Forest National Park of Hampshire: huts in rows, a sign instructing visitors to report to the Administration, a guard on the gate and a wire perimeter fence. Also neatly trimmed grass, tarmacadamed paths signed in English and Vietnamese and mature trees. Small children charge around on tricycles and an adolescent revs up a motorcycle in a park full of well-used cars. I spot a couple coming into camp with live chickens tucked in their jackets. We might be in Hong Kong, though in Hong Kong the camps are closer to civilization.

This is my first visit. At the barrier I am directed to Administration. I have sent Jane Shackman, a social worker, on ahead and she comes to warn me of 'trouble at mill'. I am expected, but the Administrator has disappeared. His deputy is racing round in ever-decreasing circles. Cars come and go as staff save themselves a few yards-worth of shoe leather. I don't mind waiting. It gives me a chance to sniff out what is going on.

An elderly gent of military bearing storms down the corridor waving keys and shouting to no one in particular that no one tells him what is going on. He is only in charge of supplies. He is only trying to do an orderly, honest job.

The Deputy Administrator rushes in, shouts, and rushes out again. I continue to sit.

I knew this was going to be a difficult undertaking but I had not reckoned on a conspiracy of silence. They know I have come to blow the final whistle on this queer, but cosy life they have established for themselves.

The Administrator arrives, apologizes, charms, telephones for tea, charms, jokes, gossips a little. I ask for a report on the camp, settlement prospects for the refugees and his proposals for reducing staffing levels. He leans over his desk as though to protect confidential papers and waffles on.

Only once before, in the early days of the refugee programme, have I had to face the smoke screen that a manager schooled in militaristic bureaucracy throws up. I feel I could write the manual. Always be polite, always agree and then hint at forces beyond one's control. Back up one's colleagues and complain with a sigh of resigned acceptance at the lack of understanding shown by an ever-so-busy H.Q. Conjure up a sheaf of reports, newspaper articles, and memos to H.Q. that have not been acknowledged. Suggest lunch. Avoid a tête a tête in a pub by claiming staff would be disappointed not to see a real-life wallah from H.Q. in the canteen.

The only way I can deal with this is by asserting my authority in a way that I do not enjoy.

How many refugees do you have in camp?

How long have they been here?

What are the settlement plans for them?

I have the answers in my briefcase and know, for instance, that the Le family, numbering about 100, have been here for well over a year. When he has confirmed what is in the records I have I will produce them to show that the decision to close this camp is based on agreed facts. I am getting nowhere when a Vietnamese resident comes to my aid.

Staff members are lounging in the office, some sitting, some standing, when an angry young man rushes in brandishing a heavy, Chinese meat cleaver which he slams into the desk. The Administrator shouts 'stand up!' In a calm voice I say 'Sit down!' Fortunately the staff takes its lead from me. In reply to my question he tells me that he and his family don't know what is happening to them. I take the details and promise to do something about his situation.

The Administrator, who has lost both control and face, resigns, clearing the way for me to begin the shut-down. One of the biggest obstacles to doing this speedily is this Le family. With the help of Quang, a wily, older, ex-sergeant major interpreter whom I have brought with me, I start negotiations. These are with the heads of the nuclear families within this extended family group, which is uncharacteristic in being ethnic Vietnamese from the North and staunch Roman Catholics from a fishing community. They want to remain by the sea. They have nearly all been in reception for about two years. BRC planned to settle them in Lanarkshire. It was going to be three years before the building would be ready.

They tell me firmly that they will not go to Scotland. I promise to see what I can do. Our RA worker gets an offer from Leeds. At my next meeting with the family I produce a map. Here at the top is Lanarkshire where they don't want to go. Here at the bottom is Sopley where they are and where we have no houses. Let us reach a compromise and split the difference. Leeds is the half-way house. I will do my best to settle them all in Leeds. They accept, and wheel out a very old lady who must be present at the sealing of the deal. The first group moves into Leeds housing and I hand over responsibility for the family to Hilary Dewhurst, an RA Resettlement Worker.

Hilary had been the project leader in Edinburgh, our youngest. The centre had been a school attached to a convent. To get it ready in time she called in the army. It was the project Princess Anne chose to visit. Normally a bevy of SCF big-wigs would have made their way North to fuss and effuse but I told them firmly that I was not going and nor were they. It was to be Hilary's day. And it was. Now she saw the Le family into Leeds houses as promised.

> So what happens next? Colin Hodgetts, settlement services director at the British Refugee Council and formerly with Refugee Action, is probably in a minority in his determination that we should be enabling refugees to build up their own self-supporting community. He wants, for instance, funding to start small businesses, which enables people to break out of that bind that says accumulation of capital means loss of social security benefits. He wants more money for Vietnamese welfare workers. But he knows, too, that research among other refugee populations shows that it takes at least five to ten years for the political groupings we are now beginning to see to turn into networks of mutual support, and that the particular cultural mix among the Vietnamese population here brings tensions as well as cohesion.
>
> So special support from the host community remains essential. (Ann Shearer *The Guardian* 22.12.82)

I realised that the plan of taking Refugee Action into the Vietnamese section of the BRC was not on. They were unlikely to provide the long-term support the Vietnamese required. So instead, I hived off BRC's Vietnamese section to Refugee Action. Then I resigned.

HOW IT WENT

Were we right to insist on small centres? Wendy Harris wrote:

> From my own experience of working in a Reception Centre, and my interviews with refugees as well as the workers on the programme, I would argue that smaller centres are much to be preferred. They offer the refugee a more secure base, providing sympathetic surroundings where they can recover from their traumas. ...Smaller centres are more conducive to successful resettlement and I would recommend them in future programmes, if centres are required, units with a maximum capacity of 70. (*The Reception and Resettlement of Vietnamese Refugees in Britain*, unpub. p.44)

The Home Office's own report reads, 'The ideal centre in terms of management and maintaining a proper relationship with the refugees should restrict capacity to no more than 100 people'. (*Report of the Joint Committee for Refugees from Vietnam*, Home Office 1982.)

One of the benefits was the ability to involve the Vietnamese in running the centre. One project leader had a Heads of Family meeting at 8.45 every morning.

> We had one particular family who in Vietnam had been very rich. They were used to servants all around them and didn't want to do anything in the centre. There was a little bit of feeling about this. It was just a matter of talking about it in Heads of Family and it was all sorted. I don't think I could have run a centre without having that support in the background.

Another advantage was that the refugees could cook for themselves, and that might involve shopping for food. Learning which shops sold what, and where special ingredients could be found was an important lesson.

Dispersal remained an issue. The Government had talked about not wanting to create 'ghettoes', for which they were later taken to task. The Home Office was accused of scaremongering and implicit racism.

> We share the concerns reflected here [in the JCRV Report 1982] about the social and psychological effects on the refugees of the dispersal policy. We are also troubled by the underlying implications of the policy – firstly, in apparently regarding the concentration of an ethnic minority group in any area as by definition undesirable because of the possible reactions of the majority community, a view which we cannot condone, and secondly, in seeing as its sole aim that the refugees become 'integrated', i.e. 'submerged' within British society, rather than retaining their own identity within the kind of pluralist society which we have envisaged in this report. (Swann 1985 p.722 HMSO)

Support groups could be a mixed blessing as befriending could lead to refugees being treated like pets. On the other hand they could be useful when it came to furnishing the settlement house. One negative element was their desire to be told the escape story. 'Their questions about the past keep the pain alive.'

Because there was an interest in how we should meet the needs of those arriving in the UK in 2015, I was invited to take part in a Radio 4 programme about the way in which Vietnamese refugees were treated (22/11/15) Most of my contribution was edited out. Was it too radical? One example: I said that it was important that refugees should not be asked about their experiences. Yes, they have to come to terms with what they have been through, but in their own way and in their own time and possibly with professional help. Those who are merely curious are a pain. Jonathan Freedland, the journalist, expressed astonishment. My observation, a report of the view of our professional social workers, was cut. Up until then I thought that the innovations we had made and the expertise we had acquired, would sell themselves. I was wrong.

Refugees want to forget. They feel they have been torn up by the roots. The loss is like the loss of a close relative or friend. The symptoms are those of someone who has been bereaved. One wakes up in a strange room in a foreign place. The details of living, which had become routine and therefore did not need to be thought about, now require conscious attention. These strange clothes have to be put on in the right order. Life is lived indoors instead of out of doors. Familiar faces are scarce. You go out to shop but do not understand which shops sell which goods. Taking a bus is a risky venture.

For the refugee the escape route is a *via dolorosa* and each stopping point a new disillusion: you find the country of first asylum, such as Hong Kong, wants to be rid of you; the reception centre sees you as a problem; your new house, though luxurious by Vietnamese standards, is not so by British standards and presents difficulties like high heating bills. You do not speak enough English. There are no jobs. The support group is friendly but does not really understand.

It can take between seven and ten years before the refugee realises that they are not going back (the myth of return) and life has to be made here. Expectations of the country of resettlement are unreasonably high. The reality of unemployment, lack of English, and isolation, which was the immediate prospect for the Vietnamese in the UK, taken with their earlier experiences and expectations, set them back.

Vietnamese mental health needs are best understood in terms of the family unit, which is extended, collectivistic, and patriarchal. Many refugees suffer from broken family status. They also experience role reversal: the social and economic power of women and children increases at the expense of men, a disruption of the traditional family structure. Communication between mental health practitioners and clients is clouded by interpretation and cultural issues.

With these things in mind we made our long-term plans, telling the Home Office that we were going to require funding for the next ten years. This desire was laughingly dismissed. With 'sausage slicing' – one little bit at a time – we managed to get them to fork out.

Like the other agencies we have worked to bring over other members of their extended families so that they can be re-united. We have promoted Chinese and Vietnamese classes for the children so that they do not forget their roots or find themselves too alienated from their parents. We have encouraged the formation of Vietnamese Associations and community groups. We helped get a Buddhist temple established in South London.

Our fieldworkers have responded to calls to help with marriages that were breaking down, to help with generations that fought each other, to help those who were depressed about the hopelessness of their situation. Sometimes they, too, for they also are refugees from Vietnam, were overcome by the depth of pain and suffering. But they recovered and continued to help others, witnesses to the resilience of the human spirit.

Some of the older people expressed a wish to die in their homeland. I understood this and argued for a programme that would help them return, another idea that met with some hostility from other agencies and parts of the Vietnamese community but which did take off.

By listening to Vietnamese community groups, recording their needs, and through devising new approaches and programmes, Refugee Action managed to sustain support for the settled Vietnamese for over twenty years, a minor triumph.

There was a period when RA entered the doldrums through a lack of funding and I took over as Chair. We were able to appoint Jack Shieh as the Director, something that gave me great satisfaction because, when I founded the organisation, I said that when we had a Chinese/Vietnamese refugee as a Director, we would have arrived. In the 1990s we had one.

At the time of writing Julia is Chair of Refugee Action. I was a trustee until 2015. I had no wish to interfere in management decisions but I wanted to ensure that the organisation remained radical – not afraid to take the Home Office to court, for example – and to ensure that the organization was being run in the interests of those who come to it for help and not the staff. Neither was difficult for we have had a great body of trustees both committed and radical, overseeing a dedicated and innovative staff.

One of the tasks that I have undertaken is to be the last port of call within the organization for those who have complaints to make. I am pleased that we were able to resolve all the cases amicably – no one felt the need to go on to an Employment tribunal.

Refugee Action has an enviable reputation for its employment practices. The 2015 staff conference I attended at Keele University was overshadowed by a decision of the Home Office to cut a major programme at short notice. Out of a staff of 160, and a similar number of volunteers, about 120 employees faced redundancy at the end of the year. Despite that, after an initial session outlining the implications and management's response, everyone turned their attention to refugee and asylum issues with commitment and good humour. I was both humbled and filled with pride, if that doesn't sound too much of a contradiction.

Chapter Twelve

In the steps of Saint Frumentius

I DON'T USUALLY READ the *Church Times* preferring invigoration to enervation, but it was passed on to me because it contained a review of the BBC's 2010 nativity play. I don't usually read job ads either, but wanted to discover how much pay organists commanded, being a part-time one myself. My eye was caught by the prominent heading of a boxed advert, 'Diocese of Egypt with North Africa and the Horn of Africa'. As I scanned the requirements for a project leader – tall, handsome, intelligent – I thought, 'This is me!' Actually it asked,

> Are you a self-starter and can you work to deadlines? Can you motivate others? Do you have a mind for detail? Can you give at least six months? We urgently need an experienced Priest to direct and coordinate programme staff at the Gambella Anglican Centre, in Ethiopia, from February 2011.

I still said, 'This is me!'

The job could have been done by a lay person but a clergyman was required because only a priest would be granted a work permit. Within minutes of showing her the advert Julia agreed that we should go for it so I emailed Andrew, the Bishop in Ethiopia, with a c.v. His swift reply was enthusiastic. We had a month and a bit to obtain visas and vaccinations. Appointed unseen!

We fly to Addis Ababa on Monday February 14th 2011 to find Bishop Andrew packing. He has been appointed Bishop of Reading. It will be some time before a successor is found. He ups the ante. Can we stay for a year, and will I supervise the local clergy down in Gambella as well as run the project? We can and, though I had not signed up to an ecclesiastical role, I will. My responsibility will be to the Metropolitan, Bishop Mouneer in Cairo, and to the ABC, the Absent Bishop Committee in Addis, a divided rule that I discover can be difficult to handle, the good bishop being an autocrat in the pharaonic mould. Preparations have included an armful of jabs and a briefcase of legalised certificates notarized at huge expense by both the Foreign Office and the Ethiopian Embassy.

How will I deal with an autocratic boss? By submitting monthly reports with proposed solutions to current problems, and requests for advice, I eventually obtain from him the ultimate authorisation: 'When you speak, I speak' and am appointed Area Dean. After six months I am given all the administrative authority that Bishop Andrew had. I can buy and sell property, open bank accounts and dismay the begging clergy by becoming both their first and last ports of call. Mouneer invests me with this power to sideline the ABC because he does not want it making decisions.

Julia, too, though not officially employed, has her brief: to keep her beady eye on the finances, making sure the appropriate systems are in place. The bishop also asks her to attend a conference in Nairobi in April on behalf of the diocese.

We befriend the two senior Head Office staff: Alemayehu (Alex), once his chauffeur and now Bishop Andrew's right hand man, and Maeza, who handles the money. We will have a lot to do with them in the coming months.

A cloud hangs over the office as efforts to re-register the Anglican Church with the government have been unsuccessful, and until registered I cannot get a work, and Julia a residence, permit. The accountant predicts a two-month delay for producing audited accounts, thought to be optimistic. In the event we have to return to London to renew our visas before permits are granted.

From Addis we fly to Gambella. As we touch the tarmac we are hit by the heat, though it is no more extreme than we have experienced in Asia. Sam, the Project Leader I am here to replace, meets us.

Gambella is a hot and humid region – usually hovering between 30 and 40 degrees both day and night, with rains that come for four months from April onwards – situated near the Sudanese border and, two days' drive on dirt roads from Addis

Ababa. There are refugee camps in the region. There has been a history of inter-tribal strife on both sides of the Sudanese border.

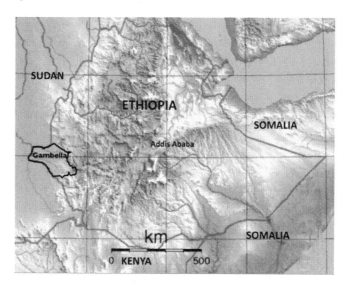

Gambella is both a town and a region. The two main tribal groups with whom we become involved are the Anuak (22%), who are slash-and-burn cultivators, and the nomadic Nuer (47%). Conflict between these two groups has an ancient pedigree, fed by the propensity of Nuer cows to consume Anuak crops. Nuer children and cows are also prey to raids by the Murle tribe that straddles the border with Sudan. Cows are wealth, are required for purchasing a bride and are therefore the target of unmarried men. A tiny tribe, the Opo, also straddles the border with Sudan. Like the Anuak they recently became Anglicans.

    None of these groups looks with favour on the Highlanders, 60,000 people forcibly settled here during the time of the Derg (1974 to 1991) who own and run most of the businesses. Everyone suffers from the fact that Ethiopian land is owned by the government, which feels free to dispose of it in whatever way it wants.

    About 70% of Gambella's population is Protestant, unlike the rest of Ethiopia which is Orthodox. There is a small Muslim community. Infant mortality is 92 deaths per thousand. Life expectancy is around 50 years, similar to that of the UK just before the war in 1914.

The Anglican Centre is on the edge of town on an unmade road. The nearly-finished buildings look smart, their yellow and grey walls topped with red corrugated metal roofs. The compound is a healthy two hectares which is mostly scrub. A volley/basketball court and a vegetable patch are part of the outline plan which we are here to realise.

Sam calls up a *bajaj*, the local equivalent of the three-wheeler Indian *tuc tuc*, and we bounce into town for a meal. We are introduced to *injera*, a pancake made of *teff*, a remarkable, somewhat sour grain, so remarkable that there was a ban on its export until 2015. We buy vegetables and salt and bajaj it back to camp.

Our new home is clean, concrete and almost new. The nylon curtains pain me but are replaceable. Other defects are more serious. Water pours through badly designed windows into the bedrooms when it rains. Gaps under the outside doors enable platoons of small creatures to invade at night. Ceiling fans have been fitted so that their arms sweep across the lights, creating a strobe effect.

Mintamir & Annabel

Darash is second-in-command but Mintamir is our right-hand woman. She caretakes the cash box. Her honesty upsets some of the clergy who bicker with her over their expenses claims. Twice they gang up to get rid of her, arguing that she is Orthodox and the job should go to an Anglican. She has been sacked once before and, fortunately, reinstated. I promote her to office manager to give her a bit more clout. She is the linchpin of the operation, dealing with public agencies, guardian of the institution's memory, bully to those who are not operating effectively and first line of defence against those who come demanding money. She has an entrepreneurial streak, owns a small shop and has just built four guest rooms. Her knowledge of the Bible, theology and English is greater than that of most of the clergy.

Teaching Mintamir is a welcome rest from struggles with other staff. We wrestle with the difference between history and myth. There is an odd moment when she says that Jesus and Paul regard music as sinful. It turns out that 'carousing' is translated as 'music' in the Amharic Bible. We wonder what other mistranslations there might be. And how loud and off-key one has to be to be guilty of carousing. You have many questions, she remarks, as though this might be a problem.

In his debriefing Sam complains about the inefficiency of local bureaucrats and the unreliability of the six guards who give 24hr cover. Do we need guards? All organisations, local and international, have them. It gives employment and is supposed to prevent theft. Our guards have demanded to be armed. One applicant for the job, when asked how he would deal with an intruder replied, 'I would kill him. I would kill him'. There's commitment for you!

In one corner of the site is the Chapel, nearing completion, with workmen plastering the walls, which are half-height so air can blow through under the thatched roof, or did.

At around 11.30am, three days after our arrival, we are alerted to a brush fire on neighbouring land. As the wind is blowing away from us there does not seem to be any danger. Vegetation around the Chapel is dampened. Unfortunately a corner of the roof catches fire and within minutes flames are shooting twenty feet into the air.

Everyone is solemn as they slowly troop back to the main buildings. Sam blames himself for not having foreseen the possibility that this might happen. It is not for nothing that the government insists roofs should be of tin. Sam wants to report the incident to Addis but the mobile phone network and internet are down, and the land line is not working. (This sort of blackout can last for days.) The electricity supply cable drips plastic. A perimeter light is a molten mess. (These lights never work again.) By 7.45pm a gale is blowing. Wind direction has changed and it is now coming from the town. We can see the red glow of a fire in the distance. Julia and I are driven to a hotel, a place of safety.

Telephone and electricity poles smoulder. One is on fire. As we pass it splits in two, the upper half bouncing, as if on a trampoline, amid an eruption of sparks.

We return in the morning. The slaughter house opposite, usually home to vultures and an ugly brand of stork, is deserted. On our side, where fire has laid waste to the vegetation, horns and jawbones litter the landscape. How the Israelites could have imagined that the smell of burnt sacrifices was a sweet fragrance in the nostrils of the Almighty I cannot imagine.

The electricity supply is extremely unreliable so we have a generator. I spot Mintamir standing on five concrete blocks disconnecting a bundle of wires from the mains and attaching them to it. If the power came back on she could be electrocuted. I am amazed that there is not a proper control switch. Sam shrugs. He seems to think I'm being fussy.

There comes a day when the power really plays up. I shut down the laptop; the lights dim. Outside I see the power lines by the radio mast showering sparks. The power stops. Then it comes back with a bang. The fluorescent tube hums like a hyperventilating bee, the lights flare, the fans double their speed and smoke rises from the TV set. I pull out the plug. Touching the satellite box I get an electric shock. Finally I find that the transformer for my laptop has blown. Now, as Mintamir's computer is bust, we are without internet access. The nearest laptop transformer is in Nairobi.

My number two, Darash, is an Anuak Deacon. The Anuak claim Gambella as theirs. Those who came as refugees from Sudan were Baptists. There being no Baptist church here they joined the Anglicans. Their priest in Gambella is Girma. I try to teach him how to take a communion service but he keeps reverting to the hymn sandwich. After we return to the UK his name is discovered fixed to a government office door, which accounts for his spasmodic attendance at clergy meetings. His house is packed with electronic equipment bought with money meant for new congregations. He is dismissed.

Darash, the real leader of the Anuak church community, keeps his head down. He must have known what Girma was up to but said nothing. His position is strong because he is related to the region's President. He runs the Health Project and the Women's Literacy Project but is a failure as a manager because he needs to be liked. What is clear from talking with him is that members of staff have made little input into, or impact on the objectives we pursue. Funders have their priorities and fundees go after the money. In general there is a preference for bricks and mortar, and for short-term projects that are likely to have measurable outcomes.

Darash cannot answer my question, What is this Centre for? An influx of refugees from Sudan began in 1996. Wood, mud and straw churches were built in Gambella town and Pinyidu refugee camp. Numbers increased and in 2004 five Gambellans were ordained. In 2006 a theological extension training programme was introduced.

The theological training material is dispiriting. Do the Nuer really need to know about Henry VIII? (And how do you pronounce 'VIII'?) 'When Christ said: "go ye therefore, and teach all nations"...he commanded his apostles to bring glad tidings, not a theology.' (Simone Weil: *Letter to a Priest.*)

Numbers grew. Bishop Mouneer procured the site for the centre from the Gambella President. Plans were drawn up and submitted to Irish Aid via CMS Ireland by Bishop Andrew.

Despite being rich in natural resources, Gambella remains one of the most under-developed and poverty-ridden areas in Ethiopia. It is a flat, swampy and hot area with a high incidence of malaria, water-borne diseases and tuberculosis. The area is food insecure for 4 months of the year due to annual flooding and drought. About 35% of the population live below subsistence level, and only 15.9% of the population have access to potable water supply. 90% of the population of the region is rural, and the main industry is subsistence farming.

The Centre would be a response to this. However, the three environmental elements in the original proposal – water conservation, solar energy and a gas plant – were all dropped because of cost. In favour of what? Guest rooms for eight, a canteen for a hundred, a latrine block with showers (useful for sports) that needs constant maintenance, a library to seat 250, a training room, a residence, an office block and a basketball/volleyball court.

How will this plant meet the development needs of the area? The Health Project and the Women's Literacy Project could be run from a small office in town. Some of the land could be used for demonstration agriculture, but that does not justify the buildings.

Nevertheless, we have to get the plant up and running.

The Guest block, canteen and training room are nearly ready. The shower and toilet block, the first to be 'finished', has never been fully operational because of unintentional misuse. Angelo, the RC bishop in Gambella, jokes that when the Catholics build, the first building to go up is the church. When the Anglicans build it is the latrines.

I soon realize that high maintenance costs are on the cards. Doors are distorting and mosquito screens are coming away because metalwork is rusting. To flush our toilet the top has to be taken off and the works operated by hand. The seat is broken.

In the library, which is badly lit, only two of the 250 seats are occupied. There is a problem with the roof. Apparently the contractor deviated from the architect's plans. There are no current school text books. They are being printed in India but the Centre is unable to obtain any.

The librarian claims the facility will not be fully used because of its distance from the town centre. We need a vehicle to fetch students. We do see an increase over the year but that is because we require those using the sports facilities – volleyball, basketball and football – to hold library cards. It is still never more than half full.

The ten machines for the computer room have not arrived. They weren't going to be ordered until the site is secure. When they do come there are queues. Disks and storage devices are confiscated to prevent viruses from being imported. There is no internet access. I load the computers with learning programmes and remove the games.

Mintamir gives her first computer lesson. The twenty-eight takers who turn up, mostly young men, are complete novices so have to be shown how to hold and move a mouse, her hand on top of theirs to guide them. I tease her about this. She doesn't care. She is chuffed at being called 'teacher'. It is reassuring to see that she has control of the class.

Dugasa, the librarian, like Mintamir, and Maeza in Head Office, is Orthodox. These are the hardest working and most honest members of staff. The others try it on, and when their fabrications and lies are exposed they just laugh.

I offer to give English lessons to some of the girls but Dugasa tells me that they are not happy to walk out from the town. We should build a library in the town, they say. My offer would only be acceptable if transport is provided. I suggest we pay half the *bajaj* fare, and that works. But the girls are right. Why was this library built? There is already a decent one in the town, permanently shut because the government cannot afford to pay staff. Why did we not consider putting our two librarians there?

My first English class gathers. We explore the difference between 'May I', 'Can I' and 'Shall I'. In pairs they have to work up a little drama. Then I baffle them with 'I was bored so I bored a hole in the board', 'I saw the saw had made a sore on his arm', and 'I knew well I was well because of the new well'. At least it convinced them that they had something to learn. There are eight girls, all bright, who have to be persuaded not to shield their mouths with a hand. Most are Highlanders whose parents value education and speak some English. Their aspiration is university and a profession.

Some weeks later Darash and Dugasa drop in with the exam results of this English group. All except one (who was pregnant) are at the top of their classes. By June I have five

English groups on three days a week, two in the morning and three in the afternoon.

We need to appoint a site manager because the one who got the job is now in prison. The runner-up in the site manager race, Pel, gets the job.

Pel the Patience Tester spends hours at his desk making lists, with short excursions to chase up the guards. He is responsible for water. Because cement is still being made a lot is being used. The float valve in the cistern is bust so the tank has to be replenished each morning by turning on the stop cock. There is enough in it for several days but the mains supply is not reliable so a daily top-up is mandatory. For a few days Pel undertakes the task. Then he forgets and on several occasions we are without and have to buy river water that comes by donkey cart in 5 gallon yellow plastic containers. He looks up from his list-making, hurt that anyone should think he is to blame. Routine is an alien concept.

On the last Sunday in February 2011 there is a great gathering as Bishops Mouneer and Andrew arrive for an Ordination service. We look on while the five deacons who are to be priested are put through their paces by the two bishops, their paces being assent to the Thirty-Nine Articles, the Creeds and the Book of Common Prayer in language which is difficult for them to pronounce, let alone understand. It all seems oddly out of place.

Bishop Mouneer, a medical doctor, holds a clinic for mothers and children and makes himself late for supper at which he quizzes the new priests about the initiation rituals their tribes put them through. The Nuer have six scars across the forehead, each with a meaning. The process is painful. By comparison, Christian baptism and ordination seem somewhat wishy-washy.

The annual Assembly of Anglican churches in Ethiopia follows. The reading for the day is the story of Jacob and the children he has by Rachel, Leah, Bilhah and Zilpah (Gen. 39.21-) and the bishops are on red, or perhaps purple, alert. They have been campaigning for monogamy – one priest was unfrocked for having more than one wife – and Bishop Mouneer is soon on his feet pitting Adam and Eve against Jacob and his harem.

The monogamy issue is a tough one. If a man's father dies he takes his mother in. If a brother dies he takes in his sister-in-law whose status becomes that of 'wife'. Does this mean there is a physical relationship between them? I am never sure, so I resist reporting these cases to Bishop Mouneer because we have no reasonable alternative to offer. Who would care for widows?

with Bishop Mouneer at Gambella

In an afternoon service Julia and I are commissioned. Bishop Mouneer declares that I have authority over the local clergy in matters pastoral and spiritual, but asking for money will be useless as I won't have any. With the departure of Andrew in the offing there are expressions of sadness. They are losing a father. Yes, I say, but with my arrival you are gaining a grandfather. There is much laughter.

After his ordination David, the only pastor ministering to the Opo people, is so moved by the ceremony that he decides there and then to give up his good government job to be a full-time priest.

The Opo have no Bible, though one is in the early stages of translation. Just how basic David's understanding of Christianity is becomes clear when, after we have left, one of the boys in his village falls out of a tree and dies. The community is traumatised and their faith challenged. They had understood that life was everlasting, that Jesus had defeated death. And now a boy is dead. (The new bishop has had to respond to this.)

The visitors depart leaving a large group of clergy hungry for material goods. Will we manage to parry their pleading?

Peter Kuel, deaf to bishop-talk, is quick off the mark with a request for money. His letter, coming before him, has greetings that would have made St Paul proud. After a request for a TV, DSTV, choir uniforms, generator, church roof, and a Mothers Union literacy programme, then this:

> For the challenges in our area the problem come from the Murle tribe so that they invaded us and loot cows and they took one child. We request our office to build our centre with a concrete because we are in the heart of the Nuer zone.

I'm not sure how building with concrete will deter cattle raiders but, in any case, as both bishops made quite clear, I have no money to give out for anything. They will get the MU literacy programme, which is being rolled out by Darash.

The clergy cannot understand why we are being so mean. We have erected and equipped these buildings at huge expense. We have laptops and indulge ourselves in luxury foods and air travel. Even though I am being paid at local rates, and we are apparently the only ex-pats who shop in the local market and cook for ourselves, we are perceived as being wealthy. And because we have medical insurance that can fly us back to the UK; because we can move on if the going gets tough; because we have a network of friends who could help us, we are indeed wealthy.

What I also can do nothing about is the difference in knowledge and understanding, especially technical knowledge. My skills set me apart. I can start the generator (usually), get a computer going, put batteries and a memory card in a camera, mend a light switch, and understand the accounts, all small tasks that seem to baffle other male members of staff.

The Indian development project that we were promoting when I was at Christian Action was one 'which grows on Indian soil and which engenders its own basic ongoing funds'. I still believe that this is the proper way for development to proceed. It will be slower but firmly rooted.

Another letter describes difficulties between two clergy. I talk it through with Darash. It is an ongoing situation with which Bishop Andrew tried to deal. Darash says Westerners don't understand the cultural niceties of such situations. There are a lot of difficulties between clergy, often because they belong to different tribal/family groups. I must tread carefully and take advice.

When the generator is stolen we call the police who have to be paid 1,000 birrs for the investigation and 1,000 birrs for the engine's return. The blame for its loss is put firmly on the guards. Pel fines the two guards who were on, or supposed to be on duty, 500 birrs and gives them a written final warning.

The second time the generator is stolen – passed through the window of the locked guards' room – the police, in response to a call by Darash to the Police Commissioner, arrest all the guards in the belief that the criminals must have had an inside contact. The officer says he will provide police to guard the place but we will have to pay them. I reply with a little white lie: I need the agreement of Addis for this and head office won't be open until Monday. I don't want the police guarding us with guns.

I phone Darash. His call to the Commissioner has led to this over-reaction. He must sort it out. The guards are released after two hours. The generator is recovered and the police require 1,000 birr 'tea money' to release it. Perhaps they have their tea at the Hilton in Addis. In Addis this sort of extortion would not happen. Here, also, such a demand can be reported and the police would be forced to retract. But, because they are almost a law to themselves, no one wants to alienate them.

A police commander, in white t-shirt, appears with a side-kick. He is furious. They intend to take Mintamir into custody for giving him a bad name by raising questions about the 1,000 birr he has demanded for dealing with the generator. Darash and Pel talk him down and I produce the cash. Philip, a literacy trainer, tells me that when he worked in government in Itang he came across these two and they are dangerous. Mintamir seems quite prepared to take them on but is restrained.

THE RELIGIOUS BIT

Each day begins with Morning Prayer, recited in mother tongues. The day Elizabeth, our Nuer cleaner, leads it the Nuer come alive. They sing the Kyrie with great gusto. Orthodox Mintamir is fascinated that Julia and I know the Greek.

It is quite a relief to be in a society where cynicism is alien, where it is possible to talk about faith and spirituality in an ordinary, down-to-earth way. Morning Prayer, rattled off in three or four languages, might be Babel in miniature. Or it might be Pentecost. The jumble of sounds puts credal statements in perspective. We are participating in a ritual in which words cease to be important. What is important in this culture is to build a relationship. So the morning greeting can be quite a lengthy exchange. One of the Mothers Union coordinators tries to teach it to me. I get about three-quarters of the way through when she claps her hands and collapses in laughter. Every time I try! The morning service is a form of greeting. We are getting ourselves onto the same wavelength, with each other and with the divine.

The clergy come in once a month for their pay and I organize a study session. We explore Mark's Gospel. There are two centres of power, the Wilderness and the Temple. Jesus retreats into the wilderness to pray. Prayer is preparation for action. Prayer without action is just empty words. Michael Anya, one of the brightest of the clergy and our sole member of the Dinka tribe, interrupts with Adam and Eve and 'original sin'. I point out that the Jews never interpreted the Adam and Eve story in this way. I treat them to a dose of Irenaeus. (The Orthodox Church subscribes to the Irenaean interpretation.) God makes humanity to be master of the earth, but this can only happen when humanity has attained adulthood. We are led astray because we are immature. We are made in God's image right from the start and strive to attain his likeness throughout our lives. Jesus shows us what is possible.

At another session I speak of the importance of silence and how we each have to find and cultivate the place of silence within us. At the heart of the universe there is a great silence. Music comes out of silence. The spiritual life is built on silence. Having a place of silence helps us to deal with anger, both ours and that of others, and I give a couple of personal examples. I suggest they might try concentrating on the breath. They might light a candle to act as a focus and a calming influence. It is a short session, no more than twenty minutes, but it has been quite intense and we break up more quietly than usual.

I share with them a wonderful description of faith in *Christianity Rediscovered*. The Missionary Vincent Donovan found that the Masai word he was using for *faith* meant *to agree to*. He talks to an elder who says that 'to believe' like that is similar to a white hunter shooting an animal with his gun at a great distance. Only his eyes and his fingers take part in the act.

> ...for a man really to believe is like a lion going after its prey. His nose and eyes and ears pick up the prey. His legs give him the speed to catch it. All the power of his body is involved in the terrible death leap and single blow to the neck with the front paw, the blow that actually kills. And as the animal goes down the lion envelops it in his arms (Africans refer to the front legs of an animal as its arms) pulls it to himself, and makes it part of himself. This is the way a lion kills. This is the way a man believes. This is what faith is.

This raises for me the issue of translating Bible passages in cultural terms. Do the Nuer and Anuak have stories into which we might tap? Perhaps my question is not understood for I get only 'Christian' answers. Nevertheless, were I here for the long haul I would want to develop Nuer and Anuak liturgies.

In January 2012 I organize a four-day conference to address issues common to clergy in all denominations. Each of our clergy invites two clergy from other churches. Thirty-eight attend. 'Peace building and reconciliation work are part and parcel of the tasks that Christ demands of the Church' claims one of the speakers, in defiance of the Government's ban on addressing Peace issues. The conference is in the hands of the priests and pastors themselves. They both plan and teach.

'Conflict' is one of the main themes: 'the nature of conflict, causes of conflict, conflict management, conflict transformation, conflict resolution, reconciliation, peace building and cultural approaches to managing conflicts. Attention is given to how Church leaders should handle conflict and division within their congregations.' This is the first time that members of different churches have addressed common problems together, and it gives them quite a buzz, leading to calls for more of the same.

The compound of the Nuer church of St Luke's, on the other side of town, is shaded by trees, the earth completely free of rubbish. I have been invited in the hope that I will give them money for the new roof and new choir robes.

The Gospel reading is the 'Temptations in the Wilderness'. I preach. Jesus is not tempted by the Devil to do anything bad, he is not tempted to break any of the commandments. He is tempted to do what is second-best instead of what is best. He is tempted to turn stones into bread. It is good to have bread. We all need bread or *injeera*. We need it to keep us going. But we need it every day. And the daily intake of food doesn't prevent us from shrivelling up with age. Spiritual food is different. Each dose lasts. So the more spiritual food we have the more spiritual we become. While the body shrinks, the spirit grows.

Then there is the political temptation: look at the leaders of Egypt, Libya, Tunisia, Algeria (all in the diocese!). They might have become politicians with the best of intentions. But power corrupts, and they begin to think of themselves as being above the law. They become dictators. Jesus rejects that way of bringing about change. I hope Stephen, *dictateur extraordinaire*, is marking and learning.

After the service we all shake hands. I am impressed by the fact that this really is a community church. The MU prays on Tuesday and practises songs on Saturday from 1-3pm. They also visit homes, the prison and the hospital. Members pay tithes. Income exceeds expenditure for the year by 1,010 birr (£40), 10% of the budget.

An hour later Julia and I are at the Baro Hotel talking about polio vaccines and development with Dr Trish, an American who is inspecting clinics in the region. About half are staffed. Refrigeration is a problem. Most units run on kerosene, which is not always available. There are solar-powered units, but she has found only one in working order because of a lack of maintenance.

We talk about our Anglican Centre. It feels too Western, especially after our visit to St Luke's. 'Pyramid Fixation' snaps Trish, apropos development agencies. People put up large, inappropriate buildings as a tribute to themselves, their Organisation, their Government. Bricks-and-mortar we can do; three-year projects we can do; long-term support for upkeep and administration is a no-goer.

There are success stories. The Norwegians managed to change farming practices in another part of Ethiopia but it was with a twenty-year programme. The Fistula Hospital, founded by Drs. Catherine and Reg Hamlin, who came from Australia in 1959, makes a significant contribution to women's health. They spent their working lives developing it. We also have one success story.

THE HEALTH PROGRAMME

Twelve of the twenty people working on the health project in Gambella town meet with Darash and me to report on progress. For three months they have been teaching basic hygiene in the *kebele* (neighbourhood wards) and encouraging people to build latrines. We find teaching in the home to be the most effective way of changing behaviour.

There are problems. Some *kebele* don't have tools, some can't afford wooden poles (it is illegal to cut wood); some live in poor areas with few men to do the labouring and need a public latrine. I ask Darash to cost tools and public latrines. I have a possible solution to the wood problem. Can he source bamboo?

This health programme is a success. 3,000 households have been covered. We will run it out again for another 3,000. It receives high praise at a regional health conference.

Toilet frame

Three months later Darash and I meet with the health workers to hear the final report of the Health Project. 7,200 families have been taught about hygiene. Ten per cent of the households without latrines have now built them. I would like, but fail, to find a funder for the building of latrines above ground. Because they require cement they are much more expensive.

A WAY FORWARD

Darash, Alemayehu and Julia return from a Tear Fund conference in Kenya. Darash reports to the monthly clergy meeting on development that has taken place in rural communities there, a scheme called 'Umoja'. It begins with Bible study. It involves all the churches working together. They study what it means to be the light, the salt, the yeast of the world. The people dream, they share their dreams, then they prioritize their dreams. No money comes from outside. The people themselves do the developing. They have built fish ponds. They have built stone churches. They have given their clergy cars. Julia remarks that it is the city clergy who get cars, not those in the villages. Darash must have been listening to a bishop boasting on a bus. I hope it won't be of Toyotas that our clergy dream.

Women develop small businesses, and some of the clergy make money on the side. I fancy that we have found a way of involving the clergy in development, the sort of development I have always had in mind.

We begin to implement Umoja and a training session is organised. Julia shows a film about it. Then Darash makes a lively speech in Anuak, translated into Nuer by a policewoman from Lare. The women laugh when he describes how, since he learnt about Umoja, he has started growing crops and keeping chickens. At New Year others were buying hens to kill and eat; he was buying them for their eggs. He has the use of some of our land which he plants and tends with enthusiasm.

THE LITERACY PROGRAMME

Darash downloads a training document for his Women's Literacy Programme that his team of four who train the women who teach it, are required to translate into Nuer and Anuak. I am amazed that an organization concerned with the development of basic literacy skills should be using such high-flown language.

How about this? 'What are the particular chosen colors thought to be appealing to the intended audience and free from unwanted connotations or problematic significance?' I translate this into plain English: 'What colours do your students like? What colours do they dislike? Do these colours mean anything?'

Two Trainers are Nuer and two are Anuak. The work does not get done because they are hardly literate in their own language.

Why have we not got literate interpreters? Darash says we are not paying enough. None of the four is up to the job.

The best form of defence is attack, they think. I receive a letter complaining about pay and threatening resignation. I accept their resignations, which takes them quite by surprise. A meeting, attended by Alemayehu, lasts two hours. They want a 'hardship allowance' like government employees. They are much better off than they would be with a 'hardship allowance', says Alemayehu. They don't understand the maths, can't calculate 10%, and don't know the difference between gross and net salary.

One of the Trainers, Philip, has AIDS and leaves to live with his grandmother in Kenya. I am sorry to see him go as he has written both words and music of the hymns sung by the Anuaks and I had hoped to try and find funding for a recording. A second, Tuach, leaves to go to university. The other two, Kim and Ochang, I plan to make redundant. By now Pel has had his marching orders and seems fairly confident that he can get another job, probably with the Education Bureau as he is a trained teacher (which is not saying much.)

Kim and Ochang can't get beyond the idea that a two-year contract is inviolable. The fact that we will have no money to pay them after March seems not to register. We are, after all, the Anglican Church, the equivalent in their minds of a gold mine.

Contracts are not set in concrete. The Government Proclamation requires that, if a contract has to be curtailed, they receive the equivalent of two months' pay as a parting gift. That is why Kim and Ochan have to leave at the end of January. The money for them runs out at the end of March, so the February and March money is their 'parting gift'. We cannot leave our successors without funds to pay them.

Mintamir is told to translate a sheet of Amharic text, embossed with purple stamps and it sends her into a fury, further inflamed by a similar letter from Pel. They have been to the Bureau of Labour and Social Affairs to claim that we owe them a year's salary. We have a day in which to put our side of the story. I write the letter which Mintamir translates. The Administrator at Don Bosco (the RC school and training project) confirms that we are acting within the law. What seems to irritate our literacy pair is that I am not fazed by their antics. But I am disappointed in Darash, their manager, who is distancing himself from what is going on.

Julia phones from Addis. Bishop Mouneer is worried for me over the court case. What court case? It later emerges that someone has been stirring it and upgraded my disagreement with Kim and Ochan to a court battle. There is a court involved, but it is the Bureau's own appeal procedure which is called a 'court'.

I go with Mintamir to the Bureau. We are told we must honour the pair's contracts.

We present a letter to the Bureau staff. The official holds it inches from his face, his eyes screwed up, his mouth turned down, as he examines it. From the ensuing discussion is appears that they do not understand what I have written or what I am saying. They won't listen to Mintamir as she is only a woman. We will have to take the matter to the Bureau's court on Thursday.

I hire a lawyer. He is young, energetic, and reassuring. We have done everything right. The Bureau usually finds for the employee and not the employer and we may have to go to the Supreme Court who will pass it down to the local high court and there the decisions of the Bureau are usually overturned. He shows me the passage in the relevant Proclamation that supports our case.

I try to reason with Kim who says that it is not about money. If we wanted to keep them we could find the money or give them another job. What job? But then he adds that even if they were offered jobs, they wouldn't accept them. He says they were given no warning. I look up my notes. On July 29th we met with Seleshie, who trains them, and discussed funding. They were told that we have no secure funding after the end of March. He said they should seek funding from Ethiopian sources. They were too busy arguing about *per diems* and chalk for this to have sunk in.

For the final meeting eight people are crammed into a tiny room made smaller by the presence of two large desks. It has the usual run-down feel of a government office. Most of the business is conducted in Amharic. Occasionally the chairman will tell or ask me something in English. He says we should give the pair three months' severance pay, not two. Will I agree to the three months? I agree. The three months must include the hardship allowance plus holiday entitlement and Provident Fund money. Agreed. He makes it clear that this is not a judgement but an act of conciliation. Kim and Ochan accept the terms, but I can't tell whether or not this is with a good grace. Pel pipes up, but is shut down by the chairman. He has no case.

The end of the Kim and Ochan saga is nigh. Mintamir sorts Ochan's Provident Account, which the bank had attributed to someone else. She has prepared a statement of what we owe them. It is not enough. They walk off leaving their documents on my desk. The end is no longer as nigh as I thought it was. Half-an-hour later Mintamir hoovers up these same documents. They have agreed to accept our offer after all. I give Pel the same deal.

MOTHERS UNION AND DEVELOPMENT

I am at the airport to meet two Mothers Union representatives. There is only one white face among the arrivals but she looks too young. Sarah Jupe is only twenty-five, not a mother, not married, not an Anglican but an evangelical Lutheran (father German, mother Finnish) belonging to one of the new churches. With her is Salome from Nairobi, a Masai grandmother, bought by her husband for five cows, a fixed rate in her tribe, who is an experienced and travelled speaker and a friend of bishops. She is both a mother and an Anglican.

Salome and Sarah have an interesting morning with our MU members. They have never before, in the Congo, Kenya or the Sudan, encountered a group with such a low level of education and self-esteem. Sarah will try and find training for our three women coordinators.

Salome says that the Masai sometimes describe God as male 'of all colours' and sometimes as female 'of all colours'. Salome's father is a Masai chief and she carries that air of authority. The Masai leap high in the air when they dance. Her demonstration causes consternation among the senior mothers. They depart with a promise to arrange further training for the MU.

Discussions take place in Addis with MU representatives from London about the women's literacy project and agreement is reached to use the experience and skills learned in the MU's South Sudanese programme. Their workers are much more sensitive to harnessing women's interests and, more importantly, their material is based on the Nuer and related languages, not Amharic. This will replace Darash's Women's Literacy Programme and be much less expensive.

In February, before we depart, three women trainers arrive from South Sudan and begin training twenty-four women,

300

representatives from each of the parishes. It is well-received and a new support system is put in place. A further course is arranged. We trust we have laid the foundations for an increase in women's literacy in Gambella and hope that the Umoja programme will link up with these women's literacy groups.

Julia and I are invited to celebrate Christmas 2011 at the Mission Centre in Pinyidu (Pinyudo) Refugee Camp near the South Sudan border. To call Pinyidu a 'camp', however, conjures up the wrong sort of image. There is no perimeter fence and the only indication that we are approaching, or even entering it, is a UNHCR sign that records the annual development in hectares from about sixty in 1994 to over twelve hundred in 2011. We have had to obtain permission to visit from ARRA, the Ethiopian refugee agency, but no one checks our credentials.

With us are Mintamir and the Revd. Isaac Pur, the Nuer Missioner who will interpret for me. In the back we have large sacks of second-hand clothes and shoes, six benches and a desk. Also a large quantity of sweets.

The area is wooded. A couple of young deer dart away from us. We pass tukuls with clay walls and grass roofs that look as if they have been here forever. The Anglican church compound is not hard to find. Outside it an all-age crowd bearing a bedsheet-sized banner greets us with a song. In the office, built around two trees, one of them sprouting leaves through the roof, we are treated to the traditional washing of feet.

There are about 9,000 Nuer and 11,000 Anuak refugees from Sudan in this camp. We are surrounded by young people and kids, dressed in their best for Christmas. These have all been born here. The Revd. Paul Pok, our host, says they are a worry to the adults for they do not observe Nuer ways, by which I think he means that they do not respect their elders. Might it not be hard, I ask, to respect parents who have no meaningful occupation? Who cannot be role models? A novel chord seems to have been struck.

Mid-afternoon, when the sun starts to turn down the heat, we bring up the rear of a procession that follows the banner, four drummers and three ranks of Mothers Union members in white dresses with dark blue sashes, to march through the settlement. We cross the paths of three other church groups processing in the same way.

To us the food here may not be that special, but that is because we do not subsist on rations of flour, oil and sugar, distributed in larger quantities than necessary so that some can be traded in the town and vegetables bought. There is also fresh milk from cows given by UNHCR. The *masala chai* we are offered is a treat for those of us who have been making do with powdered milk.

We have made a large donation for the purchase of provisions. Over the two days we are offered substantial pieces of fried river fish, cracked wheat with soft cheese, and chicken. I am treated to the twin thighs of a cockerel that was nearly snatched by a dog as it awaited its fate by the fire. I wrestle with the muscle.

she has spotted the sweets

Christmas Eve: the compound is packed with worshippers from several churches for a two-and-a-half hour service that ends at midnight. It includes a nativity play. When he discovers Mary is pregnant Joseph drags her at high speed three times round the ring. Her birthing cries are very realistic. There are no Wise Men. The Massacre of the Innocents is acted out with energy.

In the morning we move to another church compound where over two thousand members of twelve denominations are gathered, their choirs robed in bright nylon colours. This is my big moment. For forty minutes of the four-hour service I preach. Fortunately I have had plenty experience of working with an interpreter and Isaac and I find a natural rhythm.

In the afternoon Paul celebrates Holy Communion in his church. Most were Christians before they left Sudan and their religion holds them together as they wait to return home. How long will that be? When the guns are off the streets. How long will that be? The Ethiopian government reckons about five years. I sent one of our clergy to Sudan to investigate and he thought that some might be escorted back in the New Year.

This Christmas is quite different from the one we would have had in a cold Hartland. I am struck by a common factor shared with our hosts. We are all of us strangers in a foreign land.

Bishop Maurice, who was Archbishop of South America, a gentle and unassuming Englishman, is sent by Bishop Mouneer to take a Confirmation service and to sound out interested parties about what is required of the new bishop.

He uses the 'Man is the Head of the Woman' argument of the Evangelical Right, against the ordination of women. He regards homosexuality as a curable condition. He knows people who have been healed. Julia tries to hide her astonishment. We agree that the new bishop should live in Gambella, not Addis.

On Sunday Mintamir arrives at 7am with an elderly minibus and a young driver. We are ready with robes and cameras so set off for a Confirmation service at Lare, a two-hour journey. Three times we are held fast in mud. Bishop Maurice gets out to help push.

As a result we arrive at Lare mud-laden and an hour-and-a-half late. There are fifty-two, mostly adults, on the confirmation list. Seven are absent because of the weather. The church is packed and there is no reduction in the enthusiasm and energy of singers and drummers.

After the service we are given soft drinks, and spaghetti with a meat sauce. Our interpreter, a lecturer at the college in Gambella, who is here to monitor students on placement, is surprised to learn that spaghetti is an Italian dish. He thought that, like macchiato, it is Ethiopian. He tells me, with some glee, that when the rains really arrive, the water comes over the tops of the boots. The bishop's and my shoes are returned to us beautifully cleaned and polished.

The road has dried out somewhat, so there is just the occasional skid to keep us alive to the impermanence of life. When we are nearly in Gambella we are halted by a policeman with a rifle who steps out from behind a parked truck. We cannot enter the town on this road. We have to go back and come in by another way where a team is searching vehicles. We do not have enough fuel to do that. After a lot of fruitless argument Mintamir takes over and demands to speak to the policemen's boss on their mobile. He tells them to let us through.

Maurice has brought a letter from Bishop Mouneer for the Regional President, Omot Obang. Double-O One wears a sharp, light grey suit and rimless spectacles. He is surprisingly young. I hand him the letter of invitation. We watch in silence as he slowly peruses it. We are not privy to its contents. 'December!' he exclaims with distaste. The letter is an invitation from Mouneer to visit Cairo. Darash counts on his fingers. That is seven months away. 'I have training in December. July or August would be better.' The ground is thoroughly worked over and Maurice agrees to convey the message to Mouneer: July or August it will be.

Double-O One wants to know about the situation in Cairo. Is there much violence? Having been there recently for diocesan synod I reassure him. Two churches were set on fire but the trouble is local. Don't mention the proposed Ethiopian damning of the Nile, I suggest, half in jest. He becomes serious and political. Egypt has always been friendlier with outside nations. Now they must be friendly with Africa.

Maurice utters hardly a word. I get in a couple, but they may not have been heard. Suddenly there is a change in tone. 'You must get Darash a scholarship,' he tells me. He himself has an Open University degree. After twenty-five precious minutes we are ushered out.

Darash has a diploma in management. He would like a degree, but OU courses are expensive. The government only grants scholarships to high officials, and Darash isn't in government. Being a relative of the President is not, apparently, enough. We'll have to see what can be done.

Bishop Bill and his wife Hilary come to us from Tunis for another Confirmation. They are such congenial guests that we visit them in Tunis in 2012. In Pilwal we have our service under the tree. It is pleasantly cool. It gets me thinking. Services could be held outside for at least eight months of the year. For the other four months village congregations could have house churches or some other pattern that does not require a large building.

FOOD SECURITY

Hamidu, the UN man responsible for coordination, drops by. We discuss the food situation. I see no reason why there should be a recurring food shortage along the banks of the Baro river, except that it does not seem to be used for irrigation. He agrees. He visited a small farmer whose crop, in a field that lay alongside the river, was dying through lack of water. The man couldn't be bothered to get a bucket.

Bamboo is on my mind – we are planting it with the help of the research station next door – and I catalogue its benefits to the economy. We need a bamboo drive.

Two days later Hamidu calls a meeting. Fifteen agency representatives gather and we start almost on time. This is obviously serious. The Federal Government has agreed to supply food aid to 62,000 people for four months from September. But it will only be maize; no oil this year. Gambella should be food sufficient. The discussion focuses on what is needed to make it so.

Farmers plant their crops at the beginning of the rainy season. These are washed out when the river floods. At the end of the season they will plant a second crop but they have no more seed so they turn to the government to provide it. The government then comes to the agencies for help. We are given the seed distribution list for planting at the end of October. I don't know why they bother with the first crop as it consistently fails. They would then have the seed. Will the Bureau recover from the farmers the seed that they are going to be given?

I am taken aback by the reaction. What a good idea! Franz from ZOA is on board immediately. They will run with this. Why hasn't it been done before? I imagine it is because the agencies are all geared up to disaster emergencies and famine relief and not to long-term planning. Bureau officials do not want to do the work.

Funders are much more likely to respond positively if they can see a long-term strategy for improving the situation. These things must be included in the document, if only briefly, which I offer to edit. It won't be hard to improve the English. The title is an earful: *Enhancing food security in the Gambella region through the provision of improved seed in flood recession farming, together with proposals for making the region food secure.* The 'proposals' bit is my addition. 'Flood recession farming' is an odd phrase. It means farming when the water has receded, from the end of September to January. Hamidu texts: 'Gone thru doc. U captured every bit of info needed to sell project to interested partners & donors. tk u very much.' He faxes it to his bosses in Addis.

Was the flood recession farming programme successful? Julia and I had left before the results became known. Hamidu, also, had been moved. Who will stay put for twenty years?

OTHER

Good Friday is overcast, the sky lightening in the West, with a slight breeze. We have had our porridge and I sit on the porch in the relative quiet, for we can do without the generator for a while and enjoy the bird chatter. I fetch the bird book and binoculars and identify the two pairs that are hopping hopefully over the damp earth a few feet away as red-cheeked cordon-bleus.

To the side of the house a squadron of yellow and black African citrils, in scavenging mode, flits through the scrub. I think I identify a yellow-spotted Petronia. I can't identify the small, nondescript, grey birds in the middle distance. This is no day off for these nervy tots who, when a grey-headed sparrow lands among them, scatter and fly flippity flip, flippity flip. A solitary laughing dove explores the ground at a steady pace and with a steady intensity, ignoring the activity around it. High above, the hunters glide on currents of air. Six vultures perch on the top of a tree overlooking the slaughter yard. They make no contribution to the tree choir, now joined by amplified chant from the town.

A charcoal black, orange-headed lizard chases a fawn one, a pursuit with its own rules: six hasty paces forward, halt for press-ups, another six paces, another halt.

It is in this congregation of birds and lizards that I make my Good Friday meditation. It is St Francis in reverse – the birds preach to me. They bring to mind the Sermon on the Mount: don't worry about what to eat or what to wear. They feed without complaining about their limited diet; they are beautiful without dressing like Solomon.

Those who know Africa will understand that there are colours and an atmosphere to be found nowhere else. Vegetation ranges from the lush to the sun-sapped. We have planted lots of trees, including mangoes. The bananas have already produced their first crop.

One of my last acts is to close the office and guest house in Addis Ababa. It is too large, too expensive and underused. Alemayehu resigns after disagreement with the ABC and Bishop Mouneer. Maeza moves to the office at the chaplaincy.

What about the buildings? Charles, clergyman, farmer and member of the ABC and I discuss it and conclude that it should become a theological college serving Gambella and South Sudan.

Like Caroline Walker in India, I am convinced that change is necessary, but without change in national and global political and economic structures, poverty and inequality will continue to exist. As foreigners we could have no part to play in political activity in Ethiopia. 'The underlying ambivalence of our situation became apparent and we realised that only in our own country did we have a chance of being effective workers for change.' (CW)

POSTSCRIPT

The new bishop is based in Gambella, not Addis, which is an improvement. Ethiopia should become an independent diocese associated with the church in Sudan, not with the church in Cairo

Under Bishop Grant, now, there is a change of use.

Named after the first Bishop of the Church in Ethiopia, the St. Frumentius Anglican Theological College (also known as Gambella Bible College) opened in June 2015 on the grounds of the Gambella Anglican Centre. The college is initially offering a 2 year Certificate program for 20 residential students and is expected to expand in the future.

The total cost of the project is $288,680 USD of which $55,000 is still required for the chapel. It comes from outside and perpetuates a debilitating dependency.

Theological training is desperately needed. Buildings funded from outside the country, and a lot smarter than local ones, are not. I repeat what I wrote at the end of Chapter Five: 'What we should be exploring is how to be a poor church. We need to revisit Francis of Assisi: poverty is the real sacrament of seriousness.'

Chapter Thirteen

Quincecote, Cheristow

IN EARLY 80s DAYS the car journey from London to Hartland took rather longer than it does today, though getting in and out of London was somewhat speedier. Today there is a link road between the M5 and Barnstaple, and Barnstaple and Bideford. Today recently-built bridges bypass both the centre of Barnstaple and Bideford's medieval bridge, bottlenecks that thirty-five years ago could hold one up for an hour each. Driving to the West Country was an undertaking not to be embarked upon lightly. These days, however, we endure the strain of Great Western Railway trains. (They dropped the 'First' for obvious reasons.)

As, eventually, we turned off the A39 and passed through Hartland Parish – in terms of area one of the largest in England – the scenery became more severe, the landscape losing its lusciousness, the trees shrinking into dwarfitude, dwarfs that presented their backsides to the wind until, unable to bow any lower, they disappeared into the hedges, lost among bramble, holly and honeysuckle. But, ah! the sea was within sniffing distance, the smell, when not smothered by the stench of freshly-spread slurry, of phytoplankton-generated dimethyl sulphide, the fragrance of my long-departed youth.

Having decided to move to Hartland we naturally had to find somewhere to live. Because capital was modest, and income too low to repay a mortgage, we needed a wreck that we could rescue. The first property we visited, Little Barton, had been a farmhouse. The name held promise. The 'Barton' is the designation of the main farm in a settlement. Did 'Little' indicate the second-in-line? Or, less promising, did it indicate size? I puzzle in a similar way over my name. 'Hodgetts' is obviously a diminutive of 'Hodge'. Hodge is a keeper of pigs. Was the original Hodgetts small in stature, or did he keep small pigs, or perhaps just a few pigs?

We can see Little Barton across the valley now, rather more exposed to the elements than we are. When we visited, bouncing for a hundred yards down a poorly-maintained track, it had been empty for some time and, peering through the windows, it was not hard to understand why. Water lay an inch deep on a concrete floor. Anxious to see more, and without breaking door or window, we gained access. We seemed to have entered the set of some horror movie, instruments of torture scattered everywhere, for this had become the last resting place of old dental equipment, including a drill that had to be pedalled, dumped here by John Chope, the dentist, who had bought the house off the Abbey estate.

We were not surprised the estate wanted to be rid of it, and wondered what sort of landlord expected a farming family to live in these conditions. There was no inside bathroom or toilet, one weak electric bulb hung from a dodgy flex, and a general air of degeneration smothered house and barns. It had its own well, but the pump did not look promising. The outside loo lay about twenty-five yards to the side, covered in ivy, home to spiders and dead leaves. Its main interest lay in having a double-seated toilet. Had so many people lived here that they had had to crap in pairs? Or had we become privy to a peculiar Devon courting ritual?

There were numerous outbuildings in various states of decomposition, the best of them being a large barn in which I discovered several old harmoniums that added their wheezy worth to this macabre setting. This really did have the potential to spook one out. Bone-chilling, blood-curdling, skin-crawling and tooth-chattering movies could easily have been filmed here.

Despite this, we thought we might, jointly with Pete and Kirsty Rosser, some friends of ours involved in the Small School, put in an offer. We were saved: the asking price was much too high.

Our second excursion was to a cowshed and barn at Cheristow, a small hamlet to the north of the village, reputed to have been the first settlement in the parish. 'Cheristow' means 'the place of the church', and there are signs of the building in St Wenn's Acre, a neighbouring field. An Inquisition held at

'Hertilande' on June 11th 1301 lists a water mill, though where the water came from is a mystery as the single stream is modest, and when we arrived was polluted by run-off from pigs on the farm above.

The buildings we were here to inspect lay down a narrow lane which, unlike that leading to Little Barton, was tarmacked to the property though not beyond it. The only passing traffic would be tractors, muck spreaders, the occasional horse and the odd walker, though visitors using pre-war Ordinance Survey maps have arrived possessed with the belief that they could motor on. Satnavs have put a stop to that. They ignore us altogether and lead intending visitors past our turn-off to Down Farm, an upmarket spa, to the great irritation of those who run the place.

The cowshed was single-storey and L-shaped. It opened onto a small yard. The barn next to it had had two floors, but because the roof had collapsed it was protected – after a fashion – by sinusoidal, or wriggly tin: corrugated iron sheets, the victims of leprous rust. These two buildings were beautiful only in terms of their potential. I looked at them with the same sort of eye that a potter looks at a lump of clay, a sculptor a block of stone, or a knitter a ball of wool, assessing potential and envisioning a thing of beauty. Where others perceived problems I saw only promise, and it excited me.

the cowshed

Leaning on a tipsy six-bar gate we surveyed the field. The view needed no improvement. We were enraptured by a panorama that took in the tower of St Nectan's Church and the sea. This site, like that of Little Barton, was exposed to the elements but easier to shelter. We would plant trees and hedges for protection.

The Barn

The owner, John George, a local farmer, was prepared to offer land with the buildings. There was one question mark: these buildings had been on the market since February 1981 when John had been granted outline planning permission. Why had no one wanted to buy them? I discovered that a pool of water lying in the small courtyard had worried prospective purchasers. A little prodding among mud and leaves revealed a blocked drain. The only negative element was easily cleared. John accepted our offer of £13,150 for the two buildings and two acres of land and we were away, or rather, we were rapidly rooting.

Julia and I had been visiting her parents in Victoria, Canada, the previous summer. Exploring a bookshop I discovered a whole shelf of self-build books, some containing full architectural plans. I bought a couple and became infected by the enthusiasm of their authors. *House Framing* presented me with an adequate sufficiency of plans, more than 55 step-by-step construction sequences and enough information to build a dream home. I could easily see myself in shorts and steel-capped boots, with a leather oil-tanned tool pouch strapped to my waist, on the top of a ladder wielding a circular saw. I would not be wearing a hard hat. No one in the photos wears a hard hat. Such headwear is sartorially challenging – ganz inelegant! More significantly, we members of the Woodstock Nation have a laid-back attitude to protection and insurance. We like to live on the edge.

There seemed, from the photos, to be much more self-build going on in North America than here at home, possibly a consequence of less strict planning laws, but also because, across the pond, there prevails a 'can do' approach to life. Here in the UK we seem to need to place our trust in experts who, employing a stream of jargonized technological garbage, easily create a cloud of unknowing. I do my best to keep my head out of that cloud.

Yes, I truly believe that I am a 'can doer'. I suppose you surmise that I have a rather low opinion of bricklayers, plumbers, and electricians? Perhaps! You can add lawyers to the list. When selling our maisonette in Islington I persuaded Julia that we could undertake the conveyancing ourselves. Aided by a Which? handbook it proved relatively easy. However, the bank manager, an obvious 'can't doer', was taken aback when Julia appeared at the completion meeting without a solicitor.

In London we had moved to Islington before it became the up-market bailiwick of moneyed socialists because Julia's flat in the West of the city was too small for a grand piano. The estate agent had shown us a maisonette in Liverpool Road owned by a shoe designer. There was a small shop at the front that was separate from the two-floor dwelling behind. The rooms were bright, with living and bathroom floors of white tiles and walls painted in primary colours, a decorative feature that might not have been to everyone's taste. I don't know for how long the property had been empty, but with dust and webs gathering it had an unloved feel about it. It required only a little imagination to understand the potential. We offered £36,000. It was not enough.

Cycling home from work a few weeks later I called in at the estate agents. On a blackboard was scrawled 'Liverpool Road reduced to £36,000'. 'We offered that!' It was getting near closing time. I said I would hurry home and consult Julia. The agent warned me that the owner lived in France, had no phone – these were the days before mobiles – and picked up messages at the post office-cum-village shop. It might be some time before he got through to her. I rang him to confirm our offer. Ten minutes later he returned the call to tell us that our offer had been accepted. The owner had been in the shop in France when he had phoned.

We were pleased with our new purchase but the shop area was a waste of space because the only access was from the common hallway, and so it lay unused by us for some months.

Meanwhile I hired a van and picked up the Broadwood grand piano which I had bought from a former nurses' home in Essex. With a promise of beer I recruited a team of rather reluctant piano movers from the pub next-door-but-one. Despite a lot of heaving and sweating we could not manhandle the grand past the front door. It was wedged there for the weekend. The couple in the upstairs flat had to climb over it to obtain access or egress. Some things, I had to accept, can't be done, and on the Monday two professional piano movers with a trolley swivelled it through the two doorways in a matter of minutes.

Back to the shop. To incorporate it into the main part of the building I knocked out a doorway and changed the front from shop to house. When we came to sell we were marketing a two-bedroom property which earned us a bit of a profit. We could afford the site in Hartland, though we could not afford to pay builders to undertake the conversion. I would have to do most of the building work myself.

I was not completely without experience. At the Othona Community in Essex in the 70s I had built a pigsty of stone – for many years the most solid building on the site – and added a solid dairy to the wooden dining hut. And, having watched youngsters on a youth training scheme at Othona mix cement, build walls and undertake basic carpentry, I was sure I could master the arts quite quickly. If they can do it, so, surely, can I! I acquired a range of manuals to add to the books I had bought in Canada.

We needed an architect. Satish Kumar, from his time in Pembrokeshire, knew Christopher Day. Chris had converted two properties for himself. He was also involved in a parent-run Steiner school and had supervised the alterations to, and development of, the building. We went to see him and were taken by these properties. His was the philosophy of Rudolf Steiner which, simply summarized, is that square boxes made of ticky tacky result in square people who, according to the lyrics, 'all come out the same'. 'Where possible curves should replace right angles' seemed to be the marching song of the Steiner movement.

Chris agreed to draw up our plans, which he would do at the rate of £8 an hour, so we could use him as little or as much as we needed. He offered me three important principles. Firstly, a dwelling needs to appear to grow out of the landscape; secondly, think of the house as a sculpture in which to live; thirdly, when you build a house with your own hands you build yourself. Sometime later he wrote:

> A work of architecture, sculpture or painting is still only an assemblage of certain pieces of brick, timber, stone or pigment – yet their intention, given form by this assemblage, can work deep into my soul and touch my spirit so that I can recognise that in some way I will never be quite the same again – my spirit has been extended, as it were. The vibrations of music and physical movements of dance likewise remain material definitions, but can be imbued with the spirit to become art. This definition excludes much that goes under the title of art and includes much that occurs in the context of everyday life.

> Places can raise our spirits... Whatever values underlie why and how places are commissioned, planned, formed and used become embedded in them. This is embodied spirit. It's not normally visible. Indeed, only rarely are we conscious of it, but subliminally everyone 'reads' these messages. Being subliminal, they're not filtered by our thinking, so extremely potent. Like all things, these can be destructive or powerfully healing. We can't fake values or motives. They may be multi-layered and unclear, but they're there. Our own values, our ethical stance, affects whether or not our architecture acts as a Spirit Elevator. (*Building With Heart*, Green Books 1990)

At the time we did not realise how lucky we were to get Chris's services. In the two decades following our build he became an architectural guru, lecturing all over the world.

Chris visited the site only once, to measure up and to find out what ideas we had. Inspired by the plans I had brought back from Canada I thought that the open side of the cowshed that faced East could be filled in with stonework from the corner to the door, and then timber clad for the rest of the run. The side facing South would be glazed, with a passive solar roof, and would incorporate a small conservatory.

Other decisions seemed to fall into place quite naturally. It would be sensible to put dividing walls under the existing roof trusses which, with one exception, were in good condition. As the septic tank would be in the field, kitchen and bathroom would be on the West side, next to each other to make the plumbing easier.

We wanted a kitchen/dining area and a cold room. The latter should be against the North wall, that being the coolest. Thus, with a smattering of logic, decisions made themselves.

There would be a short passage with steps up from the cowshed to the barn that was adjacent to it. Half of that building would be retained as a barn and the other half turned into a music room with a large bed platform. This could be a second stage.

When the planners at Torridge District Council received the drawings they had only one question. It was not about materials. It was not about access, or space for the parking of visitors' cars. Their question was, Who is this Chris Day? They seemed happy to approve plans submitted by locals with no qualifications or training but were somewhat wary of outsiders. Whatever the reason for the planners' question, we were able to reassure them that our architect was responsible for designing buildings in the sensitive Pembrokeshire National Park, and this seemed to satisfy them.

We were lucky that we were applying for planning permission before the authorities decided that, in the conversion of farm buildings to domestic use, only existing openings could be turned into doorways or windows. Perhaps someone in power had investments in a firm making roof lights! However, once our plans received approval our only contact was with the building inspector, whose problem was not with our plans but with alcohol.

While the bureaucrats were at their exercise I was getting exercise of a different kind, wielding a sledgehammer to demolish concrete cow troughs, and flattening the floor to become the base for a concrete slab. Planning approval came through in February 1984. Building Regulation Approval had not come through by August but work had begun in March and I told them so.

Application No: 1/476/84/26/7: 'Any work you carry out prior to the granting of approval will be entirely at your own risk.' It did not seem to be too much of a risk, especially as there was a lot of preparatory work that could be done such as clearing the site, taking the slates off the roof and sorting stone.

I was teaching in the daytime. Julia was still in London earning the money to pay for wood and cement. Thanks to Satish Kumar and June Mitchell, who accommodated me and my piano, I was able to get in three or four hours' work after school. With weekends that added up to approaching forty hours a week. But still, I was going to need help.

Graham Redwood was a labourer, brother-in-law of the two brothers who farmed at the top of the lane. He was available. He had never worked on a house before, only on farm buildings, but he possessed a dumper truck and could borrow a tractor with attachments that could excavate and bulldoze. We divided the labour between us. He would do the groundwork, laying drains and installing the septic tank, would remove and replace the roof slates and would be the mason. I would be responsible for all the interior work: chippie, sparky, bricky and plumber. I already possessed a shelf of manuals and invested in a toolbox with hammers, spanners, chisels, wrenches, pliers, screwdrivers, PowerLock tape measure, pipe cutter, hacksaw, tenon and wood saws, power drill, circular saw and, in pride of place, a DeWalt radial arm saw. And, of course, a leather tool pouch to strap around my waist. I also bought a wheelbarrow, pickaxe, shovel, spirit level, plumb line, trowels, hawk and cement mixer.

The work, I am pleased to say, went according to plan. I laid the concrete base, and built the dividing walls with blocks, rather than stud, for that superior, solid feel. To add to the olde worlde ambience I distressed corners and plastered the walls with cement which, when rubbed with newspaper before it is completely dry, roughens the finish. Making the openings for the windows was somewhat hairy but with a couple of acro props and a lump hammer the job was easy on risk though tough on muscle. As the tops of the windows were to be arched I made supports of wood and hardboard and Graham constructed the stonework for the openings around them. He built the chimneys. It was then that I realised just how good a mason he is. The two chimneys he constructed are works of art.

We had some luck. Architectural Antiques in South Molton was moving premises to a disused cinema and were disposing of a pile of doors for three and five pounds each. I was able to obtain all the interior doors I needed, one of them being semi-glazed with red, blue and frosted panels that now divides the conservatory from the living room. The coloured glass glows in the morning sun. Having obtained the doors, most of which had been stripped, I could make the frames to fit them, much easier than finding doors to fit frames. We were to do even better out of Architectural Antiques.

The main room

The plastic damp proof sheet that we laid under the concrete slab had to come up the interior of the wall about 18" and had to be protected. That was fine on the South side where we were building a low wall. On the north wall it presented a problem. We decided that dado-height panelling was the answer, and Julia went off to South Molton to investigate. When she returned it was with full-height oak panelling, enough to cover the North wall and some of the East wall. She had bought it for a sum similar to that being asked for dado-height softwood panelling. How come? Firstly, because there was not enough of it to do out a whole room, which is how it is usually used, and secondly it had initials scratched in it, and a couple of places where someone had tried to set fire to it. It won't come as a surprise to know that its provenance was an institution for girls in Birmingham. It took quite some time to sand it down and polish it, but time wasn't money. It makes a fine backdrop for our oak refectory table and the six 17th century-style handmade oak stools with moulded rails and baluster and peg turned legs that I assembled from expensive kits.

The refectory table was cheap, too, because it was the odd one out, the only oak piece in a shop dedicated to stripped pine. Its length made it unsuitable for most dining rooms. It, too, appears to have come from an institution. Perhaps a brawl of students

317

snuck it out of college late one night to flog it for the wherewithal to prop up the Union bar for a few weeks.

Reclaimed wood, apart from the new tanalised battens required for holding the slates on the roof, I acquired for most other purposes: floorboards for cladding; Canadian pitch pine for windows, stairs, shelves and door frames; Canadian maple and teak for flooring The pitch pine came out of an old warehouse in Glasgow. As I write I have above me a splendid beam that has a cross section of 22 x 30 cms. The treads of the staircase are 10 x 30 cms, nice solid lumps of reddish-gold wood. In those days there was no great demand for reclaimed wood and prices were reasonable. Now you can pay more for old than for new.

Making the windows from pitch pine was the toughest of the carpentry challenges. All were designed to have curved or angled tops. At my request Chris sent detailed working drawings, essential as the profile has to be accurate if the rain is to be kept out. However, all this was far from my mind when I moved from Satish and June's to stay with David Charlesworth.

David is a Cabinet maker, acknowledged internationally as an expert on tools and techniques. He is such a perfectionist that he cannot make a living from his artefacts. I watched him constructing a revolving bookcase to hold the translated works of a prominent novelist's crime fiction. He first built a full-scale model and then spent much time and money on solving the engineering problem of having a considerable weight of books revolving on one point. I suspect he made a loss on this commission.

His finickiness is extreme when it comes to tools. I have seen him test a plane's sharpness by setting it to travel under its own weight down an inclined piece of wood, removing the whisper of a shaving. He runs week-long courses devoted solely to the sharpening of tools. Teaching, writing and making DVDs have become David's main sources of income.

In 1983 David was going through a dark period in his life. To give him support I moved into his house, Julia joining us at weekends. Together we saw him through the worst of his crisis, particularly by making sure that his students felt that they were getting their money's worth. As time went by I developed enough skills to use the tools in his workshop for the making of my windows. David's tool sharpening regime was essential: pitch pine is so resinous it clogs up blades in no time.

Being made of pitch pine I expect my windows to last forever. I was a little taken aback, then, when the glass company Andrewartha informed me with pride that their double glazing carried a twenty-five year guarantee. In terms of the life of a building, that is nothing. The manager of the firm that has now had to replace some of their glazing, for Andrewartha had a shorter life than its products, told me I was lucky. The new windows carry only a fifteen year guarantee. Nearly all modern products manufactured for the use in dwellings are sold with a limited life expectancy. Why isn't there an outcry?

Many do-it-yourselfers leave the electrics to the professionals. The only problem I had with installing the electric circuits was excavating holes in stone walls in which sockets could be inserted. Otherwise, designing the circuits is a rational procedure, though foresight is required for the siting of outlets as one has to conjure up a clear picture of the way in which space is to be used: where the tele? Where the washing machine? Where Henry, the sucker up of dust? To allay the fears of doubters, who had equally clear pictures of fires and explosions, it was only necessary to point out that my work would be tested by a qualified electrician when time for the installation of a fuse box, and the connecting of the house to the mains, came round.

One sunny day – there was a lot of sunshine that summer – I was driving through Fremington on the way to Barnstaple and I spotted a bath, a washbasin and a toilet on the pavement, supplanted, I suspected, by a suite in mint green or pantyhose pink. Mine in white for £3! The taps cost a great deal more as I wanted the new-fangled ones with ceramic discs.

It was with the installation of water works that I really began to understand Chris Day's philosophy: building a house is building oneself. Plumbing is an ideal activity for developing patience, or certainly was before the days of plastic push-fit. Whether joining copper pipes to copper pipes with soldered joints or with brass fittings, the latter requiring white tape to seal them, there is a high probability that at least one joint will leak, and probably more. The toughest challenge was the installation of radiators. This is a closed system. That means that the same water goes round and round the house, with a small header tank to top up any loss.

When all the radiators are in place and connected up, then water is let in and air is let out. It is only now that it becomes clear whether all 15 joints and 16 radiator connections are watertight. I would like to meet the plumber with a record of first-time success. He has not had to face emptying the system, a messy business as water has to be let out from the lowest point in the circuit. Dealing with radiator connections is relatively easy as that usually requires only the tightening of the nuts. For other joints one solders on. The system is re-filled. At this point leaks appear elsewhere and the whole procedure is repeated.

> If you can fill and empty, solder, fill again
> and do this umpteen times and not complain....
> you'll be several feathers nearer to sainthood than you were several
> hours before.

Chris Day proposed incorporating a passive solar water heater in the south-facing part of the roof above the small conservatory. I made a bedstead of copper pipe. A firm in Edinburgh supplied aluminium fins, matt black on one side, about 12" x 9", that clipped snugly onto the piping. This rested on the roof and was topped with glass. The water, pumped through a closed system, heats the water in a large copper cylinder. In summer we can draw directly from this. The water we get can be so hot it has to have cold water added for a comfortable shower. In winter the water passes through a second copper cylinder where it is brought up to temperature by the stove.

Our neighbour-but-one, another Graham, had bought the Victorian farmhouse and outbuildings at the top of our lane. He converted barns to holiday lets. An unconverted barn contained a wealth of bits and pieces he had picked up from auctions in the expectation that they might come in useful in further conversions. When his wife, a nurse, retired they decided to decamp to Australia. The purchaser of the property drove such a hard bargain that Graham decided to remove his treasures and asked me if I would store them in our barn until he could dispose of them. From time to time I would see a use for one of these treasures, which he would usually let me have for nothing. He was extremely generous. So our airing cupboard has oak linenfold doors, panels from a defunct pulpit. A semi-glazed door, rounded at the top, leads into the second conservatory and sits next to the mains isolating switch which is hidden behind a small carved door. A farmhouse dresser, the only storage unit in the kitchen apart from the fridge, also came from him. I really enjoyed finding uses for his odd lots.

My biggest creative challenge was the staircase from the music room to the bed platform. The maths was not difficult but the design of the banisters presented a challenge. I was using four-inch deep blocks of Canadian pine for the steps four inches above each other. For the spindles I was using 2" x 2" pine. The problem was that a spindle needed to be at the front of each step. That meant that the second one would have been only two inches away, giving the appearance similar to that of a mouth overfilled with teeth. The inspiration was to use a metal rod for the second one, a eureka moment. It is in solving problems such as this that one gets the greatest pleasure.

Dutch elm disease was no disaster for Bob and Sue, the chair-making couple in the village, for elm was eminently suitable for making their chairs. Bob had a stack of planks over 2' wide waiting to be called into service. I bought one to hold the porcelain kitchen sink and provide an adjacent work surface for which, being water resistant, elm is almost entirely suitable; the downside is its tendency to warp. By cutting slots in a piece of elm with a circular saw I made a draining rack. It was quick to make and efficient in use. I should patent it. Around the sink area floor we laid slabs of slate, cheap at the time as farmers' wives were exiling it from their kitchens. Now second-hand slate costs an arm and an overdraft.

With a wood-burning Wamsler central heating cooker stove installed, and the electric circuits tested and connected to the mains, we obtained permission to occupy the cowshed. Between it and the neighbouring barn – still a building site – a large plastic sheet provided a small degree of protection from the elements. Once installed, we moved at a more leisurely pace as we tackled the second phase, the barn.

The building inspector, not convinced that the barn walls would support the roof, asked for the architect to come up with a proposal. It would be necessary to hang the roof from a central beam. An engineer was hired to work out the specifications for it.

The north wall had to support one end of the beam but it was in such a bad state that it had to be replaced with one of concrete blocks. By placing the wood burning stove in the middle of the room and building a solid chimney for it we provided a third support for the beam. To construct this beam I made a frame from

4" x 2" wood to which I nailed and glued side panels of marine quality ply. It was almost thirty feet long, six inches wide and a foot-and-a-half deep. Great was the day when a handful of friends, aided by a pulley, helped me haul it into place.

We have tried to be ecological, using as much natural material as possible and regretting that cement had to play such a large part in the construction work. At least we could paint surfaces with limewash, at the time extremely cheap. Tamar Trading would fill plastic fertilizer sacks with slaked lime and wax at a mere fraction of the cost of emulsion. The yellow, red and brown ochre powder with which it can be tinted was also cheap. Exterior plastered walls we painted mellow yellow. The ceiling in the main room is raspberry-and-cream. Other shades of the three pigments are employed throughout the house. Where walls are likely to be rubbed against, as in the bathroom, I added the powder to white emulsion. It is helpful that, in whatever combinations they are used, earth colours will always go with each other. They also set off natural wood. I like the way that humidity alters the colour saturation.

With one exception the building inspector gave me an easy time. He required that the roof trusses be treated with preservatives known to be toxic. Chris Day advised us to use boric acid instead. The inspector was not happy to accept this. I replied that, if the local authority would give a written undertaking to accept responsibility for any illness that could reasonably be attributed to the use of the prescribed chemicals I would use them. End of discussion!

Building is done with the whole of one's body. The architect Rudolph Schwartz described the actions of the body involved in building walls, placing stone on stone, block on block, in stroking the wall with plaster and paint, in sawing and planing wood:

> Each limb of the body moves in its particular way and all of them together create the building as a second body...

> Indeed it is with the body that we experience building, with the outstretched arms and the pacing feet, with the roving glance and with the ear, and above all else in breathing. Space is dancingly experienced.

When that space is one that you have created then occupying it does indeed make the spirit 'dance'. Equally spirit-lifting is the ever-changing exterior space, the garden.

The prevailing south-west wind whistles over Stoke and straight up the valley from the sea. To protect the vegetable garden and the lawn we planted a hedge of escalonia, recommended for its tolerance of air-borne salt and widely used in Cornwall. We quartered the field with fencing and upgraded the grass to make grazing for half-a-dozen Friesland sheep which we intended to milk, an intention never realised. I do have a favourite jumper dyed in natural greens, browns and yellows and spun and knitted by Sally Gwynn, a Small School mother, from the wool. Otherwise the sheep took more than they gave, except as pets and lawnmowers. In the end, a neighbouring farm having succumbed to foot-and-mouth, they were seized for slaughter.

As Julia wanted ducks we needed a pond. We have a small one in the courtyard, shaded by a weeping Japanese cherry, which, perversely, our recent quartet of call ducks preferred to the large pond, their assigned territory. In the light of the effort that went into making it for them they have displayed a cruel ingratitude.

The hole for the large pond which Graham excavated for us was to be lined with concrete. A Czech friend whom we had met in Japan offered to help me mix and lay the lining. The summer's day was fine, but extremely hot, and before it was out he was suffering from sun stroke. As a consequence I could not complete the work until the following day. This meant there was a joint in the lining. The joint was not watertight, though the water loss was not great.

I should have used the traditional Devon method, suitable where the soil is clay. Feed, in the form of nut, roll, pellet or coarse mix, is scattered over the surface of the pond floor. A flock of sheep is then introduced. As they poddle around they puddle the clay, working it into a thick watertight paste. People only tell you these things when it is too late, and then with a certain glee. I eventually had to put in a heavy rubber lining.

Around the edge of the field we planted trees, most of which have taken their time to grow. On the other hand, a dozen pines, nine inches high when presented to us in pots by my Aunt Mona, now stand over thirty feet tall. Two have had to be taken down. Others will follow.

At the bottom of the field, down by the stream, we established a small orchard. It is now at the end of its life, being both overshadowed and overgrown. More recently we have planted a dozen cider apple trees in the lower field. Most years to date they have been pretty unproductive because they are too exposed to the Sou'westerly gales. In 2015 they gave a bumper crop, however, enough to make fifteen gallons. More regularly generous are the Golden Noble cooking apple and five eating apples which, with two barren damsons, a quince, and an ageing medlar, are on the lawn.

What had been a cattle yard we turned into a walled flower garden. That required the removal of a large quantity of stone and the importing of soil. I laid three brick paths, edged with railway sleepers to delineate the beds. Where the paths meet Katherine Leat and I made a mosaic platform with a sundial in the centre using fragments of glazed pottery begged from Branham pottery in Barnstaple. That was her 'payment' for singing lessons.

On the farm next door to us Sarah Conibear was building up a plant business specialising in lupins raised in rented polytunnels. She needed some open ground. Our sheep had gone to sheep heaven. Could she have the lower half of our field in which to grow lupins?

With lupins there is no guarantee that the seed from a plant will produce offspring of the same colour as the parent. The only way to ensure colour continuity is by taking cuttings. Sarah wanted to grow a field of lupins from which interesting specimens could be selected. In return her husband, a blacksmith – the Conibears had the forge on Ford Hill – made an arch of tall hoops for a tunnel of six apple and pear trees. These espaliers I trained a tier at a time, a foot-and-a-half a year. This avenue leads to a corner where we can sit drinking coffee or enjoying lunch beneath the vine and fig tree we planted there.

Then they shall hammer their swords into ploughshares,
And their spears into pruning-hooks.
Nation shall lift no sword against nation,
And never again will they learn to make war.
Every man shall live beneath the shade of his own vine and fig-tree,
And no one shall make him afraid. (Micah 4:3, 4)

Because of its exposure to the prevailing wind the field proved to be less than ideal for the lupin venture. Sarah moved further inland, to Woolsery, where her Westcountry Nursery is now a thriving business. She holds the National Collection of lupins and has won three gold medals at the Chelsea Flower Show.

We decided to replace our sheep with a cow. It would of course be a jersey. We were told of a woman who wanted to part with a house cow. We went to see them both. Both the woman and the cow were friendly and a deal was soon in the bag. A stainless steel pail and other necessary equipment she threw in for free. As we were leaving she said she would love to see the field in which Buttercup would be residing, and a visit was arranged.

I hurried to clear the barn, lugging stuff that we might one day use onto a storage platform. The thought of fresh golden cream on my porridge kept me at it. I fashioned a milking stand of concrete and a hay basket of wood. It would be clear to the world at large, to Cheristow neighbours and to Buttercup's 'mother', that Buttercup was going to be treated like an honoured guest.

The day of the visit was mis-chosen. It was one of the worst that winter, wind blowing rain in horizontal squalls from the direction of the sea. We stood leaning on the gate surveying the field, as we had done when we first arrived. This time, however, it was different. It took only seconds. 'My Buttercup's not coming here!' Thus ended our dairy dream.

We have had a little more luck with our ducks, but not everything has gone smoothly. Originally I had placed the duck house a quarter of the way down the field.

Kaori, a Japanese student, was staying with us. She enjoyed feeding them with corn from the dustbin store and then letting them out of their run. One morning she came rushing in as we were finishing breakfast. 'Come, you must come. It is terrible!' Running, she led us down to the duck house. There, lying sated and asleep, was a young badger. He had murdered the lot. It took him two days to sleep off his feast. We were not going to disturb him. Badgers can be vicious.

I moved the duck house so that it was next to the pond and within sight and easy reach of the house. For several years since our ducks have lived in peace and unafraid. When constructing the house I had put in a window that is about three feet off the ground, a hole covered in chicken wire, with a flap that closes over it in cold weather. One morning Julia found the wire pushed in, two dead ducks in the house and two gone. We were at a bit of a loss to decide what had happened. Julia buried the corpses. The next evening she saw a badger exhuming them, and not for purposes of carrying out a post-mortem! Thus the culprit revealed him or herself. That a badger could jump to a height of three feet with enough force to break the chicken wire, and exit the same way with a captive bird or two in its maw, was marvel sufficient to deaden some of the pain of this loss. It gave rise to exchanges among the neighbours of accounts of other difficult-to-believe acts by wild animals, without resorting, quite, to tales of the beast of Exmoor.

With the approach of retirement, and the prospect of surviving on State pensions, for none of the charities for which we worked had pension schemes, except the Church of England that is now rewarding me for six years' service, we decided to convert the barn to a holiday let. Recent regulations governing smallholdings meant that there was little likelihood of our needing it for a house cow – one is required to have at least two animals for companionship – so its only function has been as storage space for things we no longer needed or for which we might find a use. We were abashed to discover that we had accumulated six skips-worth of junk.

The Barn

Katherine Leat, the ex-pupil who helped me construct the sundial, and now an architect, drew up the plans, and I had an 'Indian summer' building project to get my trowel and saw into. Holiday lets in this area can be quite expensive. We decided ours would be cheap and, as a consequence, it is usually taken for the winter months by someone in need of housing. It is also the favourite resting place of a Tibetan Buddhist lama who comes to Hartland from time to time to teach. He and I laugh a lot.

In 2013 we decided to invest in solar panels. There not being room on the roof for them, all fifteen are in large black plastic 'buckets' that occupy about a quarter of the vegetable garden. Buckets are the installer's cunning plan. As they are technically movable they do not require planning permission. In 2015, with income from the panels, electricity cost us about £6 for the year.

I am planting up an acre of willow to be harvested in a four-year cycle. I want to build a clay oven outside for bread and pizza. As willow burns fast and furious it should be ideal for this, though we will use it mainly in our three stoves.

The house nearly complete

Enough about the house! We are one of five properties in Cheristow. We get on well with our neighbours. From the Lavender Farm and tearooms at the top of the lane we buy beef whenever they slaughter one of their Devon Reds. We usually invite friends to share some of it with us it is so delicious. In years past I would have avoided this meat for economic reasons: a vegetarian diet leads to a better use of land. However, as dairy farmers hardly make a living nowadays, and grass is the crop that grows best in Devon, beef makes some sense.

A left turn at the top of the lane leads directly to the cliffs, about a twenty-five minute walk. There one can climb down to Berry beach, not much used by visitors, or turn South to walk to Hartland Quay; North to make for Hartland Point where there is a defunct lighthouse that various wealthy outsiders are rumoured to have bought. There are extraordinary rock formations on this stretch of a coastal path that extends for 630 miles from Minehead in Somerset to Poole Harbour in Dorset.

In the bays there are grey seals, and looking West and North one can see Lundy Island and the coast of South Wales. The views are stunning, whichever way you look. On a sunny day a flat blue sea can seem out of this world, though I relish the excitement of winter winds that throw waves against the rocks and send spray to the cliff top.

Leaving the house in the opposite direction we can take a footpath through the woods to the village. In the spring bluebells fill the space between the trees. There is a badger sett at the top of the wood. Occasionally deer make a tentative appearance, disappearing at the snap of a twig. The Vale, being protected from the sea breeze, is populated by fair-sized beech trees. A calm Autumn can encourage a wonderful display of turning leaves, a yellow, gold and russet feast.

Being some distance from what is ironically referred to as 'civilization' Hartland has a certain degree of self-sufficiency, with a post office, general store, studio gallery, hardware store, chairmaker, furniture maker, two potteries, fire station, café, four pubs and a micro brewery. There are farmers and builders galore, a number of creative creatures, and a range of services. The *Hartland Post,* successor to the *Hartland Times* and the *Hartland Chronicle* (1896), keeps us up to speed with the hatching, matching and dispatching as well as the activities of the many societies and clubs.

Charlie McVeigh (the Guardian 30 May 2012) humbly proposed

...that the treacherous and – in large parts – inaccessible north-west Devon coastline is the UK's most beautiful... Hartland is a desolate, wind-swept place but the surf, granite cliffs and rock-pooling are unparalleled... This area is splendidly isolated and – unlike the beaches to the east (Saunton, Croyde and the like) – almost devoid of any organised tourist attraction...'

However, the Milky Way, the Big Sheep and other touristy delights are not so far away.

'In writing this memoir I hope to discover what I think about my life. We won't know that until we reach the final chapter.' We have now reached that point, and those Chapter One words come back to haunt me. I am not sure that I am much wiser about me and my life. Those who have observed my progress through the decades have usually thought I was mad, especially when taking on projects that others found unnerving.

I have never been troubled by thoughts of success and failure. Success is like candyfloss spun from sugar: it appears to have volume but that volume is mostly air. 'Success' is usually spelt out in conventional terms, and convention is something I have often challenged. Yesterday (as I write) was Good Friday. I took the service in my daily dress. If the altar is bare of its usual trappings, I told the congregation, I feel that I, too, should dispense with clerical costume. I broke the rules. So what?

I don't set out to break rules. I merely wish to pursue a logical path, and some policies, particularly of government, are illogical and have to be challenged. There may be obstructions on the way but these, too, are a challenge, not a deterrent. To some it may appear that in this I am pig-minded. Perhaps they are right. However, I will say this about myself: I am always open to discussion and prepared to change tack if the facts require it.

I am not concerned about material reward and have never negotiated a salary. As Director of Refugee Action I insisted on equal pay for all staff, a policy that quietly delighted me. Nor have I looked for recognition. Two of my successors have been awarded OBEs for running Refugee Action. I was delighted for them but have not wanted that for myself. The only reason I mention these things is that I believe they are indications of a proper understanding of the teachings of Jesus. I take the Sermon on the Mount extremely seriously. Yes, I am divorced, and in that I have failed to live up to the teaching that I take to heart. So I won't avoid censure by claiming, as some do, that the Sermon is a counsel of perfection intended only to apply in the short period between Jesus' crucifixion and his return in glory to oversee the kingdom. My deepest wish?

> To be humble, reverent, grateful, content;
> to temper desire that the heart be pure -
> this is the greatest blessing.
>
> To lead simple lives in a beautiful land
> reflecting on selfless examples -
> this is the greatest blessing.
>
> To possess a heart unperturbed by the world,
> untroubled by grief or deep passion -
> this is the greatest blessing.
>
> Those who act like this never suffer defeat,
> all roads they may travel in safety -
> theirs is the greatest blessing.

(From the *Kuddaka-Patha* & *Sutta Nipata*)

Made in the USA
Charleston, SC
09 August 2016